PENGUIN BOOKS
THE JAM FRUIT TREE

Carl Muller completed his education from the Royal College,
Colombo, and has served in the Royal Ceylon Navy and Ceylon
Army. In 1959 he entered the Colombo Port Commission and
subsequently worked in advertising and travel firms. Muller
took up journalism and writing in the early Sixties and has
worked in leading newspapers in Sri Lanka and the Middle
East. His published works include, *Sri Lanka—A Lyric, Father
Saman and the Devil* and a link language reader for students,
Ranjit Discovers Where Kandy Began.

At present he is working on his third novel. He lives in Kandy
with his wife and four children.

D1636782

Carl Muller

THE JAM FRUIT TREE

PENGUIN BOOKS

PENGUIN BOOKS
Published by the Penguin Group
Penguin Books India Pvt. Ltd, 11 Community Centre, Panchsheel Park,
New Delhi 110 017, India
Penguin Group (USA) Inc., 375 Hudson Street, New York, New York 10014,
USA
Penguin Group (Canada), 90 Eglinton Avenue East, Suite 700, Toronto, Ontario,
M4P 2Y3, Canada (a division of Pearson Penguin Canada Inc.)
Penguin Books Ltd, 80 Strand, London WC2R 0RL, England
Penguin Ireland, 25 St Stephen's Green, Dublin 2, Ireland (a division of Penguin
Books Ltd)
Penguin Group (Australia), 707 Collins Street, Melbourne, Victoria 3008, Australia
(a division of Pearson Australia Group Pty Ltd)
Penguin Group (NZ), 67 Apollo Drive, Rosedale, Auckland 0632, New Zealand
(a division of Pearson New Zealand Ltd)
Penguin Group (South Africa) (Pty) Ltd, Block D, Rosebank Office Park, 181 Jan
Smuts Avenue, Parktown North, Johannesburg 2193, South Africa

Penguin Books Ltd, Registered Offices: 80 Strand, London WC2R 0RL, England
First published by Penguin Books India 1994

ISBN 9780140230314

This book is, as the author claims, a work of 'faction' and, while fixed both
historically and chronologically, remains fiction, based on fact, embroidered and
distorted in order to protect the characters herein. All names, save where obviously
genuine, are fictitious and any resemblance to persons living or dead is wholly
coincidental.

Typeset in Palatino by Digital Technologies and Printing Solutions, New Delhi
Printed at Repro India Ltd., Navi Mumbai

*To Professor ASHLEY HALPE, Dean, Faculty of Arts, University
of Peradeniya, Sri Lanka and his wife, BRIDGET—my dearest
friends and my greatest inspiration*

Contents

Contents

PART ONE
The Flowering

The sky was as blue as an Eskimo's nose on the morning that Sonnaboy cycled sedately to work. A large man with big fists, grey eyes set wide in a broad, brown face, a largish nose that swept down from between bushy eyebrows to just short of a rather petulant mouth and a chin that kept saying 'to hell with you' in a language all its own, Sonnaboy was pushing thirty-five and, in his home in suburban Dehiwela and in the Ceylon Government Railway Running Shed in Dematagoda, was a force to reckon with.

Cecilprins von Bloss had a principle he firmly abided by. Keep the wife in the family way. Women, he maintained, stay out of mischief when they are 'carrying'. Siring a string of children was, to the old reprobate, child's play. In those fine old days a meal of rice and curry, a cup of tea and a cigarette cost a mere nine cents—and the best samba rice with beef, two vegetables, *sambol* (a relish made of ground coconut, chillie, lime, salt, chopped onions, tomato and peppercorns, eaten with meals), a pappadam and *mallung* (chopped leaves, basted with grated coconut and seasoning) at that—and an assistant postmaster's job was 'public service' with all manner of perks and pensionable to boot. All a husband could wish for was to come home from office, drink great quantities of tea, consider his fat wife who sprawled on the lounger fingering her rosary and check the time. Cecilprins was a creature of habit. Leave the General Post Office at four, take the 4.18 train to Dehiwela, reach home at five. Sometimes Maudiegirl had a bun on his plate with his tea. After a bath at the well, carry his sagging rattan chair to the porch where he would sit, watch the road and waggle a hand at passers-by. Neighbours would pop heads over walls to say 'how' and 'do you know what?' and Cecilprins would say he knew and nod and slap at his ankles as the early mosquitoes swizzed around.

Boteju Lane, Dehiwela, had a fair wedge of assorted citizenry. Old Simmons who hated dogs, and the Bennett woman with one big filaria leg, and the Fernandos who moved away one night after the Rodrigo boy fucked their daughter. Cecilprins enjoyed his porch evenings. He got, he knew, respect. He was an assistant postmaster and always wore high, white, starched collars and a cravat as large as a table napkin. And such a man, too. Thirteen

3

children. Must be the Dutch blood in him. Or was it German? One couldn't be specific.

When the mosquitoes became too demanding, Cecilprins would go indoors and take the little key he kept on the altar where an old Palm Sunday coconut-frond cross lay propped between two sputtering oil lamps and a frayed St. Anthony's scapular. Over the little altar was a quite spectacular picture of the Sacred Heart of Jesus, all scarlet and butter-yellow with a heart that was crowned with tongues of flame—thirteen points of flame, Cecilprins noted one day and remarked on and the whole family counted and solemnly agreed that Papa was right and thirteen had to mean something. Maudiegirl clutched at her rosary and called on the Blessed Virgin to witness. 'See, will you, how Jesus is telling to me. Thirteen fires in His heart like thirteen fires in my stomach, no? Thirteen children I give and every one of you make me suffer.'

Cecilprins would take the key from the altar, open his special cupboard, pour himself four fingers of whisky, top that with water and say 'Cheers' and take a deep swig. Maudiegirl would watch and sniff. 'Small sip is good for my rheumatics, no?' and a carefully measured tot is dispensed, which the old lady would dispatch in a twinkling.

Dinner was a humdrum affair, usually. The children would straggle in at odd times. Terry was in Singapore. He had gone into rubber, and the broker-house he worked for had sent him to their Malayan office. He wrote long letters about tiger shooting and his bungalow and Malay servants with their red caps and the enormous snakes he encountered. Sonnaboy would snort and smack a fist into a palm and stalk off to the well. He liked coming home before dark. Stripped to his jocks he would make quite a hullaballoo drawing and dashing water on himself while the servant-girl next door would creep up to peer through the thatch. Sonnaboy would take out his cock and waggle it at her. He was proud of his penis. It was, he knew, bigger and stood stiffer than Dunnyboy's or Totoboy's. He made an elaborate show of soaping it as the servant girl crept closer to watch, and he thought of Elaine and how they would be married soon. Thin girl, Elaine, not much flesh on her thighs, boyishly undeveloped, small breasts, tight little bum. Yes, Elaine was just right. Like a boy. And Sonnaboy liked boys.

Elsie, his sister, would come to the well. '*Chee*! What you are doing! Wait, I'll tell Mama.' But she would go to the store-room where the rice and flour was kept and rub and rub until her bloomers were wet between her legs and would then emerge panting and run to the bedroom to say a feverish Hail Mary.

Yes, a nice, ordinary family. Terry and Dunnyboy, Leah and Elsie, Totoboy and Anna, Viva and Patty, Ruthie and Vinto, Fritzy and Marla and Sonnaboy who was the youngest and quite the strongest in a clutch of eight strong sons. Three died, however, before reaching their teens. Patty and Vinto succumbed to pneumonia and Fritzy fell off the neighbour's roof where he had perched to steal guavas. Of all the family, Dunnyboy was near inconsolable at their passing. He was the eldest and the strangest. Routed from school in disgrace, he never found work. Strong as an ox, too, and not a man to tangle with, with a twelve-year-old mind in his strapping, adult body. Viva was lean, whip-strong and calculating. Totoboy a gregarious, sunny fellow with pianist's fingers and a great talker.

The girls were all big-buttocked and round-thighed, each promising to be fat and fifty like their mother. The fat clung to their bottoms even as teenagers and they bustled invitingly as they walked and Dunnyboy would squeeze them gently over their knees and rub against their behinds and couldn't stop the trembling in his fingers. The small Boteju Lane house had two and a half rooms, actually, and the boys would lump in one and the girls in another and there were no doors to shut between any of them—not even when Cecilprins would cover Maudiegirl at eleven each night and she would wheeze complainingly as he jerked over her and the girls would listen and shiver deliciously and Sonnaboy would crawl softly on hands and knees to peer into the darkness and discover what being married was all about.

'They're doing, no?' Marla would hiss when he crawled past their mats.

Sonnaboy would nod and Leah would sigh softly and go to the chamberpot to raise her nightdress and squat and do pippy. It was

Dunnyboy who would want to play papa with them and crawl over to meddle with them and rub his cock against their legs. But that was the night and everything was all right at daybreak when they rose, stacked their pillows, rolled up their mats and emptied the chamberpot in the lavatory and dressed for Mass. St. Mary's Church was a few blocks away. They would check their Missals and the Saint's day and mark the epistle and gospel with holy pictures. The girls wore veils and the boys snapped loops of elastic under their stocking-hose to keep them in place below the knee. And so, each morning, Cecilprins von Bloss and his family would go to church and Sonnaboy would go to the vestry to put on a red cassock and white surplice and serve at the altar. Father Romiel would beam on them and wish them a blessed morning and they would say hullo to old Mr Capper and Mrs Vanderputt and the Rozairos with their three straw-haired daughters.

'Come go,' Maudiegirl would urge, 'told, no, the *hopper* boy to come by seven.' And sure enough the *hopper* boy would come with his basket and Maudiegirl would count a quantity of *hoppers* (a type of thin griddle cake made of flour and fermented coconut water) for breakfast and tip the packet of *sambol* into a tin plate and note the account in a little book. The boy would whistle and show yellow teeth and pick at a sore on his hand. And it was another day. Cecilprins to the G.P.O.; Totoboy to the liquor merchant's where he counted stock and wrote all manner of squiggles in ledgers; Leah to a florist's where she arranged posies and bouquets and smiled at vinegary customers; Anna to a pharmacy where she spent long hours cooing with a Sinhalese gentleman who was something in the radio station, a Buddhist, and who rode a Raleigh bicycle. He was a fastidious little person, scrawny and a regular fusspot. He was the only one Anna knew who wore bicycle clips at the bottom of his trousers. All the others, she said, including Sonnaboy, just shoved the bottom of their trousers into their socks. Sonnaboy would grin. Mostly, he wore short trousers to work anyway. Viva was a salesman. He would wait at the top of the lane for the company van and make a great show of checking stocks of milkfood before setting off each morning. And Sonnaboy would wear a grimy cap, khaki shirt and shorts and climb on his bicycle to take the long road to Dematagoda. He said he was the only labourer in the family. A cleaner in the railway. A grease monkey. For eight hours a day he cleaned and greased huge steam locomotives, tenders, the couplings of carriages, frothy wads of cotton waste tucked in his pockets, gunk on his overalls, tarry oil on his neck and elbows, coal dust in his hair and grime under every fingernail. He carried nine cents for lunch and cigarettes and a snapshot of Elaine in his wallet. He was doing okay. Seventy-nine cents a day was a good 1930s salary for a man. Because the British nabobs favoured the 'educated' Burghers, he knew that someday he would become a locomotive apprentice and actually ride the rails. One day he would be an engine driver but in the meantime he would marry Elaine and spend all his off-time in bed with her.

Oh, all in all a robust, brawny, bawdy family, praising the Lord, church-going, singing their Aves with the same gusto as they would eat, drink and fornicate. Ruthie and Marla went around with sailors. They took to smoking cigarettes in long holders and were the first in the neighbourhood to wobble forth on the new high heels. Maudiegirl was suitably shocked. When Marla painted her lips it was the last straw.

'Jezebel,' Maudiegirl panted, 'go and wash your mouth!'

Marla glowered and minced away.

Ruthie went off first. She had married a sailor, she wrote, and Cecilprins went to the British Admiralty office in Galle Buck and was told that the sailor in question was a Goanese cook.

'What is this? Goanese?'

'An Indian, sir. From Goa.'

'Goa. That is in Italy?'

The writer petty officer was amused. 'Goa is in India, sir. No need to worry, is there? Your daughter is over twenty-one.'

'But she is a bloody fool, no? You don't know what her poor mother is saying.'

Sympathetic noises did not help, but that was all the Royal Navy could offer. Cecilprins came home boiling mad. He waylaid Marla, sailing out with lipstick liberally daubed across her wide mouth. 'You also!' he stormed, 'Bringing all these sailors home. Goas. That's what they are. You think I want Goas in this family. Heads together putting . . . vulgar talks talking. Can't be like decent people and listen even to gramophone. And smoking cigarettes. Go inside and change!'

Marla wailed and tried to escape. The old man grabbed at her, tore the sleeve of her dress. Her screams brought the neighbours tumbling to the gate. Sensing that now was the time for a father's outraged dignity, Cecilprins raised a hand like a latter-day Moses. 'Go!' he thundered, 'You are not my child. Go to where the devil is waiting for you. Go!'

Maudiegirl charged out like a hippopotamus delivering an urgent telegram. 'My little girl,' she screeched. 'From here you came,' she bleated, smiting her abdomen, then turning to her husband, 'How you can drive her away like this? She who I carried and brought forth. I gave her name from Bible, no? My baby. You come, babba, and I make nice cup of tea.'

Outside, a sea of faces watched the drama keenly. Old Simmons urged Cecilprins to forgive and forget. Village women from the tenements broke into a babble of Sinhala. Cecilprins grew grand in purpose and intent. 'You disgrace my name,' he bawled. 'Stay if you want, but you are not my child. If you go now, don't come back, do you hear?'

Marla stood, bent in shame under the jam fruit tree. All of Boteju Lane was now jammed against the gate. Slowly, she crept past her glowering father and ran indoors where she broke into a storm of weeping. When Sonnaboy came home and heard of the day's shenanigans he did what brothers do. He seized Marla by her hair and cuffed her across the face, once, twice. Early next morning Marla was gone. And she never was heard of again. She seemed to have walked off the face of the earth.

And so, at the time this chronicle begins we have father and mother von Bloss, sons Terry, Dunnyboy, Totoboy, Viva and Sonnaboy and daughters Elsie, Anna and Leah. Eight lives to consider in all the pages ahead. Eight lives and the lives they begat and the changing times and fortunes in a changing country. Today, in this year of grace, one thousand nine hundred and ninety-one, none of them are alive. They are all, doubtless in some great, cloudy boudoir in the sky. But let me hark back to that blue morning when

Sonnaboy pedalled to work. Life held few complications for him. He had his nine cents, his picture of Elaine, he had pumped air into his tyres and the Galle Road had few cars and charabancs to bother him with their exploding exhausts and chug-a-chug engines.

Rickshawmen scudded along, carrying ladies with gaudy parasols. He free-wheeled past the Holy Family Convent at Bambalapitiya and saw, as he claimed, a vision. Actually a roly-poly schoolgirl, fresh, round-cheeked, with a white pith hat on her head of dark hair. Dark eyes looked impudently into his and she turned into a lane leading to the sea. Sonnaboy was entranced. And glad to realize that true femininity could arouse him. He had always liked boys, to touch them, stroke them, feel them grow hard under his fingers. This was what had drawn him to Elaine. Her thin page-boy hair and figure was more male than female. Braking, he watched the girl walk down the lane, enter a house. He followed, noted nameboard and number. Through the curtains fifteen-year-old Beryl saw him turn around at the gate. Such a big, husky man. Her heart fluttered and she ran to the kitchen where Florrie da Brea saw her daughter's flaming face and immediately grabbed an ear. 'What are you up to?' she demanded.

'*Aiyo*, nothing, *anney* (a Sinhala expression used loosely in conversation to express pain, dismay loss or grief). Let go, Mummee, it's hurting.'

Florrie was not satisfied. She had had her share of shame and her children were a trial ever since Clarence had died. She sighed, pushed her youngest away and poured out a cup of tea. 'You want tea?'

Beryl was feeling her ear. 'You hurt it,' she complained.

'Good. Don't think I don't know you, miss. You're up to something. Can tell by just looking. So what you are up to now?'

'Nothing, *anney*. Fine thing, no? Just coming from school and getting scolded. Can I cut some bread?'

'You leave the bread, will you. If eating now won't have enough for dinner. Here, drink your tea and go and change. Are your knickers dirty? You know very well can't give those things to the dhoby woman. If dirty put in the tub to wash.'

'*Chee*, as if I will wear dirty knickers. You must see Elva's. They're filthy', Beryl giggled and nearly choked on her tea.

'Never mind Elva,' said Florrie severely, 'You mind how you talk about your elders, miss.'

'But it's true, Mama.'

Florrie cuffed her daughter almost absent-mindedly. It had been hard since Clarence died, God rest his soul. What was to be done? Every All Souls Day she would go to the cemetery and grumble at his grave. 'Eight daughters you gave, do you hear, and three sons and the two who died. So I gave you thirteen children and you stay to bury two and then leave me. Fine thing, no? Eleven to see to and everyday something to put fire on my head. How to go on like this? You tell me how. But what do you care? You are dead and you think the pension and the Widows and Orphans is enough? Thank God five girls married. Useless buggers, I know, but what to do? Now only Millie and Elva and Beryl. And Elva is worst. You must see how doing the la-di-da with the boys on the road. How to control, *anney*? And Millie working in the NAAFI and going in the night to Sailors Institute to dance. Now Beryl also fifteen and got breasts and have to tie cloth on those days. You sleep. What do you care? Just because I come on your birthday and Christmas and say a decade, and light a candle you must be thinking we are all right. What to all right? Only the boys are all right. But that Henry is drinking and drinking and Charlie has married that Hazel somebody and she thinks she fell from the sky. Fine thing, no? to come and tell all this to your grave. That Beryl is in bad age now. Yesterday she catch the dog and slowly putting her finger inside and feeling. Servantwoman saw and shouted and came and told me baby is putting finger in dog's hole. I gave her tight. Whole trouble is that next door dog came last week and do the job to our dog. Then Beryl see them stuck and asking Soma, and Soma telling her God knows what. I think that Soma telling her too much unnecessary things. Whole time Beryl talking with her in kitchen. *Aiyo* (Sinhala expression used in much the same way as '*anney*'), I don't know, Clarence. Why you die and give me all this trouble I don't know. Now must go. Our father, who art in heaven, hallowed be Thy name . . . .'

It had to be the act of a middle-class God. The thirteenth child of

Cecilprins and Maudiegirl and the thirteenth child of Florrie and Clarence, deceased. Sonnaboy returned home, bathed, got into his best clothes and cycled back to Nimal Lane, Bambalapitiya, to number 19, and rapped at the gate. There were no frills about his calling. He was thirty-five years old, a government servant and on the list for consideration as an apprentice driver. Florrie was taken by the grey eyes and the candid manner of his calling. She shooed her daughters indoors and invited him to sit. Sonnaboy was not there to mince words. He wished to marry Beryl. Was that her name? A nice name. So he was twenty years her senior. His parents? Everything was laid on the table for Florrie's dissection.

'But you don't know my daughter even.'

Sonnaboy nodded. 'Can I see her?'

Florrie said no. She was a schoolgirl. A good girl. An innocent girl. She must study. She was still a child. Her little *patiya* (Sinhala for 'tiny tot' or smallest child). 'Sin, no, to marry a girl this age. What she know about anything?'

Beryl, listening behind the inner door, frowned. Elva pinched her, almost made her squeal. 'What she know,' Elva hissed, 'I'll tell Mama how you go to that Lauries Lane house after school. Taking money from that man there. What are you doing with him?'

Beryl tossed her head. All that old man did was sit her on his lap and feel her legs. She regretted ever having told Elva about it. They listened together as Sonnaboy offered to bring his parents. Tomorrow?

Florrie was flustered. If only Clarence was here to deal with this huge fellow and his big hands. Such a big, bulgy man. But a railway man. That's a good job. Pension, too, and later maybe government quarters to live in. But he's thirty-five. That's not good. May die soon and leave my Beryl a widow with children. 'Must ask Saint Anthony,' she muttered as she watched Sonnaboy pedal away.

The girls came out. 'Mama, who is that?'

'You mind your business, will you. Nobody can come and even fart in this house without you asking why. See, child, if have a candle in the whatnot.'

Elva nudged Beryl. 'Mama is going to pray for you.'

Florrie took the candle crossly. 'See the time Millie went to work and still not coming. I don't know why somebody won't come and marry you big two. That fellow coming here sweet as you please and saying never mind the school, he wants to marry Beryl. Cheek, no? I have told you girls a thousand times don't encourage every loafer on the road. Otherwise how he know this place to come like this? See, will you, how nicely he walked in. As sweet as you please. Must be knowing your father is dead. Here, light this. I must ask Saint Anthony to help me. Better he take you, miss,' poking the candle at Elva, 'You are almost twenty-five now.'

Beryl was outraged. She had never had a suitor. And here was a knight on a bicycle and her mother wanted to fob Elva on him. 'But he wants to marry me,' she wailed.

'Who said so? Walls have big ears.'

'But he saw me after school.'

'Shut, shut. You stay in the kitchen when he comes again, miss. Marry. You're only fifteen. What you know about men? How you can make babies at your age? And cook and wash his clothes and what you do when he comes drunk I like to know. See how big he is.'

Elva ran to strike a pose before the long wardrobe mirror. A slim, willowy beauty, to be sure. Narrow-hipped, neatly tapering calves and ankles. She had put a good many boys to flight, but this Sonnaboy struck her as someone to be wary of. There was something brutal about being so big. Why, his muscles rippled under those short sleeves. 'Will I do?' she asked, making large eyes.

Beryl was on her in a fit of fury. 'He wants to marry me,' she cried seizing a fistful of hair. Elva screamed and Florrie waded in to slap both soundly.

'You wait,' said Elva darkly, 'I'll tell.'

'So tell. As if I care. If you tell, Mama will quickly say to marry him.'

Elva was annoyed. She was the elder sister. She must marry first. What will people say if Beryl married first. 'They will call me an old maid,' she cried.

'Serves you right,' said Florrie. 'What about that Koelmeyer boy?

And who's that other fellow. Forsythe? Came every day. Why they don't come now? Why you want to get all high and mighty, ah? See that Peterson boy. From this high we know him. Used to ring the bell for Angelus in church when he was small. Now he is in Mackinnons. Good job. He wanted to take you for his office party. How many times he came.'

'But Mama, he is awful. Only want to go to the beach and hold hands.'

'Because he is gentleman, that's why. Not like some fellows. Even this fellow. See how he come to talk with me. Because he knows his place, that's why. No hanky-panky nonsense. Telling the parents first. That is why I even talk so long with him. Because he is well-brought up. And railway man. He will be good husband for you. Tomorrow I will go to Kanatte and tell your father and he will be happy to hear. Beryl, stop that long face business and go and tell Soma to make some tea. Don't you pout at me, my girl. I'll pout you on the other side of your face!'

And while Florrie skittered around aimlessly, talking to herself, and Beryl rattled cups and stamped her feet in the kitchen and poured out her woes to Soma, and while Elva was making up her mind that Sonnaboy would make an eminently suitable husband, the cause of all this domestic pother was soaping himself at the well and emerged, reeking of carbolic to tell his fond papa and mama that they must accompany him the next day to meet his future bride.

'But you're engaged to Elaine, no?' Maudiegirl objected.

'I don't care,' said Sonnaboy, 'I love this girl.'

Cecilprins fussed over the name. 'Da Brea . . . da Brea? Sounds like Portuguese to me. Who is the father?'

'Father is dead.'

'Hmmm. But old lady is managing. Must be all right. Never mind, can see tomorrow, no. How's the house?'

'Not bad. Like this. Two three rooms, I think.'

'Then can't be badly off. But you go and tell Elaine, do you hear? Her father is good friend of mine. Damn shame if they get angry because of your nonsense.'

*

Eric de Mello worked in the General Post Office too, and was a mite lower in rank to Cecilprins who had his own desk and keys to drawers he could lock and, glory be, his own row of pigeon holes where he would stuff odds and ends. Each pigeon hole had been carefully labelled 'Standing orders', 'Memoranda', 'PMG's Circulars', 'Queries', etc., and Eric marvelled at this edifice of efficiency.

Eric shared a counter with a Tamil clerk named Naiswamy and a freckled Burgher lad named Raux who was easier called Rooks and who whistled tonelessly all day. Eric lived in Dehiwela too—in Station Lane—and was always on the platform to greet Cecilprins. He, being younger would always swing aboard first and secure a window seat, back to the engine, for Cecilprins, which was his first humble duty for the day. You see, Eric had his eye on Elsie and cultivated the father quite atrociously. It did not strike him that, as a couple, he and Elsie would cut quite a ludicrous figure. He, thin as a pipecleaner, slightly stooped with an air of permanent defeat; she, a healthy, strapping woman with calves and upper arms bigger than his thigh. He loved her to distraction. He needed someone to domineer him, even beat him, as his mother still did, yet, to tend to him, for Eric could never tend to himself. His was a world full of stumblings and bumblings, and odd socks and shirts buttoned wrong and leaving umbrellas in buses and sitting on his spectacles. Yet, he had his own little vice: the Ceylon Turf Club, and although he sometimes forgot and carried the race paper home and was soundly pummelled by his mother for venturing on this road to eternal damnation, he was mad on horse-racing. A sad, timid soul, he would resort to stealing from his own pay packet to put a fifty cents each way on horses who always insisted on raising their tails and refusing to finish.

'Canteen!' mother Aggie would bellow, 'What's this canteen nonsense? I give lunch packet and ten cents every day, no? And you have train season-ticket, no? So what for you going to canteen and eating and drinking God knows what? And four rupees cut from your pay. Four rupees! Can buy eggs and meat and pay the baker and get kerosene oil, no? with that money. You are waster like your father. Don't talk! God in heaven, what is this son you give me. I feed him and darn his shirts and only yesterday I cut cardboard with my own two hands to put in his shoes. And I think today he bring his pay home to his old mama who is slaving and grinding away with no rest from morning to night and four rupees gone for canteen. Canteen!'

Eric would cower near the sofa with its ghastly purple flower pattern and say, 'I'm sorry, Mama,' and Aggie would charge him like an enraged buffalo and twist a fat forearm around his neck and drag him to the centre of the hall, pummelling his head with her fist and breathing like an overworked bellows. Eric would yelp and struggle feebly, then stand still and inhale his mother's body smell as she whacked him, then pushed him into a chair and tucked in her hairpins.

'Think that I do this for your own good,' she would puff. 'Responsible you can be if you want. When I die and go what you will do, I don't know.'

Eric didn't know either. But Mama had whacked him and that was balm to his soul. Mama loved him.

It took a long time for Eric to summon the courage to tell Cecilprins of his intentions. The latter was impressed. Runty little fellow, to be sure, but steady, obliging, respectful and good son-in-law material. Could be kept in order, too. So Eric was invited home and he came with a tin of Bluebird toffees and made eyes at Elsie who glared back fiercely and scattered toffee wrappers in the veranda. Close up to his goddess, Eric was positively inflamed. Such a bosom. He could bury his head in that while she beat him and she was welcome to beat him every hour if she wished.

Mother Aggie was pleased. She was always impressed by the von Blosses who had produced such strong girls, each built like a pack-bull. When she learned of her son's intentions she swatted him affectionately and taking out a large bunch of keys, opened the kitchen safe and cut him a large wedge of love cake. 'From Christmas I save this cake,' she breathed, 'to give you one day you make your poor mama happy. So today you take a piece. You marry that girl. I will say a rosary for you.'

Eric, overwhelmed, cried: 'Mama.'

'My sugar ball,' Aggie cried—and that was perhaps the only maternal endearment Eric ever received. Aggie passed away that night with a sneer on her lips and Eric found a pillowcase full of money the old lady had stashed away and had a grand funeral with a band and two Tamil women he paid fifty cents each, to wail at the cemetery and beat their foreheads in the dust.

Cecilprins had had his reservations about Aggie. Now that she was safely interred his last doubts were dispelled. His Elsie would be mistress of a nice home in Station Lane. Eric would have to wait a decent interval, of course, but that couldn't be helped. 'I think six months is enough,' he told Maudiegirl.

'*Chickay* (Sinhala expression conveying contempt or disgust), that's not enough,' said Maudiegirl, heaving herself upright in her lounger. 'Poor mother in the sand and no time even to say twelve masses. Must wait one year, no?'

'You're mad, woman? When he coming here every day. Now not even talking in the house. Putting chairs under jam fruit tree and who knows what he's telling to her? Putting ideas in her head, must be. Everybody going on the road can see also. Tell, will you, to be like normal.'

Sonnaboy regarded his sister's boyfriend with contempt. '*Soththiya* (Sinhala word meaning a weak, effeminate person), no? Bugger can't even stand straight.'

'You don't worry, will you,' Maudiegirl would frown. 'He does better job than you, no? Have brains in his head.'

Cecilprins was assured by Father Romiel that there was no harm in an early wedding. 'I'm sure the poor soul would like an early wedding.'

'But what will people think, don't know.'

'Think of the poor soul,' the priest murmured.

Cecilprins bridled. 'What poor soul? My Elsie is all right. I'm giving her almirah and the old sewing-machine. A Pfaff. Only needs oiling. And some pots and pans and some money also. She will be all right.'

'No, no, I'm meaning Mrs de Mello. Surely she is now in heaven, waiting to see her son get married.'

'Oh.'

'Yes. So when shall we fix the day.'

'As you like, Father. Maybe two-three months.' Poor soul. Hah! Must tell that to Maudiegirl.

Elsie was delighted. 'So now we can get married,' she told Eric and seizing his hand thrust it between her legs. She deplored Eric's lack of spirit. She expected him to be more forthcoming. Like Dunnyboy, for example, whose nightly predations were clockwork regular. When Eric rose to go, he held the *Morning Leader* strategically to hide the bulge in his trousers. He felt, at last, a man.

*

George de Mello was Eric's cousin, and when he heard of the latter's marriage plans he called to check out the lay of the land. George was a crafty piece of work. Old Papa de Mello, who kept milch cows and was known in Kandana as a real bullshitter, was inordinately proud of his Georgieboy. 'Such a mind he has,' he told wife Mattie, 'and not even thinking of girls. Only work, work, work. Like his father, no?'

Mattie would shrug her bony shoulders and scorn reply. If goaded to reply she would sniff and say, '*Apoi*, yes. If doing well, like the father. When Barbie painting toenails, you say like the mother. Easy for you to talk.'

She would then sweep away to the kitchen and bang away at the pots and pans. Papa de Mello would twist the tops of his pajamas into a knot, tuck it in and bawl: 'So what for you putting parts, woman. What your temper for? See, can't even put a elastic on my pajamas.' And having got that shot in he would clump out to give the man who was cutting grass for the cows a piece of his mind.

George de Mello was a perfect crow of a man. Hooked nose, sunken cheeks and sly eyes, he was a cold fish. From the firm of Bosanquet and Skrine, general importers, he moved to Delmege Forsythe, shippers, where the pickings were infinitely better. The shipping firm took him in as a tally clerk, and he found the port and shipside job one of vast potential. He scorned bus and train. The old Ebert Silva buses were a nightmare to travel in anyway. The hard wooden seats hurt his back and his long, spindly legs were always in the way. So he had his own rickshaw man to carry him in state to work each day and bowl him back. It was a long trot to the most enthusiastic of rickshaw-wallahs, but George's arrivals and departures in so regal a fashion impressed his fellow-workers no end. Yet, he remained a small, mean man and not above stealing or cadging what he could, given the opportunities galore on board cargo ships and merchant packets.

Thus would he bring home boxes of Cadbury's Roses one day and tins of Black Magic another. He made it a point to cadge a bottle of whisky or Martell's Three Stars from ships captains and swiped what he could from purser's cabins. He found that he could tally cargo consignments so well that there were always a couple of tins of this or packets of that, which belonged to nobody and were naturally, his. His dedication pleased his bosses no end. When he came to see his cousin Eric, he was senior tally master and the port of Colombo sang his praises in fifty different sharps and flats.

'You know,' he told Eric, 'high time I also got married, no?'

Eric nodded like a puppet. He had always admired George. Even when they were children he always bowled and George always batted. Eric never had the courage to ask to bat. Today, however, he felt almost equal to his beady-eyed cousin. He was one step ahead, wasn't he? He was going to marry. George was not.

The thought irked George. 'What do you know about getting married, men? You know what to do?'

Eric's lips trembled. He thought about how warm his hand felt between Elsie's legs. 'Of course I know,' he croaked, 'What you think I don't know? Foo, I know all about that.' Then he elaborated: 'My Elsie also know. And she wants to do even now. But better to wait, no, until the wedding.'

George was not impressed. 'You're a bloody fool, men.'

Eric was used to being called so. He didn't mind. Together they went to Boteju Lane and George was introduced and Leah came in after work and George was all eyes for this florist's assistant. His conversation with Cecilprins was forcefully loud; lots of swagger about the docks and the harbour workers he controlled and the ships captains he knew and how the firm of Delmege Forsyth would surely fold up tomorrow if he walked out on it. All this, naturally, for Leah's benefit, who listened and sighed and brought him a cup of tea and said she had never been to the port or seen a ship close up.

George was in his element. 'I can arrange,' he said, 'You can come on board with me. I have permits for visitors, no? Anything in the port I can do and anywhere I can go. I'll tell when big ship comes and we can go.'

Maudiegirl hauled Leah indoors and propelled her to the back verenda. 'I'll port you. You're mad or what? All coolies there and those ships fellows big cads. Go and wash the grinding stone and clean the fireplace. Listening to all this nonsense. You know what happened to Nellie, no? Went to visit ship and how many fellows got round her. What you girls thinking of, I don't know.'

Cecilprins expelled noisily when George left. Pukka fellow, no?' he told Maudiegirl. 'One to talk. Two hours boasting, boasting. And damn cheek, no? Telling will take Leah to big ship. And in front of me! Not even asking. Just telling. Because he is Eric's relation I keep quiet. Tchah! Feel like chasing both from here. What for he bring that fellow I don't know. He coming to see Elsie, all right. What for he bringing his family people also?'

But the next evening George turned up with a box of chocolates and a Swan fountain-pen for Cecilprins. Eric and Elsie, under the jam fruit tree, were surprised to see him walk in and George just nodded at them and proceeded to soften up Cecilprins and Maudiegirl. 'Just passing. I was going to Mount Lavinia to see a friend. So I was passing your lane and I had this and said those people so nice and take me in their home and give me tea. Here, this is for the ladies. From Switzerland. See, have on the box, Swiss Chocolates. And this is for you. Brand new, in box and all. Only got yesterday in shipment. Very good pen, I think.'

So he was invited to sit and half an hour later Cecilprins said, 'Your friend must be waiting, no?'

'What?'

'In Mount Lavinia. You were going to see, no?'

'Ah yes. But never mind. Can go another day. You have nice jam fruit tree. Must be very old.'

Cecilprins melted visibly. 'When we came here, birds must have dropped seeds from the wall. When it started growing owner said cut it. Said the roots will go under the house and break the floor. Told the bugger to clear off. I pay rent, no? What I grow is not his business. When the children start coming it is so high and see today the size. Now forty years. Whole garden it shading now. Always I telling, that tree like this family. Always flowers, always cherries. Enough for everybody. All the children eating and boys in the lane climbing the wall and eating.'

Nobody then considered the philosophy behind those words. But in truth, the jam fruit tree was so symbolic. The ever-bearing tree. And never-dying, too. Like the stout Burgher women of the age: fruitful, tough, always in bloom, earthy. Like the men too. Hard-working, hard-drinking, as lusty as life itself. Such a tree: always sprouting, reaching out, spreading over the leaf-strewn earth with its umbrella branches. It was the jam fruit tree that first gave the young ones an awareness of each other. Totoboy would climb and Anna would stand below and look up his short trousers and sing out: '*Chee*, I can see.'

'See what?'

'Your birdie. It's hanging like a big worm.'

'You wait till I come down, will you.'

'I'll tell Mama.'

'So go and tell. Good for you to look, no? You also come up and show yours.'

'But I haven't birdie like you.'

'So never mind. You climb, will you.'

And between the branches, hidden in the masses of foliage they explored and wondered at the difference and the wind sang ribald songs and all was right with the world.

George never knew, but it was his chance remark about the jam fruit tree that made him more acceptable. Old Cecilprins thawed enough to even offer him a 'small sip' and was even more gratified when this was politely refused. 'Only on Sunday I take,' George said grandly. 'Put a tot before lunch. Weekdays, when working I don't touch. When having big job with all these ships must be always clear. Those dock workers big rogues. Take your trousers even, if not looking. Some job, this is.'

He came again and again. And he dispensed pilfered ships stores lavishly. Tinned mackerel, a bottle of Booths, spools of Coats thread, whatever he laid his hands on in the port. But all his swagger could not give him the gall to broach the subject of Leah whom he took to seeing at the florist's and giving her little packets of caramel and tins of Schweitzers cocoatina.

It was on the day that he brought a bottle of Tarragona and a twelve-pack of twenty under proof Irish whisky (and only the good Lord knows how he got it out of the port) that the Boteju Lane house became positively merry and Maudiegirl kept complaining of recurring rheumatics. Leah, emboldened, sat next to George and said she was tickled by the way the hair grew out of his ears. With the old Irish to break down fences, even Elsie hustled Eric to the bathroom where she raised her skirts, perched on the edge of the cement sink and told him to put it in. Poor Eric, scared out of his wits, fled, and Elsie sulked, said she had a headache and went to the bedroom to cry a little. Sonnaboy walked in and was annoyed. 'What the hell is all this? Look at Totoboy. Drunk and mouth open. Whole damn house in a mess, no?' But he swallowed a tumbler of neat whisky and went in to wash and change. George was happy. All he now had to do, he thought, was to corner the old man and pop the question. But, poor idiot that he was, he decided on another course of action. Had he cornered Cecilprins that day he would have gained ready consent. But George had to do it his way. He would go home and write a formal letter. That, he thought, would impress the old boy no end.

When the letter arrived two days later, Cecilprins and Maudiegirl went into a huddle. They were feeling pretty low about the revels of the day before yesterday. Dunnyboy said how he saw George squeezing Leah's breasts and Totoboy had slept in his chair all evening and did not go to work the next day. Maudiegirl slapped Leah who shouted: 'Fine thing, no. Take all his presents but bad for him to touch me.'

This plunged them into a new awareness of the situation. 'Tchah, damn shame, no? Damn shame for us,' said Cecilprins. 'Now see, writing, and saying want to marry Leah. He and his port. Can come to make us drunk but can't come to discuss like gentleman. Writing letter. All this Eric's fault. Bringing him here in the first place. I suppose now he waiting for me to reply and say here my Leah, take and go.'

Anna, ever the practical soul said: 'Tell Sonnaboy. Catch and give him good pasting.'

Maudiegirl shuddered. 'You're mad, *anney*. He go to police and tell how he gave us things and damn shame for us, no? Write and tell not to come again. Tell that Leah already promised.'

'Or tell Eric to tell him not to come,' said Elsie.

'And where, pray, is Eric? Two days now he not coming. What you do to him?

Elsie blushed. 'Nothing, *anney*. All your fault. Drinking and drinking. Now he not even coming.'

'So good,' said Cecilprins fiercely. 'Fine son-in-law he be. If put two drinks he running home. If going to be like this better you don't marry.'

'Chut,' said Maudiegirl, 'All your fault, no? Taking his whisky and whole night snoring and smelling like tavern. Tomorrow you tell Eric in office that Elsie very upset. Will come running. And better you write to this George, no? Tell not to come again. Tell will return his whisky. Have some put-away money in the tin on the almirah. Can buy from Cargills and give Eric to give to George. What to do? When have girls always this trouble. From all over coming like as if have bitch in heat.'

So a letter was written and George, ripping open the envelope eagerly couldn't believe what he read. He was furious, and when George was furious he threw caution to the winds. This, he determined, was injustice of the rankest. What wrong had he done? Those girls were just waiting for someone to get under their skirts. Hah! Old fools with their rosaries and starched collars and all high and mighty. I'll postmaster him. Then, with incredible venom, he actually made a list. At the top he wrote, one bottle Tarragona invalids wine and the twelve-pack of Irish. Then, licking his pencil he added the following:

1 packet Jordan almonds
3 tins Schweitzer's cocoatina

2 packets milk paste chocolates
1 tin Yeastman's baking powder
1 box Fry's chocolates
1 tin East India coffee
1 packet Harvest's egg powder
2 boxes Congou tea
3 tins Dorset butter
1 ball Cheshire cheese
2 bottles Mason's beef tea
1 tin Isinglass golden syrup
1 packet pudding powder
1 Swan fountain-pen with filler
1 bottle calf's foot jelly
1 tin Abernethy biscuits
6 tins Paysandu ox tongue
1 tin Julienne soup
1 packet Osborne biscuits
1 bottle Bengal Club pickle
2 cakes Rimmel toilet soap
1 flask Hennessy brandy
1 tin Rowntree's cocoa

He scanned the list and furrowed his brows at it. 'So much I give and not a word to thank,' he gritted, 'useless buggers, I'll show who I am. Think they can take and take and then kick my backside, no.' He went to his cousin Jembo with a martyred air and related how shabbily he had been treated. He produced his list and Cecilprins' letter. Jembo's eyebrows shot skyward. 'Damn fool, no? to give like this. Damn good for you. When I asking for bottle for my birthday, you remember? What did you say? Ah, now you're coming running. But good for you to give these people all these things. Why you go to give all this? Once in a way you give girl some toffees enough, no?'

Jembo was a bull of a man. Built like a wardrobe. Nobody messed with him because he was so big, so nobody knew what an arrant coward he was. Crafty George saw distinct advantage in confronting the von Blosses in Jembo's company. One look at

Jembo and they will take cover. They reached Boteju Lane rather late that evening and while Jembo stood under the jam fruit tree, crossed his arms over his chest and made menacing faces, George paraded the veranda, flourishing the offending letter and brandishing his famous list. 'So what I do!' he thundered. 'All because of Leah, no? Because I loving her I bring you things out of my goodness. All from my hard-earned, no? How you know how I sweat to buy these things I bring to show I am kind person only thinking of you. Not like other people who only give the girl, I give for everybody. And for that I get slap in the face. Nice way to treat people, no? Pudding powder!'

Cecilprins, growing whiter, tried to calm him down. 'We only think you must not get serious on Leah,' he stammered.

'Beef tea!' George yelled.

'We not mean insult, child . . .' Maudiegirl began.

'Egg powder!' George roared.

'You give all back, right,' Jembo growled from the garden.

George was hitting second wind. He tore Cecilprins letter into shreds and flung the bits all over the veranda. 'That's the way I take your insult,' he hooted. Maudiegirl clutched her heart. The van Dort family were perched on the side wall lapping up the show. Then there was a bang at the gate and Sonnaboy strode in. He didn't have to be filled in with past history. Neighbours on the wall, a strange ape in the garden and George in the veranda shouting his head off.

He never did like George. One big hand closed around the back of George's neck in a grip of iron and the noisy little cockerel was hauled off the veranda and down the steps. Something like a sledge struck him, numbing the entire left side of his face. Jembo uncrossed his arms, dropped his lower jaw and only stayed long enough to give a high squeak of alarm. Then he was through the gate and legging it for the Galle Road like a champion sprinter. George, he decided, could take the thrashing for them both. And George did. He was propped against the jam fruit tree and methodically pulped. George did not know it at the time but he was in the hands of a true craftsman. And Sonnaboy excelled in his craft. Then it was time for everyone to jump on his back and cling to him and somehow drag him off before murder was done, but not before he had scooped up the thinly-screaming George and hurled him through the gate where he lay for all the world like a rag doll after an injudicious encounter with a steamroller.

Leah, whose screams were positively operatic in quality and pitch, pushed past everybody to put her head on George's breast and declare that she would kill herself, so there. The neighbours applauded vigorously. This was better than the Bioscope. Sonnaboy strode to the gate. 'Can he walk?'

George moaned.

'Good. You still want to marry my sister?'

'Grooooh.' A lot of Leah's hair seemed to be in his mouth.

'Good. And you try any more nonsense after you marry her and I will come and hammer you every time. Did you hear?'

'Oooooooh.'

Maudiegirl kept gasping as though she had swallowed a lobster. '*Aiyo,* mother of mercy, take him inside, child, put some embrocation. Blood coming also. Where that other fellow? Who that other fellow. Didn't even tell his name, no?'

So George was dragged in with scant ceremony and Leah fomented his face and Maudiegirl brought cottonwool and flavine and George moaned that he couldn't stand erect and Leah said I know, I know, you lie back, will you, have big bruise on your ribs also. 'Where else it paining,' and she made a great show of tending on her poor martyr and seized the chance to take a close look at this man she was going to marry. Cecilprins came in with an enormous pair of green striped pajamas and a banian, 'Here, you change and give your clothes to wash. Trouser knee also torn. Can darn, no?'

So Leah washed and darned and brought him beef tea—his beef tea—and asked him where it hurt. 'There,' he said and she would feel the spot and venture lower down and say, 'Here also?' and he would nod and her hands would slip to his hips and 'Here also?' and soon she was squeezing his cock and exclaiming at its size and that it would do very nicely, thank you.

*

Totoboy first saw Iris Holdenbottle through an alcoholic haze. Nothing to write home about, was Iris. Quite the bawd, but clever with her fingers, needle and thread and sewing-machine. A bossy, loudmouthed fishwife of a woman. A bargiwallah, as the Indians say, and with a temper that kept her in a permanent state of explosion.

This is a poor way to tell a story, to be sure. I have not really laid the groundwork for any of the characters so far woven in, and for this, I beg your pardon. Let me do so now.

Ceylon—the island known today as Sri Lanka—was first invaded by the Portuguese in 1505. After 150 years of Portuguese domination the Dutch moved in for another 150-year spell, after which the British took over around 1815. The Portuguese employed the sword and the Bible to good effect. There was not much difference between missionary zeal and the poniard's steel. Then came the Dutch with their law books and ledgers, their *kokjes* (a preparation of creamed flour, wrapped around a special mould and deep-fried; this is now adopted as a special Sinhala sweetmeat and called 'kokis') and *breudhers* (a dough cake baked in a special ring mould with plums and sultanas and a traditional cake for Christmas breakfast) and fondness for building houses with stoeps, which were open verandas and which the Sinhalese called isstoppuwas. When the business-minded British barged in they gave the country coffee and tea, rubber and coconut, roads and railways, Queen Victoria and how to shake hands and play cricket.

The native Sinhalese were a pretty insular lot. Pretty haughty, stuck in their ways and while putting up with all these foreign comings and goings, stubbornly clung to their way of life and scorned all else. The Portuguese and Dutch took little notice. All they wished was to bleed the island of all it had: spices, salt, elephants and ivory, sandalwood, gems, bamboo and arecanuts. The Portuguese did much the same but in addition, baptized here, there, everywhere. And in the wake of the militia came the settlers—a new race of people who worked their way into the country's canvas; descendente of the Portuguese and Dutch, mixtures of both and then a goodly range of hybrids. It was like

26

what was mentioned in the Book of Genesis, how the sons of Heaven came down and found the daughters of the Earth fair. May this same Heaven forbid—for the sons of the Dutch found Sinhalese and Tamil girls to their liking and the British, who ramrodded the plantations went in among the natives too. The result was a hotch-potch that was, for convenience, classified as Burgher (from the Dutch 'burgher' or townsman). The brew was further spiced by other foreign types who drifted in and out with each East Indiaman that sailed in—French, Germans, Persians, Indians, Afghans (who became very serious-minded money lenders) and Scandinavians. A few Chinese were also added into the pot. They settled down, went around on rickety bicycles shouting, 'Nooooo-dles,' and otherwise taking pretty Malay girls to bed in Slave Island where they lived with Dutch artisans, clerks and craftsmen.

Indeed, the first Dutch civilian workers who chose to try their luck in this new outpost were those who came to provide ancillary services to the stockaded forts. The main fort in Colombo (still called The Fort) was served by the assorted denizens of Slave Island, and the most sought after of them was the cobbler. As long as the army marched, the cobbler was in business. Which is why, to this day, the Sinhalese will derisively refer to a Burgher as a shoemaker—deemed a deadly insult—and worse still, a cockroach, which is deadlier still although, for the life of me, I cannot determine why the name was given.

The Burghers found immense favour with the British because their mother tongue was English, although they thought Dutch and spoke English which did nothing to phraseology or syntax. Yet, they were regarded as those of 'European descent', posed no communication problems and were a far cry over the Sinhalese who were of ill-disposition, morose, apt to fawn and bootlick and then do a Brutus. So it was that while the true people of Ceylon, the Sinhalese, were the subject race, the hewers of wood and drawers of water, the vast contingent of Burghers, all nondescript, no-roots, fair-skinned hybrids, became the white-collar workers, the police inspectors, the fire chiefs, foremen, storekeepers, managers, executives, assistant superintendents on estates, administrators, and formed an upper stratum in the social hierarchy. Did I say fair-skinned? Scratch that. There were white Burghers and brown Burghers, black and grey Burghers. It all depended on where the wild oats had been sown. But the names clung on, even if a Van der Wert or a Van der Houten had blue eyes in a very dark face.

It's hard to find a 'true' Burgher today. The type this story deals with are very much the real McCoy. They hailed from Mutwal and Modera, Chilaw and Negombo, Galle and Batticaloa. But they were as adaptable and as hardy as the cockroach (maybe that's what earned them the derisive) and they believed in living life to the full. Old sayings are still heard around the country. One insists that 'Burgher buggers became beggars by buying brandy bottles' while a Sinhalese doggeral goes:

> *Kaapalla, beepalla, jollikarapalla,*
> *Heta marunoth hithata sapai*
> *Ada jollikaralla*

Which, in homespun Sinhala means: 'Eat, drink and be merry and even if we must die tomorrow, don't let it worry you because you're having a good time today.' (Who said Shakespeare had no Sinhalese blood in him?)

And the names: A glorious mixture of Portuguese, Dutch, British, French, German and God knows what else. The Schumachers will stoutly uphold that there never was a shoemaker in the family tree. The Van der Pootens don't know if this was originally a dirty word. There are the Almeidas and the Bartholomeuszes and the De Vallieres; the Grays and the Ingletons, the MacHeyzers and De Witts and Barbetts and Wittenslegers. The von Haghts claim a teaspoon or two of German blood, the Brohiers are proud of their Dutch uncles, the Dabares are not sure of anything. The Van der Walls don't like to hob-nob with the Van der Putts who are always reminded of the day some ancestor was hauled into courts before a British judge who asked for his name.

'Van der Putt, my lord,' he said.

'Eh? Van der who?' The judge had this hearing trouble.

'Putt, my lord.'

'Eh? What's that?'

'Putt, my lord,' the man bawled.

Frowning, the judge told the clerk of the court to advise the accused to keep a civil tongue in his head and that he, the judge, need not be told when to or when not to put, he, the judge, being perfectly capable of making such decisions himself.

My readers will still meet the Burghers in Sri Lanka. They are the Herfts and the Meerwalds and the Gingers and the De Kauwes; the Arnoldas and the Martenstyns, the Van Cuylenbergs and Van Langenbergs, the Breckenridges and Barsenbachs and Rulachs; the Edemas and the Direckszes, the De Zylvas and De la Zilwas, the Missos and the Modders, the Heyns and the Toussaints. Such a ding-a-dong, ring-a-bell roundelay. Every blood infusion and transfusion made them stronger, more virile. They are not as fussy today as they were at the turn of the century. Cecilprins' father would have fed him rat poison if he sought to marry a Sinhalese or a Tamil. The intermixing today has become something quite fierce and a whole generation of Nathanielszes with Aryan eyes and Dravid lips bear witness to the undoubtedly Sri Lanka connection. And, my friends, I ought to know, for I am part of this polyglot Burgher clan myself!

Well, having got all that off my chest, let me now return you to Totoboy who saw Iris Holdenbottle at old Vere's daughter's birthday party and considered her the girl of his dreams despite the tipsy state he was in. Totoboy was popular. He had this knack of sitting at a keyboard, sighting carefully and then breaking into a risque song while syncopating furiously. What is more, the piano miraculously matched the song and young ladies were quite taken up by his performances. All over Dehiwela, no party was ever thrown without Totoboy being pressed to attend, and which he gladly did since he believed that liquor was best consumed when it belonged to someone else.

Iris Holdenbottle was dark-skinned. Nobody wished to tangle with her. Old De Niese had once poked a finger between her ribs and said: 'Where's that servant woman your father used to go with?' And she grabbed the pair of scissors from her sewing-table and chased the man for about half a mile. She was no great looker either. High cheek bones, a big lower lip permanently set against the upper, and eyes that froze the marrow. But she had a figure that could stop a regiment in column of route. Totoboy leered and leered and weaved up to her. 'Want a small drink?'

Iris was touched. What she wanted she usually took. No one offered. The lower lip unlocked a fraction. 'Get a arrack. Horsepiss, this whisky.'

Totoboy gaped. The local arrack was never served. Too lowly. Matured from the toddy of the coconut flower, it was only secured, and surreptitiously at that, for the servants at Christmas and to give the latrine coolie a snort when he came to the gate on New Year's Day to salaam and ask for baksheesh.

Latrine coolie, you ask? Well, yes. In those days many homes had no drainage, sewerage or water service. Not even the best of them. So the lavatories had squatting plates and buckets—and each day around ten a.m. the coolies (also called bucket men) would come around with their carts (universally known as shitcarts for want of a simpler name) and carry away the nightsoil. Their visits would scent the air, true, but were they not vital in their service to the community? Totoboy did not think so. One day he had borrowed Sonnaboy's bicycle, gone carousing, and when wobbling back the following morning, collided with a bucket man. Violently separated from his bicycle, he found himself astride the shitcart, which sobered him up in a trice.

'Bucket man's drink,' he muttered, as he went to find his host, Socks Joachim.

'I say, Socks, you have any arrack, men?'

'My God, why? Who asking. Some bloody street-fellow? Where? I'll kick the bugger out.'

'No, no. Nobody came. Just tell, will you, if have.'

'Must see, men. Last time brought bottle for firewood man. Will look and see.'

'If have bring a glass, will you.'

'Here, hold these patties. I'll see.'

The arrack being there, Totoboy took a stiff one to Iris who actually smiled. 'You good fellow,' she conceded, tipping ginger ale into the arrack. 'Not like other pariahs here.'

Bunny Mottau took umbrage. 'Pariah?' he roared, 'Who the pariah you're saying? That's the trouble asking black bitches to come. Don't now how to talk.' Iris hit Bunny on the head with the bottle of ginger ale and the party immediately took on a new dimension.

One is inclined to draw a veil over the events that immediately followed. The general pandemonium was made of several mini-events, each contributing to the overall chaos. Bunny Mottau lay bleeding on the floor as if in the eye of a cyclone that raged around and in which Totoboy tried to drag Iris away, and Babyboy Nathanielsz punched Miko Sampson in the throat and Pippie Nellie threw glasses at the fishtank. Soon everybody was hitting everybody else and ladies raised their skirts and fled shrieking, some to the road, others to bedrooms and the rear garden, where Dolly Loos tried to climb a fence, got snagged on the barbed wire, and bayed at the moon. Iris, surprisingly, went meekly. Totoboy had her out and on the Galle Road quickly enough, which was most creditable considering the state he was in. Inside there was confusion of breaking chairs and the sound of unpleasant thuds and screeches and someone saying 'graaaah' as though he was being garrotted. Socks Joachim wanted no part of it. He crept underneath the dining-table and waited out the storm. 'This what happens when give arrack,' he told himself dolefully.

'Pukka party, no?' said Totoboy, 'Where are you living?'

Iris smiled. 'You can come with me. Not far.'

'Pukka girl you are,' said Totoboy. 'Oh the head you hit. Stitches for sure.'

Iris whooped and swayed. 'Getting giddy. Must be breeze, no?'

'That's the way,' Totoboy said wisely, 'Here, I'll hold you. What way?'

Iris pointed uncertainly. Totoboy put an arm round her waist. Anchored together they found the going better. True, they did a couple of half circles and found themselves walking in the opposite direction but it added to the fun of clinging on to each other. 'Nice girl you are,' said Totoboy, 'You like to be my girl?'

Iris sneezed and said she would. And Totoboy grinned and saluted a pillarbox and never imagined at the time the mess he was going to make of his life.

*

Anna, who was quite taken up with her Sinhalese gentleman and his trouser clips found the affair progressing to the point when the said Sinhalese gentleman had declared that he saw no reason why they should not get married. 'You go to your church and I will go to temple, and you hang your holy pictures in the house, never mind.'

'You're mad, *anney*. Papa will kill for sure. You can become Catholic, no?'

The Sinhalese gentleman, who rejoiced in the name of Dionysius Richard Colontota frowned. 'I thought of that,' he said, 'but then my people kill me.'

'So what to do, *anney*. These days in our lane, top market man's son also coming behind and saying he love me. Sending me *aluwa* (halwa) and *konde kavun* (a small knobbed honey cake) also and Mama went and had big row. She said to boy, "If you don't stop will break your legs." You think Mama keep quiet if I tell about you? Will come and break your legs for sure. And my brother. You don't know that Sonnaboy. Only wanting to hammer somebody.'

Dionysius Richard Colontota set his jaw. 'Ho! you think I am afraid. If coming to hit you, think I keep quiet? I say hit to see, and if hit I also hit.'

Anna chewed her lip. She did not want to dampen the man's enthusiasm. The trouble was that if Sonnaboy hit first this poor fish would be in no condition to hit back. Rather, he would be in dire need of a stretcher and an ambulance. This romance was fraught. The complications could sweat pounds off her, and Anna, quite the dimwit at the best of times, was still wise enough to see the future as somewhat bleak.

'Have idea,' she said, 'You go to GPO and see Papa. Good, no?'

Colontota squeezed her hand gratefully. Anna surprised him at times. Just when he was certain that her physical charms amply made up for a singular lack of brains, she would come up with a nugget, thus raising her several notches in his esteem. And Colontota would do better than that. He would write and beg an appointment . . . or type. The office Remington would do nicely. And why not the office stationery too? So he snaffled a letterhead and pecked away industriously and Cecilprins was startled at the missive which read:

Honoured Sir,

Please be good enough to give the undersigned a little of your valuable time in order that the undersigned could discuss with your goodself a matter of importance. The undersigned awaits the favour of your reply and remains, honoured sir,

Your faithful servant,
D. R. Colontota
Department of Accounting—Radio Ceylon

Cecilprins waved the letter at Maudiegirl. 'See, will you, some big shot, must be. Sinhalese name, but must be England educated, no. How he writing undersigned, undersigned, undersigned and your faithful servant. Polite is not the word. So what he want, don't know. Matter of importance, it seems.'

'So tell him to come, *anney*. Without knowing what how to tell?'

'Must show I am busy, no? Even he must know. That's why saying valuable time. Wait, woman, must think and write carefully. Tchah, damn shame haven't typing thing. He typing and I handwriting.'

'So ask Totoboy to type in his office and bring, will you.'

'That bugger? Don't know what he got in his brain these days. Won't come after work even. Where going I don't know.'

Cecilprins excelled himself:

May it please your honour,

Your letter to hand is duly noted. The undersigned will be pleased to give you a little time on Monday, August 12, if your honour will make his presence at 10 a.m. at the General Post Office, Colombo. The undersigned will receive you at the main counter. I am your honour's servant,

C. von Bloss
Assistant Post Master
Department of Posts and Telegraphs

Anna learned about it and sniffed. 'What is all this my honour your honour business. And undersigned and all. Fine pair you are to write. So go on Monday then.'

Colontota nodded. 'Must put tie,' he said.

So Dionysius Richard Colontota called at the GPO and Cecilprins was suitably impressed. Mauve tie, white shirt and brown trousers made Colontota like something in a medical exhibition. Like the cross-section of some virus, perhaps, but Cecilprins thought it natty.

'Mister von Bloss, sir?'

'Mister Colontota? Sit, men, sit. So you got my letter, no?'

'Yes, Yes. Thank you, thank you.' He sat and had this urge to scratch his nose.

'You said important thing. Must be, no? Otherwise why you writing anyway. And coming also.'

'It is about Anna.'

'Anna? Anna who?'

This becalmed Colontota. 'Anna who,' he said.

'That's what I'm saying, men. When you say Anna how I know who?'

Colontota began to sweat. This lack of brains seemed to run in the family. 'Your daughter, sir. Working in the Dehiwela pharmacy. I know her.'

Cecilprins sat upright. 'You mean our Anna? How you know her? You are Dehiwela person?'

'No. I stay in Wellawatte.'

'Ah, close by, no? Whereabout?'

'High Street bottom.'

'Nice area. My friend Gauders living there. You know the Gauders? Big girl ran away with the dhoby man.'

Colontota shook his head.

'My gosh, everyone know them. And the de Kretsers. Twelve boys in that family.'

Colontota gave in and rubbed his nose. 'About Anna,' he said faintly.

'Anna? Ah, you mean our Anna. So you know her, eh? What's the trouble? She give you wrong medicine or something? Always telling her be careful when working there. If give wrong medicine can die also, no?'

'I am friend with Anna. Now about one year.'

This stopped Cecilprins cold. 'How you mean one year,' he asked eventually, 'She only working one year. She not saying anything like this.'

'Only friend,' said Colontota hastily, 'but she very nice girl and I think if Anna so nice her father and mother must be very nice people also. Such a nice girl she is. So polite and look after customers and saying thank you, come again, can I help you and always neat . . . .'

'You mean our Anna?' Cecilprins was certain the man was making a ghastly mistake. 'Some other Anna you're meaning, surely.'

'No, no, Anna von Bloss. Your daughter and I am mad for her.' (There, that's got it out at last).

'You're what?'

'I want to marry her. I am important man in radio station. Good post. Accounts section. Have property. Have another small house in Battaramulla also. You come anytime you feel like it and see my house.'

Cecilprins stared. 'You are—you are Sinhalese,' he croaked.

'But I am like you people. Educated good and Cambridge Senior also. Not like other yakko fellows who are waiters in GOH and peons in Kachcheri. My parents have paddy fields in Gampaha, and coconut and jak and buffaloes also.'

'Buffaloes,' said Cecilprins weakly.

'Six-seven buffaloes.'

'But my daughter cannot marry a Sinhalese. We are Burgher people, no? How to face if I gave our Anna to a Sinhalese? Funny thing, no? Walking in sarong all over house and putting wooden clogs and going to temple . . . my God, going to temple! You are Buddhist, no?'

'Yes, that not problem. I let Anna go to church and everything. Even Anna say that is all right.'

'Who? Anna?'

Colontota was sure this conversation was doing a sort of loop-the-loop. Just when he felt he was getting somewhere it spiralled back to Anna who or who Anna. He had a long ride back to Torrington Square and the midday sun, considered favourably by mad dogs and Englishmen was not his idea of fun. 'So what do you say,' he asked, trying to bring matters to a head.

Cecilprins stared. 'What I say? What to say? One year you see our Anna and not a word from her. Wait till I catch her. And fixing up everything behind my back, no? You go temple, she go church. You put sarong and go tok, tok with clogs on legs and she put housecoat and cooking country rice and dry fish for you and when you take to paddy field won't know what those buffaloes will do—'

'But . . . .'

'But, but. But what? What but, men? Have Sinhalese girls, no? They know how to drive buffaloes, no? and pound rice and wear cloth up to here and bathe and go to temple with you. What you want our Anna for? Just wasting my time, no?'

'But I love her,' Colontota bawled. 'How you can stop us? She almost thirty, no? I will see her anyway.'

The Burgher blood went on the boil. 'You try, will you and see what will happen. Break your bloody legs. Coming here and threatening, ah? Because I decent enough to spare my valuable time. This is government office. I send report to your office and then see how you catch it.' He jumped up and Colontota shot up in alarm and scooted. Never knew with the old bugger. Might send a report. Leaping on his bicycle he pedalled off madly.

While all these dramatic events swirled around it was scarcely noticed that Maudiegirl kept preparing and applying all manner of home-made remedies to various parts of her body and kept wheezing and clumping around the house like an oversized policeman in dire distress. Home had become a sort of assizes with fevered discussions, consultations, arguments and crosstalk on Totoboy's latest and totally obnoxious choice of soulmate; on Sonnaboy's determination to marry a schoolgirl and the wild threats of Elaine and her gargantuan brothers; on George and Leah who were hell-bent on getting married next month, next week, next day if possible; on Anna's 'Nonsense, damn nonsense, no?' and on Elsie's venturesome habit of sneaking off to Eric's home and coming back humming 'Bluebells of Scotland' in E minor. Viva, too, seemed to have something on his mind. At first, nobody gave him much thought. He would come home with a packet of postcards and religiously post one each day after cramming the back of it with a script so small and fine that it looked like something those fellows do who engrave the old Testament on the head of a pin. Nobody wanted to even look at these curious missives. 'When I just look I get a headache,' Totoboy declared. Viva was a mingy man. He always had this miserly streak in him . . . and he was in love. In his peregrinations as a purveyor of milkfoods he had met an acid-mouthed, buxom female with a screwed-up nose, and a permanent film of sweat on her upper lip. A slatternly girl who was the daughter of a strange man who claimed to be a Pentecostalist, and stood at street corners and threatened passers-by with his Bible. He could have named his daughter Bathsheba or Naomi or even Eve, but his wife, who took one look at what she had brought forth and expired, (or so he said) had gone to Abraham's bosom in the month of October. The baby was named after the birthstone of that month, the opal, but papa Ludwick changed it to Opel, doubtless influenced by the new Reckard cabriolet newly in the market.

Opel grew up to be the worst of that funny mixture that is the result of grandpa running off with the Sinhalese bicycle-repair man's daughter—a Sinhalese—and son Patti Ludwick bedding Missie Moraes who had umpteen pints of Indian blood in her. Opel Ludwick was a swarthy, fierce-tempered 'Burgher' of completely convoluted ancestry. She also had hips one could put a saddle on. It was the hips that sealed Viva's fate. She would walk due north but those hips would swing east-west with minds of their own, making her buttocks bounce provocatively. Opel, too, liked the idea of being courted by a fellow who rode around in a van, hob-nobbing with merchants and shopkeepers and being very industrious. Papa Ludwick was gratified. This was better than that fellow Holmus. Pukka bugger that Holmus. Spelling his name Holmus and saying he is Hollums. When it was beyond all possible doubt that Viva was hooked, he told his neighbour: 'Lucky to get boy like this for Opel, no?'

The neighbour, Pantis Perera said that his son Kukku would marry Opel any day,'and we next door and all.'

Papa Ludwick smiled. 'But this good Burgher fellow, no? After all, we also Burghers,' and Pantis spat betel juice and scowled.

'See how now getting big for the boots,' Pantis told his wife, 'saying they are Burgher. Only name. *Thuppahi* (half caste) Burgher. Never mind. Can find Kukku good girl. Better than that half-caste next-door one.'

As has been recorded, Viva was a miserly fellow. While enraptured with Opel's pelvic perambulations, he wasn't going to put his pocket in jeopardy. He embarked on a strange and perhaps the cheapest form of courtship ever: the humble postcard. Each morning he would write the damndest things he could think of on a postcard and send it to Opel. It never occurred to him that Opel might need a microscope to read his tiny script. At first Opel was, in her own words, 'stuntified'. What the hell was it, anyway? Papa Ludwick squinted and ventured that it must be a 'tax department thing' but grew easier when he read 'my dearest Opel' and the 'Vivi' in a miniscule flourish at the bottom, 'Vivi? Who the hell is Vivi?'

'Must be that Viva, no? Mad, *anney*, to write like this. Have to hold it far otherwise get squint.'

'What is he saying?'

'Apoi, how to tell when can't even read. Like in sardine tin, no?'

Papa snorted. 'Sardine tin? Sardines better off. Like lice on your head. Give to see.'

Opel tried one eye, then the other, then both, screwing them up until they were fair competition to her nose. 'All nonsense, *anney.* Saying he love me and can kiss even my toes and getting something up his something when near to me and then something stamps . . . no, stars and . . . and *aiyo,* I don't know, putting big words . . . motions? No—'

'Motions? Why, he having bad stomach or what? Let see, child; here, hold to the light . . .'

'Ah,' said Opel, 'emotions. What is that?'

Papa shrugged. 'So what he wants, anyway?'

'Nothing. Simply writing. Stars, moons, he adore me . . . want to worship me. Saying I am angel and how he cannot sleep and wants to kiss me everywhere . . . .'

'Chee, what he thinking? Nowadays fellows no shame. If come today you behave yourself, you hear? And wash your toes. Walking all over without slippers even. Boys thinking funny things these days. Kissing toes. I didn't know your mother had toes until I married her.'

Viva would roll up at six, beaming, the love-light like 100-watt bulbs in each eye. 'You got my postcard?'

'Yes,' Opel simpered.

'My morning gift to you. What better thing I can give, you tell me. Putting my heart on postcard. Every day I send you one. You can collect and keep.'

'But so small your writing, Viva.'

'What to do? All my love I sending, no? You think I just write dearest Opel, I love you, Viva, and that is enough? Wasting whole postcard, no? Now see, I post one today also. Will get tomorrow. And I post 'nother one tomorrow. So everyday postman come with my love. How's that?'

Opel simpered again. This man was devastating. 'If like can kiss my toes,' she murmured, 'Washed nicely and put powder also.'

That night Papa Ludwick gave Viva a fistful of tracts and a beat-up Bible. 'You take home and read,' he said, 'You put everything in the hands of the Lord and he give you strength to smite everybody. See that David in Chronicles. He got the strength of the Lord. So he goes knocking about the country smiting everybody. Wait, I show you . . . here, Chronicles 18—see, David smite the Philistines, the Maobites, the king of Zobah. Then the Syrians come to fight. He smite them also.'

Viva listened patiently. He didn't see the point in going around smiting everyone. That was Sonnaboy's department. But he took the tracts and the Bible home and, if the family history can be credited, sealed his poor mother's fate.

As earlier recorded, Maudiegirl had taken to medicating herself. Anna had, over the past two weeks been told to bring all manner of things from the pharmacy. Maudiegirl would mix compound camphor liniment with soap liniment and rub the mixture on her chest and then rub a flannel, thick with the stuff, around her neck. 'Touch of the quinsy,' she would croak and lower herself into the lounger groaning 'Uppaday' and digging out her rosary. At other times she would heat up camphorated oil and keep massaging it into the base of her neck. What is more, she had the bed moved from its position between the doorway and the window.

'What for you moving the bed, woman?' Cecilprins would want to know.

'Getting draught. Air coming from doorway. Some more coming from window. Bad, no?'

And when Cecilprins found Maudiegirl sprinkling chloride of lime on the bedroom floor he grew concerned. 'Something wrong with you, no? Better if I get doctor.'

'Just don't waste money,' Maudiegirl would moan. 'What can doctor do? Just come and look and go and tell to rest. Who doctor for everybody in this house all these years? I, no?'

Cecilprins had to admit that this was no boast. Through the years, from whooping cough to worms and measles and all the ills a family is heir to, it was Maudiegirl who had worked her miracles of healing. Her poultices were the talk of Dehiwela. Her liniments (mustard flour and spirits of turpentine) should have been patented. Nobody got colds. Maudiegirl's cold cure was positively awesome. Besides making the sufferer swallow thirty drops of camphorated sal volatile in a cup of warm water every hour on the hour, she would mix camphorated spirit in boiling water, then wring a sponge into it and apply the steaming sponge to the nose and mouth. 'Breathe in deep,' she would growl as the sponge was thrust under the nostrils. Then to the mouth! 'Swallow the steam!' To make sure none of the healing steam escaped she would also drape a large flannel over the patient's head. Operation over, she would then apply the sponge to throat and chest. Colds? Nobody dared get a cold in the von Bloss household.

Cuts were treated with Friar's balsam or diluted tincture of arnica. Burns were rubbed over with soft soap, then coated with olive oil and flour. Wounds were treated with sanitas and water or carbolic acid and water or Condy's fluid and water. Small cuts got a dusting of dried alum powder. Dill water did the trick for heartburn or flatulence, and whenever Anna over-ate, which was often.

Around the home, too, Maudiegirl had the formula, the recipe, the answer for almost everything. She would take the yolk of an egg, a spoon of treacle, a little isinglass, half a tumbler of water and a big lump of lampblack and stir the whole into a gooey mess that would become a waxen cake in time. And it was the finest shoe polish. Even when shoes became so scuffed that an archaeological restoration was indicated, she had the answer. Black ink and the white of an egg. She would go over the shoes with a soft sponge dipped in this mixture and they were as good as new.

Leah would bring flowers home from the florist's and put them in assorted vases around the house. They lasted longer, Leah said, than if at the florist's. Maudiegirl would simply drop a lump of charcoal or a small piece of camphor into the water. Sometimes Leah would carry home a sorry-looking bunch of cut flowers.

'From whose grave you took,' Viva would cackle and Maudiegirl would bustle up and take the wilted, woebegone specimens and say: 'Never mind, child, you go and boil some water, will you.' She would plunge the stems into the boiling water and by the time the water cooled each flower had perked up considerably. They no longer draggled. They stood at attention. Maudiegirl would then snip the ends off each stem and put the flowers in fresh, cold water and they were ready to bloom for another two days.

Yes, Maudiegirl, like all good Burgher women of the 1930s was a wonder when it came to anything and everything in and around the home. She made her own linseed oil, turpentine, vinegar and spirits of wine. Shaking the mixture well, she would apply it on the furniture with a linen rag and then polish with a duster. She had her special rust and stain removers and special concoctions for cleaning wood, brass, metal; she made starch and a gum that was hyper-effective in mending broken glass and china. She was the only one around who made her own linen bleach and no one could clean a mirror the way she did. She would damp a sponge with spirits of wine, clean, and when dry, dust the mirror liberally with whiting. One of the boys would be pressed to scour the mirror with a soft cloth. This done, Maudiegirl would go to her kitchen cupboard for a bottle of blotchy powder. This was the snuff from the wicks of burnt candles, carefully collected. 'Only top of wick snuff,' she would say explaining that at the bottom of the wick where the candle melts around, the snuff is greasy. The particles are patiently scraped into a fold of paper and tipped into the bottle. Then, when the whiting has been well worked out of the mirror and the surface has already begun to glow, the candle snuff is carefully dusted over. A silk handkerchief is then produced for the final polish, and the result was truly spectacular.

She was the only woman who could wash silk . . . and this, mind you, was an art much sought after in an age when every woman had a goodly store of silk gowns. And she hugged that secret to the end. Only when she lay dying did she ask that her girls wear their black silk dresses to the cemetery. 'And don't forget,' she whispered, 'After filling the washtub, put pint of gin in the water and then wash. After washing, keep dry in the shade, not in sun, and iron from inside, not outside.' So that was how she did it!

Poor Maudiegirl knew she was very ill. And everybody was all mixed up in their affairs and Cecilprins was apparently mixed up in all of them too. 'If can see one girl even married,' she said, and Anna, being the eldest, found the spotlight turned on her.

'I die and go and cannot see even one married,' Maudiegirl would grumble and Cecilprins would make the old rattan chair creak and say: 'What's this silliness you're saying. If anything wrong with you can bring doctor, no?' But he knew. Deep inside. Over fifty years of married life and all it stood for was not lost on this man. 'Anna doing the dance with Sinhalese fellow. So what to do? You want Sinhalese son-in-law, I suppose.

Maudiegirl glared and let loose one of those rare shafts of wisdom that was based, even if she did not know it, on pure logic. 'So never mind. You thinking we are special or something? Good to go to top market buying *bombili* (the dried 'Bombay duck'—a thin ell-like fish that is found in abundance in Indian waters) from Sinhalese man. Good to get children's bicycle made by Sinhalese man. Good to eat rice and curry and *stringhoppers* (steamed circlets of flour—a favourite breakfast dish in Sri Lanka) like Sinhalese man. When want to cut tree in the backside you call Sinhalese man, no? Firewood bringing Sinhalese man. Plucking coconuts who? Dhoby who? All over people Sinhalese, no? Father telling in church love the neighbour. See, will you, who neighbour is. Sinhalese, no? Never mind if Anna wants to marry that Colon somebody. Can write, can typewrite, even. And in the radio, no? How he do such good job if he not good man? That day you telling how you chase him from office. How if you can go to his office and he chase you? He put switch and then everybody hear on radio. Now Anna old also. And all the other girls also getting old. You want to put them in convents? And when I die who will look after Dunnyboy? He mad a little, no? If children marry can even give small room to Dunnyboy to stay also. What you're thinking, I don't know.'

Cecilprins heard her out and grew terribly afraid. And Anna's happiness became the need of the hour.

'That bicycle clip fellow still coming to see you?'

Anna was not going to admit to anything. Colontota turned up as usual but he wasn't the same man. Jittery, she thought. Didn't even hold her hand. He would keep looking over his shoulder and wanted assurance that no other member of the von Bloss family was within a quarter-mile radius. But he kept coming, and as Anna correctly estimated, 'If coming then he still love me.' Which was correct, but she was not going to trust the home folk any further.

'Nobody coming to see me and I'm not going to see anybody and if anybody come anyway that's not anybody here's business.'

Eventually it was impressed on the angry woman that Bicycle Clips was not out of favour. 'Nobody saying anything against, no?' said Totoboy, 'That day Papa say he got angry because he seeing you so long and even you not saying anything. Going on behind the back, no? From the start should have told. But that's never mind now. Papa is all right. Ask and see if you like. You tell that fellow to come here and see how Papa will say hullo and give chair to sit.'

Anna was doubtful. 'Easy to say. Saw what happened to George? When Mister Colontota come that Sonnaboy will hammer for sure.'

Sonnaboy came up wearing a towel. 'Hammer whom?'

Totoboy hastened to explain.

Sonnaboy grinned. 'You tell to come. And tell to marry you. If all you buggers hurry up and get married I can also marry, no?'

So, after an hour's cajoling, twenty-three minutes coaxing and fourteen minutes of earnest assurances that nothing would happen to him that would merit plastic surgery, Colontota entered the von Bloss home.

He was, as Leah noted, 'dressed to kill' and the entire family awaited him while 'our Anna' wore her Blessed Virgin blue dress with the French lace edging and Cecilprins polished his spectacles for the umpteenth time and Elsie sulked because Eric had been told to stay away because of 'important family business and not for him to come and listen'.

Maudiegirl, reclining on the lounger had insisted that the large Victorian print titled 'Two Strings to her Beau' which hung in the living-room be replaced with a picture of our Lady of Perpetual Succour. A picture of St. Cecilia playing the organ was brought from the bedroom to a spot near the altar. A calendar advertising Brand's Gravy and Giblet Soup was sent on temporary transfer to the kitchen and a shocking picture of Saint Lawrence being roasted on a gridiron by a bunch of unshaven Roman soldiers was installed.

'Must show we are good Catholic family,' Maudiegirl said, 'And you remember to tell about Anna going church and all. Sunday, First Friday, Feast Days, everything,' she warned Cecilprins, 'Put the foot down. All well and good getting married but if she going Godless afterwards I will curse from my grave, wait and see.'

Everything went swimmingly for the first one hundred and seventy-six seconds. This was the period of 'hullo, hullo' and 'How, men?' and 'No harm if you call me Colon but Anna always says Mister Colon,' and Cecilprins saying, 'That's because my girls always brought up to show respect.'

Sonnaboy sized up the visitor and there was something about the fellow he didn't like. He decided that this particular bull needed to be taken by the horns, firmly. 'Never mind all that,' he said, 'Are you going to marry Anna or not?'

That's when Colontota made his big mistake. It flashed upon him that the family now wanted him to marry Anna. So he was at an advantage, eh? Good. Now he can make the old man squirm . . . .

'That day your father is very rude to me and saying he will break my legs and all. And after I do the right thing. Went to see him to tell. And he telling me to find Sinhalese girl and throwing my parents' buffaloes in my face. If I marry . . . .'

'What do you mean if? Why you came, then, came to if and but? You want to marry Anna or not?'

'But—'

Sonnaboy rose. 'Again you're saying but. Asking simple question, no? Tell, will you, like a man.'

Colontota paled. 'What I mean is how quick to threaten me as if I doing something wrong. I do nothing bad. Now I think your father sorry he talk to me like that.'

'So why you come today, then? Asking for the last time if you going to marry Anna.'

'But have lot of things to sort out,' Colontota objected, 'That's why I came.'

'Can do all that afterwards. First must know if you want to marry Anna, no?'

'If your father—'

Sonnaboy's right hand shot out, a fist closed over the front of his shirt and tie and Colontota was hauled out of his chair squeaking in alarm. 'Wasting our bloody time. From time you come only iffing and butting. You think you can play games here!' Colontota was shaken violently and he kicked out in desperation. Thud! The blow seemed to send the top of his head into his shoulders. Anna's screams split the welkin as she leapt upon Sonnaboy's back. Totoboy tried to intervene, received a whallop on the side of his face and lost interest in the rest of the evening. Colontota was hauled around the veranda and lambaced at half second intervals and the stream of Sinhala invective was effectively dammed by a punch that split his upper lip and dislodged a tooth. Finally, when it was deemed that the neighbours had been sufficiently entertained and that Colontota would survive although any possibility of kissing Anna would have to be shelved for a fortnight, the man was dragged in, laid on the divan in the hall and fomented with a hot towel and dosed with brandy, which added to his misery since that was the first and only time in his life that an intoxicant had been poured down his throat. He kicked out feebly, then flopped back to lie as stiff as a board.

'He's dead,' Anna howled, 'I knowed it, I knowed it. Everybody promise and I tell to come and now you kill him. I'll jump in the well. Let go! I going to jump!'

'So jump,' Sonnaboy snarled.

'Hooooo! Now want to kill me also.'

Dunnyboy wanted to know what was the four-letter word for what a diva sang in an opera. He was not interested in the proceedings. Lately he had decided that fame and fortune lay in winning the enticing cash prizes offered for all-corrects in the Sunday newspaper crossword puzzles. He would hunch over the puzzles for days, filling words that had to be from some Martian dialect and energetically scratching his testicles for inspiration.

Old van Dort put a head over the wall. 'Oi, Sonnaboy, who that fellow you clouting?'

'Damn bugger, saying he won't marry Anna.'

'Never said that,' Anna screeched, 'I jumping in well now.'

'If you don't shut up I'll put you in the bloody well.'

'Hooooooo!'

Van Dort liked to get things straight. 'But that other fellow you clouting last month . . . .'

'Who? Ah, that George? Saying he will marry Leah.'

Van Dort frowned and bobbed out of sight. 'Bella,' he told his wife, 'funny business going on. If say will marry get a hammering.

If say won't marry get a hammering also.'

'You keep quiet,' Bella advised, 'Let hammer anybody. Not your business, no?'

'Real one that Sonnaboy. Now want to put Anna in the well.'

Bella considered this for a moment. 'Not so easy, I think. She too big for well. Will get stuck halfway.'

Elsie told Anna, 'Good thing told Eric not to come. If saw this he put the bolt and won't come back.'

'Hoooooo! Hoooooooo!'

Cecilprins said: 'One more hoo from you and I give you hoo. See to that fellow and tell to stay and eat dinner,' he looked at Colontota, 'If he can, that is.'

Colontota couldn't, of course, but he stayed; and employing the golden rule that discretion is the better part of getting ground to powder and being ignobly buried under the jam fruit tree, made a painful declaration of marriage and agreed before the picture of the Sacred Heart to give Anna licence to pray and follow her road to the many palaces of the Father's kingdom and have an altar at home and say the family rosary and that even if they were to have a 'registry wedding', he will go with Anna to the church to get Father Romiel's blessing. Furthermore all the children must be baptized and be Catholics and have godfathers and godmothers and Sonnaboy said he would be godfather for the firstborn and everybody drank to that and did justice to Maudiegirl's chicken curry which was excellent.

Thanks to Maudiegirl's ministrations (an application of lard and essence of lemon) the various swellings and the lip deflated considerably, so that as the evening progressed it was easier to understand what Colontota was saying. Anna held his hand and kept on saying 'Poor man, poor man' until told severely to shut up and Colontota, eager to please, said, 'Yech, shubbub,' and Anna burst into tears and wiped her nose on the end of the tablecloth.

Father Romiel was as mad as a hornet. When Cecilprins told him that Anna was to marry a Buddhist and that there would, naturally, be no church wedding, he shook his breviary under Cecilprins' nose and said that he, Cecilprins, was sending his daughter to hell. 'The imps of hell will torture her for all eternity,' he thundered, 'and you will also be there, burning forever, and the imps of hell will pour boiling oil in your eyes and tear your burning flesh with fiery whips and you will suffer forever and ever and what fires of torment will burn inside you when you see your poor Anna coming to that everlasting pit of pain!'

Cecilprins listened entranced. 'But how to see her if coming or going, Father.'

'How to see? You will be there! Hell will be your prison forever! The imps—'

'That's what. Those imps things. They pouring boiling oil in my eyes. So how to see after that?'

'You are joking, ah!' the priest roared. 'You are breaking the laws of God and Holy Mother the Church and coming to joke? At this age, with grown-up children. You must pray. I will pray for your damned soul. Marriages are made in heaven, in the sight of God and the angels and saints and the blessed Mother of God. Are you trying to make your daughter's marriage in hell? If there is no blessing of the church and the marriage is not sanctified before the altar of God on high, you and your daughter will burn forever!'

'With those imps. Father, what are these imps? Haven't anything about imps in prayer book.'

'Never mind the imps!' the priest roared again, 'You must not allow Anna to marry a Buddhist.'

'But already given my word, no? One year he coming round her and Sonnaboy hammer him also and lip like a bicycle tube. Now, anyway, everything fixed.'

Father Romiel's eyes were frozen. 'Then why you coming to me? You think I will give absolution when you commit this sin with your eyes wide open? You are the father. You can stop this.'

Cecilprins shook his head. 'Only came to ask if you will bless our Anna and her husband after the wedding. Will bring them to church and you just put some holy water and say something. That way she happy to know she have blessing and she go to church and everything like normal, no? And all the children she baptize and take to church and be Catholic. We fix everything, Father. Actually came to tell you not to worry. Only to ask this small favour that you bless them.'

'And you really believe this man will keep his word? How can you tell. Once they marry he is the master. If he does not allow Anna to go to church?'

Cecilprins chuckled. 'Then Sonnaboy hammer him again.'

The priest inclined his head. 'Yes, I see . . . hmmm . . . . But that does not absolve you from blame,' Father Romiel said severely. 'You are denying your daughter a church wedding. She is not marrying in the presence of the Lord.'

'But you teaching that God is everywhere, no?'

The good Father glared. 'Don't you tell me where God is and God isn't! That's for me to say. But for what you are doing you will be denied the sight of God forever. And Anna should know better. Are you sure she will continue to practice her religion?'

'Sure I'm sure, Father.'

'And all her children will be baptized and practice their religion and go to Catholic schools.'

Cecilprins nodded.

'Oh very well. You bring the couple to the mission house and I will bless them. Who knows, if Anna is a good and devout wife and a good Catholic and he see her go to Mass and take the children to church and saying the family rosary every day he may also become a Catholic.'

Cecilprins pounced on this. 'That's what I also thinking, Father. And he not bad fellow. Well off also, and in the radio. Two houses also. Only thing, Father, see and put extra holy water on him. No harm if emptying the bottle on the bugger.'

'And where will the couple live?'

'Wellawatte.'

'Ah, then I must send a note to Father Grero at Saint Lawrence Church and tell him to visit and make sure that Anna comes to church. You bring me address.'

Cecilprins promised.

'And you tell Anna to come and see me. Must give her some instructions on being good Catholic wife.'

Cecilprins promised. He was relieved. He had dreaded the encounter but it had turned out well. The only thing that worried him were those damned imps. Hell, he mused, must be a hell of a place.

At home he made it a point to tell Anna: 'You see what your poor papa has to go through for you? Because I let you marry that Colon I will have to go to hell. Already writing the ticket, I think. And have things called imps to put fire on my head and boiling my eyes in oil.'

Anna paled and Maudiegirl gasped painfully.

'And not for little while, no? Father said for ever and ever. Non-stop boiling my eyes. And all because of my children. What to do?' and the brave martyr reached for the altar and took his cupboard key. A small drink would help. Imps! Hah!

A burgher wedding can only be described as a BURGHER wedding. The very thought of all that had to be done gave Maudiegirl a new lease of life. Invitations to be printed at Cave and Company; Leah's florists to provide the flowers and little posies to be pinned on to the tablecloth; Grosvenor Caterers to provide those little porcelain blue boxes to hold cake; crackers and fireworks to be bought and stored safely in boxes of sawdust; Anna to be fitted out with shoes, underlinen and a visit to Whiteway Laidlaw's first floor salon where bolts of cloth were purchased and carried away—tulle, silk, organza, muslin, flannel, chintz, lace to trim aprons, satin, assorted linens and something called broadcloth which was apparently an all-purpose textile for a multitude of uses. Haberdashery was a must, and then there was bargain hunting in the Pettah where Parsee merchants and fat Babus behind counters sprang to attention as the von Blosses descended on them like the Assyrians of the poem. Moolchands was singled out for ribbons and bows and buttons and corset laces; F.X. Pereiras for stockings and garters and Carwallios for Sunday bonnets and a smart 'picture hat' with the necessary hatpins and hair pins and small squiggly things which Maudiegirl insisted were 'hair-holding combs' and nobody contested the declaration. Then to Pearlrich for shoes and slippers and warnings to Anna to walk like a lady and not like Colontota's buffaloes and 'waste the heels in no time'.

It would take several pages to record the frenzied preparations in the clothing department only. The menfolk had to be decked in sharkskin and they insisted on Arrow shirts. From collarstuds upwards everything had to be spanking new with shoes from

Cargills and ties from Motwanis (and handkerchiefs also), and Maudiegirl went to Keyzer Street where a tiny shop she knew gave her heaping quantities of press studs, dress tape, thread, gauze and whalesbone, stiffener, perilaster, a length of gingham, pearl buttons, clips, edging and fancy bordering.

Maudiegirl decided that Anna should be outfitted to launch married life in the manner born. This made Cecilprins cringe. By the end of the first week he was shuffling around moaning, 'Pauperised, pauperised, that's what I will be.' And it looked as though he was right. Outfitting Anna meant not just her wardrobe, wedding gown, veil, shoes and headdress. The most amazing collection of utilities was assembled: housemaid's brushes and dusting brush; a chamber pail, scrubbing brushes and long hair brush; toilet covers, dusting sheets, special silk squares for polishing, a china bedroom ewer and basin, a clothes-horse, bed clothes, a counterpane, two feather pillows, butter dish, egg cups, salt cellar, butter knives, bread knife and bin, a hot-water urn, crumb brush, knife tray, hearth brush and even that necessity of the age—the dress stand. It is nigh impossible to record the full inventory, not with the way Cecilprins kept moaning and saying, 'You're mad, woman, all our savings gone, no?' Maudiegirl would quiver. 'You think I live to see others getting married? This only wedding I see, so this is all I have to do for my eldest, no. You go on this way and I go and lie down and die. Must be you want that.' And with that threat wafting in the air she went out and added a sandwich tray and candlestands and an altar statue of the Virgin and all manner of whatchmacallits and gew-gaws.

Yes, Maudiegirl did her daughter proud. The wedding, in the Colombo Registry was a dull affair. A special car was hired and bedecked with ribbons and bits of coloured crepe and many went in buggy-carts and a lot of assorted sisters and cousins and uncles in tussore and tweed and some with umbrellas and some with coats and sarongs and hair scraped back into topknots. Totoboy had begun his personal revels earlier than warranted and stank of gin and kept stumbling into everybody. The ceremony was a soulless affair. The registrar, a Burgher named Jonklaas, was not entirely in approval and kept bumbling over Colontota's name. Eventually they all signed and were duly witnessed and Viva lit crackers outside and startled the skittish bulls who nearly took off with the buggies. While all this history was being made, while Maudiegirl cried and hugged Anna and declared to the world that her 'big *ukkum baba* (baby that is nursed at the breast) was gone and now felt like all her ribs taking', while Colontota's people clucked their sympathy and Maudiegirl embraced each of them in turn and went around weeping on every shoulder that presented itself, a team of neighbours and shanghaied 'lane women' were busy in the Boteju Lane home cutting, chopping, basting, baking, roasting, boiling, frying, mixing, mangling, dicing, slicing, grinding, pounding, frying, flouring, garnishing, tossing, icing, salting, stirring, whipping, turning, pouring and making several rear rooms, the rear veranda, store-room plus kitchen into a vast theatre of the culinary arts. Others from 'down the road and cross the lane' were sweeping, dusting, polishing, scouring, cleaning, mopping, rubbing and scrubbing. Even the gate had been scraped and washed and old van Dort had to be forcibly prevented from painting it for, as Sonnaboy pointed out, 'If paint don't dry people coming will rub and clothes go to hell, no?'

Maudiegirl and her brood—that is those who did not accompany Anna and Colontota to the Times Studio for the photograph—rushed home to organize that monumental business of the wedding lunch. Cecilprins checked the liquor. People dashed in and out until his head swam. He didn't even dare to ascertain who they were. They just bustled and jostled around doing all manner of things and, he had to admit, the old home had never looked so good. It was almost eleven when the newly-weds rolled up with Leah in tow and a sister of Colontota's and a sweet-faced flower girl who was Colontota's sister's daughter. In the kitchen, Maudiegirl determined that there was time enough to give the lunch of the century—as everyone declared it was—and she outdid herself in fullest measure.

It hadn't been easy. Cecilprins who trotted along with a look of acute agony had sworn that 'all the other buggers can elope for all I care' and had sincerely prayed for such relief. The visit to Elephant House for the food, was worse than an eternity with those imps.

He couldn't understand. 'Married so long and now you getting completely mad. You trying to bury me in mat when no money left to buy coffin.'

Maudiegirl took scant heed. If pressed to explain she just said, 'That's the way,' and Cecilprins would open his mouth and trot behind her, quite forgetting to close it. When Maudiegirl ordered a whole side of beef he nearly had a stroke. 'From hock to shin,' he groaned, 'half a bloody bull!'

He got no sympathy from Sonnaboy. 'Half only? Can eat a whole bull.'

Only Elsie pointed out that even a regiment of invitees couldn't possibly consume it all. 'Will have food for a month afterwards, wait and see.'

'My godfather! Half will spoil and have to throw, no? Mad, mad, completely mad.'

Maudiegirl added a shoulder of veal, a haunch of lamb and a leg of pork. 'Can get sucking pig,' she said, 'but never mind this time,' and promptly bought a turkey which seemed, to Cecilprins, had started off being an ostrich and changed its mind halfway.

The arrival of the newly-weds did not go unmarked or unsung. The whole population of Boteju Lane, even Mrs Bennett with the big leg stood in the road to see the old Austin pull up followed by divers conveyances which included bicycles, buggy carts and the Colontota clan in a rattletrap Ford that broke wind apologetically every fifteen yards. Waves of applause, whistles and cheers rolled up and down wind. Totoboy, as merry as a sandboy, lurched out of a cart trailing long strings of red and green Chinese crackers which he lit and did a jig with, while all the pi-dogs from the tenement garden dashed into the crowd and old Simmons climbed the nearest wall and cheered, 'Damn good. Fire some more. Bloody animals everywhere. Chase the buggers off. I hate dogs. Coming behind and biting.'

Maudiegirl shot out to embrace Anna, and Elsie and Leah bundled up her train and they all tottered through the gate with Colontota picking up arum lillies which Anna was shedding from her bouquet. Urchins whooped and Totoboy burned his fingers and howled, and Sonnaboy shepherded the Colontotas inside while Cecilprins stood, arms outstretched, spectacles gleaming. Every adjoining home had been stripped of its chairs and tables for the occasion. Dunnyboy had also dressed for the occasion, but in togging-up and finding no belt had, instead, knotted one of Viva's ties around his waist. He liked the effect and was much commented on by the Colontota menfolk who considered this a masterful way to hold up a sarong.

The order of the day demanded a claret cup and cheese biscuits with assorted carbonated fizzes and Maudiegirl's famous home-made ginger beer. All through the previous night the gingerbeer had kept popping corks with little pistol-shot bangs as the bottles lay in their tubs of water. The plums had grown fat and sleek in the effervescent mixture and they now floated in each glass like round, smooth dog-ticks, ready to burst tangily between the teeth. After everyone held a glass of the decoction of his or her choice it was noted that none of the Colontotas accepted the wine.

'Hell of a hat, no?' Cecilprins said, 'These not drinking people.'

'Then what about meat?' Sonnaboy asked casually, 'Buddhist fellows in railway not eating meat.'

'Oh my God,' Cecilprins exploded, 'Call that Colon and ask if true.'

Colontota nodded gravely. 'Why? Anna not tell you? She knows we don't eat meat. Only fish.'

Sonnaboy shrugged. 'What about your people. All fish-eating only?'

Colontota nodded again. 'And won't drink. Only my father. But he won't drink for anybody to see. You can call him quietly to the back and give a drink if you like.'

Cecilprins was not impressed by Colontota senior's drinking habit. He was thinking of the side of beef, the turkey, the haunch of lamb, the leg of pork, the shoulder of veal. He smacked his forehead and rushed to the kitchen that was looking like a base camp in the Crimean war. 'Want fish,' he panted, 'all those buggers won't eat meat.'

'What buggers?'

'Bridegroom buggers.'

Maudiegirl stared. 'Call Sonnaboy and Viva,' she said crisply.

When Sonnaboy sped to the Dehiwela fish market he had explicit instructions. 'Buy, child, big seer head and shoulders only and one red mullet.' Viva was despatched to the Elephant House outlet in Wellawatte in the bridal car, ribbons, crepe and all and caused quite a sensation when he pulled up at the Wellawatte main junction where he was seen carrying a large salmon and a clutch of smoked herring. Maudiegirl tucked up her sleeves. 'Now lunch get little late. Anyhow can manage. Must send Anna and Colon to church, no? Call that Anna here.'

Anna, sweeping in in a wave of white satin and lace and cheese biscuit crumbs in her bodice was worried about this visit to Father Romiel. 'Will scold for sure, *anney.*'

'Don't talk rot, child. Papa going with you, no? Only give blessing and tell Colon also to kneel, right?'

Colontota had also hoped that this church business would be forgotten. Senior was curious. 'Where they want to go now?' he asked, 'Without eating, even, going for honeymoon?'

Cecilprins tried to explain.

'So that is Anna's church. So what for my son going. *Apoi,* if head priest in temple hears about this, *thoppi* (literally 'big hat'—a colloquial Sinhala expression meaning that it will be a disaster) for us also'.

'So you also come and see,' Cecilprins invited, 'and not even going inside church. Only to mission house where priest live.'

Colontota's mother, a doll-faced woman with a derririere that had Dunnyboy in ecstasy, smiled. 'If not going inside church then no harm. What your priest will do?'

'Give blessing. And pray that they have happy married life. That is good thing, no?'

Senior nodded slowly. 'No harm if I come also?'

So Cecilprins, Anna, Colontota and his father and sister chugged to St. Mary's where Father Romiel emerged only after the mission house bell had been rung thrice, and looked them over narrowly. 'Smelling of spirits you come,' he told Cecilprins severely. 'So this is the couple? Wait a minute,' and he popped off to pop back wearing a purple stole and carrying a carafe of holy water and sprinkler.

'What's that thing?' Colontota senior asked.

'For putting water.'

'Water?'

'So kneel,' Father Romiel said and Anna sank to the floor while Colontota looked uncertainly around. Cecilprins prodded his son-in-law in the ribs. 'Kneel, men, going to bless you, no?'

Colontota knelt and behind him his father knelt as well and grinned: 'Put for me also.'

Father Romiel stared. 'Who is this?'

'That is bridegroom's father.'

'And he is also Buddhist?'

'Yes, Father.'

'So you see? He has more respect than you. Wants to receive my blessing with his son and new daughter. And you standing and smelling of alcohol. Kneel down all!' the priest roared and Colontota's sister and Cecilprins dropped to the floor as though someone had given them smart kicks behind the knees. Calling on the Lord in Latin, Father Romiel sternly asked that He look upon this bunch of misfits and favour them with His divine mercy and did a histrionic *'in nomine patris'* and emptied the dispenser, dashing it this way and that until he had soaked them all considerably. 'I bless you because this is all I can do,' he said, regarding the empty carafe ruefully, 'You, child,' addressing Anna, 'chose to marry this . . . this . . . a Buddhist and have denied yourself the grace of a sanctified marriage. But I will pray for you and may God have mercy on you. So now you can go,' and that unpleasant duty over, he hopped off and they all got up and Cecilprins said, 'Foo! Like as if he poured with a bucket.'

Back home Anna was told to get out of her bridal dress 'otherwise sure to spill some curry on it, damn careless woman, no?' and a bunch of ladies huddled in the bedroom to watch the bride change and finger the lace and feel the satin and say ooh and aah and giggle and whisper. Mavis Lappan couldn't contain herself. 'So what you do when he coming to sleep in the night?'

Anna turned scarlet. *'Chee,* men, as if you don't know.'

'Yes,' said Lalla Boniface, 'but Sinhalese fellows have black ones, no? And long also.'

'So never mind. Anyway, Mister Colontota not so dark,' said Anna.

'That's sure, quite fair he is. Must be doing same way like Burghers, no?'

'I don't know, men . . . here, take out this hooks 'n' eye . . . I'll just wait and let him do.'

'*Anney*, you must tell us when you come again, right?' and all twinkled with laughter and Anna kept blushing and saying 'all right, all right' and Dora Markwick sighed and said, 'I also feel like going with Sinhalese boy. Or Muslim.'

'*Chee*, now because Anna marry Sinhalese, everybody getting mad or what?'

'Burgher boys nice, men. But when marry only want to drink and do. Can see, no? Even my mama say can't with Papa. Only last week she telling that she tired of going to maternity home and Papa don't know when to stop.'

'Yes, men. And when coming home drunk won't even eat and sleep. Same thing at home,' said Bunty Todd, 'Whole time squeezing his thing and saying where's your mother. No shame, men.'

And while all these delicious titbits were tossed around and Anna wore a pale-blue silk and Maudiegirl charged in to carefully take away the wedding dress for airing and wrapping in blue crepe paper to keep it fresh and white, the drinks had begun to circulate with a vengeance and Colontota senior had made several trips to the back room where Totoboy plied the poor man with all manner of 'rheumatic cures'. It turned out that a lot of other members of the clan were also willing to imbibe, provided their drinks were sufficiently disguised, so the weirdest concoctions were on offer to be snapped up, tossed down the hatch with equally weird grimaces and loud lip-smackings.

Colontota senior would weave in, squint and point at the rows of bottles. He went, apparently by the colours. 'Give that and . . . that,' and Totoboy, ever obliging, would go half and half on sweetened Irish gin and vintage port. The old man would swallow this in a long gulp, vibrate like an electric eel on the prod and steer an erratic course back to the revels.

And revels they were. The band had arrived: three boys in bow ties, two fiddles and a tom-tom and Jessie Ferdinands produced a harmonica and Finny Jackson played the spoons, clickety-clack on his knees and a rollicking kaffrinja set everybody in motion with Colontota's uncles hitching up their sarongs and jerking around shouting 'adi-ji! adi-ji!' and the ladies holding the sides of their skirts and high-stepping to the beat. Colontota said he did not know how to dance, which announcement was greeted by shouts of disapproval because the wedding couple simply had to take a turn. So he was dragged to the floor where he clutched blindly at Anna and the fiddlers played a sonorous 'Daisy, Daisy' in three-four time and Anna humped him around quite unceremoniously. Totoboy, quite unblushingly, cut loose with the parody:

Daisy, Daisy, show me your grassy land,

until Maudiegirl clouted him across the ear and everybody grinned and ladies covered their smiles with their fans and Anna dragged Colontota feverishly around the floor as though she was sweeping the kerb. Dunnyboy, meanwhile, had been put out of action on Maudiegirl's strict orders. The good woman, who had her eyes everywhere, noted her son's fascination with Mrs Colontota's beam-end and wisely plied him with a huge whisky saying, 'Drink all like a good boy,' and Dunnyboy, after years of Mama's castor oil and Epsom salts and white mixture, obliged without a murmur and went to sleep with his trouser buttons open. 'Saw him opening his Galle Face. Shame, no, if took out his thing in front of everyone.'

So the fiddlers scraped away and everybody cavorted around as merry as could be and snatches of this, that and the other rose to the rafters and all manner of yokels walked in from the lane and hung around under the jam fruit tree to watch and point and cackle and say,'What about small one for us also.'

Merriment hit a high spot with 'Hands knees and boomps-a-daisy' with the 'boooomps' bringing hips and buttocks into swivelling contact and the ladies getting the better of the men every time. George de Mello flapped his arms like a penguin on pension and bawled:

Hai, ho, sister Bubby's brand new bicy-kell,
All the buggers coming round to ring the bloody bell.

Totoboy, in a state bordering delirium tremens was howling:

Nearer my God to thee, nearer to thee.

until Sonnaboy told him to shut up, 'You thought this is a bloody funeral, you damn fool!'

Viva insisted that there was a voice breathing over Eden and old Simmons was giving a gamey rendition of 'Sweet Violets'. Then, as if on signal all began:

O Danny boy, the pipes, the pipes are calling . . .

while Cecilprins insisted that somebody must sing his favourite, 'Come into the garden, Maud', and Maudiegirl would blush and said, 'Good for him to say, with all the work in the kitchen.'

'All the work' was the understatement of the year. Never had a kitchen in a Dehiwela home been so overworked, so hectic, yet so perfect in what it produced. Maudiegirl had this passion. A meal, be it the humblest of sorts, had to be a work of art. On the wall beside the big, circular kitchen clock was her famous card, much admired and much copied out by all the ladies of Dehiwela who had been privileged enough to visit her kitchen. On the card were Maudiegirl's Golden Rules, and deserve mention:

- Without CLEANLINESS and PUNCTUALITY good cooking is impossible
- Leave nothing DIRTY. CLEAN AND CLEAR as you go
- A time for everything, and EVERYTHING IN TIME
- A good cook wastes NOTHING
- An hour LOST IN THE MORNING has to be run after ALL DAY

- Haste WITHOUT HURRY saves worry, fuss and flurry
- Stew BOILED is stew SPOILED
- STRONG fire for roasting; CLEAR fire for broiling
- Wash vegetables in THREE waters
- Boil fish QUICKLY, meat SLOWLY

With such inspiring admonitions, it would be natural that for this wedding lunch, Maudiegirl outdid herself. Each hour by roaring fireplaces—not all roared, though, some hissing, some spitting, others burning placidly, almost morose in mood—made her face redder and redder until she looked as well done as Saint Lawrence in the picture. When the tables were covered and chairs pushed and pulled around and guests swarmed around to push and pull each other around as well, Cecilprins rose to say grace and nobody took any notice for flushed, blousy women, their breasts bulging over low-cut jackets began to stock the tables with grave dignity. The old faithfuls were there: great bins of yellow rice studded with cashew nuts, plums and stoned French olives; pappadams in lined wire baskets and deep plates of steaming almond soup. The latter, Maudiegirl said, 'Was to settle all the drinking and give good appetite,' and even the Colontotas quaffed deep and long and never minded that twelve pounds of veal and a large chunk of lamb had been boiled for an eternity and the gravy strained off as the base for the soup.

'Shah! Very fine this soup. What have in it?'

'Over three pounds almonds, child. All pounded and putting also cream and eggs and cloves. How you like it?'

'Pukka. Can drink bucketful.'

'*Apoi,* if drinking like that, how to eat. Have fish for you people and beef for others. Only fish had to do in big hurry because how to know you not beef-eating, no?'

Old Colontota was gallantry plus. 'If fish like this soup, I eat everything you put here. Wait and see.'

Dispensing with further polite conversation—although the chronicler must mention that George de Mello fell asleep between the sixty-third and seventy-fourth minute with his face in his plate of pork—it must be emphasized that Anna's wedding lunch was a smash hit. The head and shoulders of seer arrived in Italian sauce, garnished with finely-minced devilled pork and lettuce and lemon and tomato slices. Over the whole, Maudiegirl had brushed garlic vinegar and a coating of cream and a dusting of powdered sugar. She tried to warn the Colontotas about the pig meat in the garnish. She was blithely ignored. When the salmon arrived, brushed over with egg, basted in butter and floating in thick anchovy sauce, their cup of happiness spilled over. The salted herrings in their bed of bay leaves, with their red-gold skins after an open grilling and sprinkled with Cayenne pepper, were greeted vociferously; and the red mullet, too, had been grilled in oil-paper wrapping, which held Maudiegirl's special mixture of parsley, pepper, salt, lemon juice and a tumbler of sherry.

It was a masterful, monumental, marvellous mastodon of a meal. The distinctive brown gravy made the meats simply delicious. Home-made bacon sauce, brandy sauce and, of course, the Dutch Sauce (tarragon vinegar, flour, butter, yolks of eggs, lemon juice and water) went equally well with the meat and the fish. There was Tartar mustard for the pork and brown onion sauce for the turkey that couldn't have looked better in its bier of mushrooms and fried breadcrumbs. The side of beef had given rise to a host of preparations—curried, broiled, a fricassee, an aromatic stew, a ragout, roast ribs and Maudiegirl's special salt beef which, twenty days ago, was a twenty-pound round of flank, shiny with treacle. Maudiegirl had kept rubbing in the honey and turning the beef for days, after which she had carefully wiped it and begun the thankless task of kneading in the saltpetre and salt, turning and pressing in the preservative until just last week she had rapped it with her knuckles, given a grunt of satisfaction and begun the smoking and boiling which took all of three days. Then to the large press (who could boast of a salt-beef press today?) where it lay, palpitating until the wedding morning.

There were rissoles and baked veal, neatly-stewed fillets of veal and a special mince with macaroni and large dishes of young carrots and new potatoes. The lamb was braised and part of it went into Maudiegirl's favourite Dutch Stew with side dishes of asparagus. And there was excellent pickled pork and stone jars of ground mustard relish with large peppers, spring onions, finely sliced carrots and lean, fiery chillies just turning red. And so they ate, and belched, and ate again and Cecilprins could hardly believe that so much could be consumed by so many so quickly.

The shadow of the jam fruit tree lengthened slowly, falling across the boundary wall and it was time for Anna and Colontota to leave. Already a bullock-cart was trundling its way to Wellawatte, piled high with all manner of boxes and packages—the brushes and candlestands and pails and basins, the wedding presents, and piles of wrapped-up clothes and linen and curtaining. Cecilprins, feeling quite reckless, had thrown in the household egg-rack and tumbler-rack, and the umbrella-stand in the veranda. 'You take and go, will you, never mind us.' Viva rode the bullock-cart to show the carter the way while Totoboy, totally useless after consuming enough liquor to sink the *Queen Mary* was sleeping the sleep of the replete.

They drove off to Colontota's home after a screeching farewell where Maudiegirl struck her breast and declared: 'Lost to us now you are,' and, 'For this, no, I bring you up for 'nother man to take and use,' and Leah and Elsie bawled and Maudiegirl cuffed them and said, 'What for you crying? Tomorrow day after you also go and leave your poor mama alone, no?' And they all boo-hooed and clung to each other and Colontota looked uncomfortably around and felt like a criminal.

Such a show! But earlier, when the tables had been cleared Maudiegirl had dragged Anna to the bedroom and given her a big rosary with a crucifix as large as a handgun and said: 'Now say your prayers every evening, did you hear, and three Hail Mary's when Angelus goes and when it is time you first ask the Holy Mother to help you and then don't be too forward, miss. Just lie down and listen to what he say. Don't try to show you know all about it. Just do what he tells. And when he get inside you cry and tell it paining, remember, because that make him very proud because all these buggers the same. Telling love, love, but very happy when hurt you. Thinking they big men if make the wife suffer. And will pain, anyway, but not much so don't worry because this is first time, no? Nobody getting inside you yet, no?'

Anna, red-faced, gulped. 'No, Mama.'

'That's good. Worried I was about that Dunnyboy, but he little mad, no?'

Anna gulped again. Dunnyboy had had his moments but she was quite certain that as a *virgo* she was pretty well *intacta.*

'That's good. These Sinhalese people funny about these things. Coming in the morning to see if have blood. *Hopper* woman telling me yesterday. But I told that Colon, if his people coming between and telling anything will send Sonnaboy to hammer. And he tell his people won't come too much. They go back anyway and only you and he in house. And getting servant woman also for cooking and pounding and grinding and washing *chatti*-pots (earthenware cooking vessel) and all, so you have easy life I think. Only you work also and don't just sit in chair like pudding and get fat. Already you too fat and some men like when young but when getting old what?'

When more crackers had been lit and the entire lane had reassembled to see them go and all manner of snide remarks had been made (old Simmons' stock advice: 'Just keep your mouth shut and your legs open, child. That's the only way to be good wife. When my Dora died undertaker had hell of a time putting her legs together.') and old shoes, tins and lumps of blue rag were tied to the rear bumper of the Ford, Anna and Colontota got in and everybody rushed round the car, fighting and elbowing furiously and the driver honked madly to clear the way as they waved and waved and slowly moved through the maelstrom of grinning faces and jerking arms and legs and bodies that weaved in and out, and mothers scooped up children to point and sing, 'There, there, they going,' and shouts of 'Don't break the bed' and 'If he too small never mind, tell to call me'.

So Anna and Colontota went away to a childless marriage and only Father Romiel looked pleased and said it was the judgement of God and Maudiegirl wept and said, 'How my Anna unbearable? Must be that Colontota,' while his father shook his head and said, 'If married girl from here will have big stomach every year. What to do? Worked in pharmacy before getting married, no? Must have swallowed something. Big pig she is. Always eating. Don't know if when hungry ate pills in pharmacy. Saw how ate on wedding day?'

Mrs Colontota did not hold with this. 'She is good girl. And see how she is looking after him. Everyday buying slice of seer and making nice *mirismalu* (fish cooked in condiments and water without a coconut milk base) for him and not just spending. If they are happy what do we care?'

'But what about me?' Colontota senior would growl, 'When I be a grandfather?'

'For what you wanting to be grandfather?'

That stymied the man. 'Must have grandchild. Everyone here expecting, no. But that Anna still not expecting. See how here even the buffaloes having young.'

Mrs Colontota would have none of it. 'What people here are you talking about? All because you going all over the place boasting, that's what. Just keep quiet. Son is happy. How do we know? Maybe he don't want child now itself. If the buffaloes putting young you go and be grand-buffalo.'

In Boteju Lane, also, other crises had to be met. Viva brought home Papa Ludwick and Opel and the hullaballoo of that visit was talked about for months. To her everlasting credit Opel took no part in the gory proceedings and embraced Maudiegirl and cried and said, 'This my life, no? *Anney,* my mama die and then papa bringing people home with bibles and things with bells and whole night shouting hallellooiya and going doh-doh-doh-doh-doh and praise the lord and rolling on the floor and saying the angels holdings lamps for them to see and pointing to the roof and shouting Manuel, em-manuel like mad peoples. And now poor Vivi also caught by Papa to do this.'

Maudiegirl said, 'Don't worry, child, that Sonnaboy will settle,' which Sonnaboy did, to be sure, in the best way he knew. He was, some minutes before this exchange, making mincemeat of Viva who was embracing the jam fruit tree and yelling blue murder while Cecilprins danced around shouting 'Your older brother, no? Hitting your older brother, no?' and then rushing to the kitchen for a firewood stick and being pounced on by Maudiegirl and Totoboy and dragged to the store-room shouting, 'Let go! I break his bloody back!'

This was a crackling family row. And all because of Papa Ludwick who came in like a lamb, got all worked up, made a blithering ass of himself, ravaged the home, and, when Sonnaboy went for him, took off like a rocket, racing up the road in open-mouthed panic.

It all began in a most civilized fashion. Viva let the light of his life indoors and said grandly, 'This is Opel, who I going to marry.' In the hubbub Papa Ludwick strode to the altar and was eyeing the holy pictures, the statue of the Virgin and all the other trappings with a jaundiced eye. This, he decided, needed immediate rectification. His Pentecostal gorge rose. Swinging round he roared: 'Exodus twenty-four and five!'

'What, what,' Cecilprins said, 'Who this fellow you bringing, Viva? Asking riddles or what?'

'Exodus twenty-four and five,' Ludwick roared even louder, 'No making these graven images of anything that have in Heaven or on the earth or even in the water and no bowing and serving these things because God say he getting jealous and put curse on your children and children's children and children's children to fourth generation.'

Cecilprins blinked. Totoboy blinked. Sonnaboy stared.

'Who—who—what this fellow saying?' Cecilprins said, 'Who is this?'

Viva leaped forward. 'This is Opel's papa. He is Pentecost . . . like me.'

'Like you? Who? You?'

'I! Me! I now Pentecost. I finding way to Heaven and can lie down in still waters and all and giving my soul to God straight, and what he saying is right. Graven images. Putting altars and pictures and saying that is picture of God. All this abom—abomy—something. Kneeling and saying useless things everyday. See me. Now I biding in the Tabernacle. Yes! Tabernacle of the Lord . . . .'

'Praise the lord!' Ludwick thundered.

'. . . and all are brothers and sisters and we are not deaf adders. Deaf adders! That's what. Have in the psalms about these deaf adders who saying Hail Mary, Hail Mary and not hearing when God trying to tell to stop all these rubbish prayers.'

The family listened open-mouthed. Viva was decidedly mad. Sonnaboy was the first to rise and glare. 'What do you mean rubbish prayers. Our Father and Hail Mary you're calling rubbish. You learning all this from this sonovabitch?'

Papa Ludwick rushed to the hat-rack where Cecilprins' walking stick hung from a peg, seized it and, before he could be intercepted, struck out at the picture of the Sacred Heart. 'Praise the Lord,' he roared, while Leah and Elsie screamed and an altar lamp toppled, splashing and dripping oil. Somehow Sonnaboy was not quick enough. He did manage to land a hefty punch into the small of Ludwick's back and the latter-day prophet yelped, dropped the walking stick and dived for safety behind the settee. Sonnaboy lunged and Ludwick leaped aside with a yell of terror, tripped over a stool and shot into the garden. Sonnaboy charged after him and at his heels trotted Viva shouting Halleluia.

That, for Viva was most unfortunate, for Ludwick, with an incredible display of agility, doubtless born of desperation, actually vaulted the gate, fell heavily on the road, picked himself up and took off like a bolt of lightning. Viva, alas, was in line for the dispensing of summary punishment which he received in fullest measure.

The upshot was that Viva left home with a pale-faced Opel while an equally pale Cecilprins shakily helped pick up splinters of glass and take down the picture that had received a nasty crease across the heart, obliterating many of those points of flame as though the Saviour was trying to tell all and sundry that Maudiegirl's thirteen fires were ready for a diaspora. That good woman's face was a study of tragedy and she just sat and trembled as Sonnaboy rampaged through the house, tossing everything of Viva's—his clothes, ties, shoes, suits, his pads and stockbooks—into the garden. 'Take everything and get out,' he snarled at the fallen Viva who was wheezing painfully and whose knees trembled so that he could hardly pick himself up and first clung to the jam fruit tree, then to a plaintively sobbing Opel. Sonnaboy, still seething like an ill-tempered volcano strode to the firewood shed at the bottom of the lane and hauled out a bewildered firewood man who was told to bring along his handcart. Into this Viva's belongings were unceremoniously dumped and the man was told to go to wherever the chosen son of Heaven wished him to go.

To Opel's of course, to a storming malevolent Ludwick, who, with hand upraised and open Bible, relegated the von Blosses to the lowest pit of hell. 'Pour out thy wrath upon the heathen,' he bawled, 'Help us O God of our salvation . . . thought my heart will burst after running like that. Saw the eyes? Like devil's . . . keep not thou silence O God for lo, thine enemies make a tumult and they that hate thee have lifted up the head . . . my God, don't know how I jumped that gate. But the Lord put out the hand and saved me, brother . . . O my God, make them like a wheel, as the stubble before the wind . . . God preserved me, brother Vivi, saw the hand of God scooping me up. Sent an angel to lift me over that gate. Praise the Lord, brother, say Amen, men . . . persecute them with thy tempest and make them afraid with thy storm . . . dogs on road also chasing when I ran. And people saying rogue, rogue, also. God saved me, brother. Put wings on my legs for sure. Alleluia! What's that fellow with that cart. Why he waiting outside?'

Opel was able to explain and Ludwick frowned and scratched his head and looked at Viva's puffy face and shuddered. Truly God had had an eye for him. There, he thought, but for some amazing grace, go I. So Viva was helped in, walking like a stork with arthritis and his worldly possessions carried in and old Pantis Perera watched from his gate and told his wife: 'See what happening now. Looks like fellow coming to stay. Cart of things also. Damn shame, no? Not even married and living with that Opel now. How if our Kukku got caught?'

'That's what telling,' his wife said, squeezing past, 'Move a little, will you, to see. *Chee,* don't know what he is thinking to do like this. That fellow living Dehiwela, no?'

'What Dehiwela? Now living here, I think. You should have seen how Opel embracing and taking inside.'

'And cart also came?'

'Yes. Full of things.'

'*Anney,* don't know if got married even. These Pentecosts not like others, no. Everything doing in hurry and praying also fifty miles an hour.'

Pantis Perera considered this darkly. 'Yes, you're right maybe. But this time in evening? Tell you what? Later I go and say hullo and see.'

Old Ludwick, despite his deep involvement with things ethereal which, after all, gave him some clout among the other half-wits in his group, was earthbound enough to know why his neighbour came calling. He also knew the sort of bush telegraph that operated in the neighbourhood. Viva lay in the spare room, laid up with the shivers which Ludwick diagnosed as the immediate aftermath of being in direct line of a cataclysm of seven-point magnitude. But he wished the fellow would not keep emitting long groans every so often. He had stiffened up in all sorts of places but the mouth was still in business.

'So how men, when saw cart I thought you shifting or something.'

Ludwick smiled. 'No men, brought that Viva home. Have to pray over him, no, all tonight.'

Pantis Perera's eyes widened. 'Why, got sick or something?'

'No, no. That is usual thing in our mission. If getting married tomorrow, have to bring boy home and pray over him. How to know otherwise if he is ready? This marriage business sacred thing, no? Now he in room in touch with holy spirit and telling all his sins and asking for Lamb of Salvation to wash his dirty soul and make all clean. Can hear him crying sometime and in very bad state, I tell you. How to tell what these young fellows nowadays up to, no? Opel also praying in her room and asking to wash him clean and take all his sins.'

Pantis couldn't understand this rigmarole. Heaven, it seemed to him, was operating some sort of a laundering service. But he admitted to the niceties of the situation which only Ludwick's God, in his mysterious way, could condone. Funny things Pentecosts do.

'So why you not tell that they getting married tomorrow. And us next door and all.'

'But that not the way with us God's children, no? First to wash and clean and all night praying, then take to Tabernacle for vowing to live in light of spirit as husband-wife, then union with God and telling Holy Spirit to give grace for making word flesh and then coming home.'

'And then you put party?'

'What party? We no drinking and giving cake and all, no? Party will have in Heaven, men, when angels all rejoicing about marriage of God's children. This world have nothing for us, men. Only Kingdom of Heaven waiting and place kept for us. Right hand of God we will be.'

Pantis mumbled and left. 'All these fellows God-mad,' he told his wife, 'Lucky escape for our Kukku boy. That Viva making noises as if someone smashing his toes with rice-pounder. Getting salvation, it seems. Lamb is washing his soul. Must be paining like hell.'

Papa Ludwick decided that, like Washington, he could not tell a lie. Having cleverly put off that evil-minded Pantis, he had to now make the fiction fact. He swept into the spare room grabbed Viva by the shoulder, got a howl of pained protest and took scant heed of the man's obvious sensitivity to a laying of hands. 'You listen,' he said, 'First thing tomorrow you dress up and come with Opel to Tabernacle. You two get married. Opel! Opel! Where's that bloody woman, ah, tomorrow you get married, you hear?'

Opel would have liked, of course, to have a wedding gown and the trimmings. Girls are born to marry, true, but she seemed to be having marriage thrust upon her. And at the Pentecostal mission of all places; with a pip-squeak registrar hauled out of Dickman's Lane to make it legal and a couple of loonies banging their heads on the wall and shouting 'Praise the Lord'. She presented objections.

'But Viva going to work, no? And have to see doctor also, I think. Look, will you, his state. Like run over by train.'

'Never mind that. If can't marry you tomorrow, out he go! That Pantis fellow came to see just now and you think he keep quiet? Wife will tell the Bakelman's and they will tell the Mullers and the Landsbergers and the Silvas and the whole damn area know he stay the night here. Fine how do you do, no? You're the one who will get it, wait and see, everyone casting remarks. If put the face out will laugh behind the back and say you keeping man in the house. You know, no? how they put together talks!'

'But, Papa . . . .'

'What to buts? You want to marry him, no?'

Opel nodded.

'So then you marry. I'll go to registrar's house now and tell to come to Tabernacle in the morning. Can send rickshaw for him. And you sit in veranda and wait. If anybody looking they know you sitting alone. Otherwise make another story that I go out and leaving you alone with him. And don't get up until I come, do you hear? Put the lamp and read the Bible. I'll go and come soon.'

And so were Viva and Opel married and the couple lived with Ludwick for two months after which the milkfood company asked Viva to handle distribution and sales of its products upcountry and he took Opel to Bandarawela, a mountain resort about 4000 feet up in the central tea district. He informed the family of his fortunes and of his Pentecostalist marriage and that he was now a senior sales agent and also a prayer leader and an important member of the Pentecostalist congregation upcountry. Heaven, he declared, was surely his, and he would pray for them that they may see the error of their ways and come with suitable humility to the throne of the Almighty without recourse to all the idolatry and meaningless ritual of priests and bishops and some Roman pope who hadn't the foggiest who the von Blosses were anyway. Denouncing the faith of his fathers was as nothing to Viva who had long outstripped Ludwick in quoting chapter and verse and spinning Heaven like a roulette wheel to suit his purpose. He saw great potential in being a tub-thumper for the Lord. He dismissed Sonnaboy as an agent of the devil, Totoboy as a creature of unrighteousness and a drunkard to boot; called his father rude names and his mother a glutton for the things of the flesh. Sin, he wrote, had a stranglehold on them and all the wiles of Satan crepitated in Dunnyboy who was a depraved lout. On Judgement Day, he was certain, God would strike them down and send an angel with a fiery sword to drive them down, down, into the pit and there would be a gnashing of teeth and he would watch their agony with a beatific smile on his face and only then would they know the truth of God's word. He added lashings from the Bible—all about brimstone and fire and how the sea will become blood and how the demons will take the von Blosses, poor sinners, and torment them for all eternity.

Elsie, who was making preparations for her own wedding, took the letter from the postman, recognized the handwriting and ran to Maudiegirl. 'From Viva a letter,' she announced, 'Open to see.'

Maudiegirl said no. 'If for Papa then he must open, no? Not for you to poke the nose.'

A white-faced Cecilprins read it.

'So what saying?' Maudiegirl asked.

'Nothing. Living in Bandarawela, it seems.'

'Nothing? All those pages. Then why your hand shaking and face like bedsheet? Give to see.'

'No, no. He Pentecost, no? All Bible stuff. And such small writing. Hard to read even.'

'Never mind, let see, will you. Think I don't know that Viva? Must be scolding for what happened.' And the old lady seized the letter and read it all and lay back on her lounger with a little moan. She refused to budge. Just lay there, the letter on her lap. Sonnaboy came in full of glad tidings. He had been raised in rank to apprentice driver. Ninety rupees a month. A fortune. Now to get that da Brea woman to say yes. Noting his mother's distressed face he raised an eyebrow at Cecilprins.

Sonnaboy read the letter. 'I'll go to Bandarawela and bury the bastard,' he exclaimed.

Maudiegirl opened her eyes. 'Mouth! mouth!' She cried, 'Who you telling bastard? Your brother, no?'

'If he real son will write like this? Cursing us. Cursing the religion. All these years went to church and first communion and everything. He's a bloody bastard!'

All the venom of Viva's letter seemed to take form and perch, like some evil black bird on Maudiegirl's shoulder. She saw nothing of the days to come. No tonight, no tomorrow. Her heart thudded painfully and her legs felt numb and it hurt to breathe in and out. Her son. Her flesh. Such hatred and spite in his words. And how could this be? Could one who professed to love God so much hate so much?

Cecilprins told Sonnaboy: 'You go and tell Doctor Loos to come. She being like this not good.'

Sonnaboy went. At the gate he said, 'All the doctors won't do any good when I catch that Viva,' and he cycled slowly, thinking that somewhere a switch had been thrown. The family was coming apart. 'This won't do,' he gritted. 'I'll keep them together, even if I have to hammer them everyday.'

Maudiegirl took to her bed that evening after the doctor came and went, and never got out of it again. Anna and Colontota were summoned the next morning. Eric and George came too, and even Iris Holdenbottle. A telegram was despatched to Terry in Singapore and Viva was telegraphed in Bandarawela. All the morning, with her daughters around her and Dr Loos fussing around and shaking his head and Father Romiel gliding about in his cassock and also shaking his head, Maudiegirl seemed the least concerned. 'Know I'm going to die, no?' she said, 'So you girls listen and don't interrupt. You get married and see to your poor papa. If he living here then come to see in the evenings. If Sonnaboy marry can live here with that Beryl but I think that Beryl not marry now itself. And that Iris must not live here. Sure to fight with Papa.'

Cecilprins stood, looking bleakly at his wife and not caring what he would do for he could not imagine what it would be like with her gone. But he did assure her that he would live on in Boteju Lane with the boys until they married and that Elsie would marry and take in Dunnyboy and Leah would marry next and then Totoboy could set up home with Iris if he wished but why Iris of all women no one could understand. When Sonnaboy was ready to marry, Cecilprins could give up the house and live with any of the children and Anna said that Papa was always welcome and Leah said the same while George made some rapid calculations and said, 'Yes, but that is later, no?'

'Like to eat some rice *conjee* (thin rice porridge),' Maudiegirl murmured, 'With small piece of jaggery. Have in top shelf tin in kitchen cupboard,' and Leah rushed off to make the porridge while Father Romiel told the rest to kneel and led prayers and gave Maudiegirl his crucifix to kiss and asked if she would like to confess. Then he shooed everyone out and sat beside her, listening to the faint voice as Maudiegirl tried to remember if she had lately transgressed the laws of God. After the blessing she actually tried to raise herself up as Leah brought her the *conjee* and the room filled again. Friends, neighbours, relatives filed in just to stand around her and press her hands. Nobody spoke. Even old Simmons, garrulous at the worst of times, was silent. Maudiegirl swallowed two spoons of the *conjee* and lay back. 'That's nice,' she whispered and closed her eyes, opened them again to seek out Cecilprins and raise a hand to him. He held on to it as the children closed around and Father Romiel told all to kneel as he anointed her and made the sign of the cross on her eyes, mouth and on her breasts and then, with hands under the covers anointed the other openings in her body, sanctifying it, lest evil invade her in these dying moments. Gently, Cecilprins, his hands trembling, placed Maudiegirl's rosary between her fingers and her eyes flicked from him to her children, one by one. They drew closer, touching her, willing her to stay, and she smiled, a large tear trickling down her check, shuddered and gripped her husband's hand.

And so she died and the shrieks and wailings and the broken sobs of the men were terrible to hear. And only Sonnaboy, dry-eyed but with an ache in his heart that could not be eased, said: 'Viva never came. Never forgive him for this. Papa, Viva never came.'

Cecilprins looked at his youngest with unseeing eyes.

'Viva never came,' Sonnaboy grated, 'He killed our mama and he never came.'

PART TWO
The Berrying

Such a crowd there was . . .

The chronicler finds it difficult in the extreme to paint in mere words the many details of Maudiegirl's funeral. Satisfied beyond all doubt that Maudiegirl had died in a state of grace and that her soul was now travelling first-class to Paradise, Father Romiel gave ready consent for Barney Raymond, morticians, to transport the body in its handsome coffin, with the ornate brass carrying grips and the specially-inscribed brass plate bearing the name of the deceased, to St. Mary's where a catafalque was set up in the middle of the main aisle, towards the arched doors. Sonnaboy worked all morning, placing a few potted palms around the catafalque and with the help of friends and neighbours, hanging a large black flag on which were the white letters RIP and a cross, and lining the route from home to church with the little black flags. The motor hearse was a grand-looking vehicle and the wreaths came in to fill the hall were Maudiegirl lay, and overflow to the veranda. Raymond's men, with quiet efficiency, washed and prepared the corpse and the smell of formalene clung cloyingly in the air even when it was all over and Maudiegirl was arrayed in flowing white with her rosary draped around her hands and her prayerbook also placed, at Cecilprins' insistence, and which held a mezzotint of the family. She was a perfect picture of repose. Her hair had been carefully, lovingly combed and the bandage around her jaw removed. Stout and marbled in death, she seemed to have shed many years. Even the care lines at the ends of her mouth had disappeared. Lamps burned all the night as she lay with the family keeping vigil. The doors were kept wide open and people came in at every hour to cross themselves, whisper a prayer and embrace the sad-shouldered family and then sit and fidget and ponder on the mystery of it all.

It is an open-house business, actually, and the girls were kept on their feet, serving innumerable cups of tea and plates of biscuits and wondering why there was scarcely time to weep. Totoboy, weak creature that he was, found solace in the bottle and drank fiercely. He was far in his cups when the hearse took Maudiegirl to church and was unable to even help to carry out the coffin. He watched his mother's body leave, sat in the dining-room and bawled with a great feeling of helplessness until Sonnaboy came in to shake him angrily, drag him to the bathroom where he was held firmly by the scruff of his neck and pushed, spluttering and crying, under the tap. 'Clean up and get dressed,' Sonnaboy snarled, 'You are coming to the cemetery even if I have to drag you.'

The service was a melancholy one. With Maudiegirl under a special black drape and the tall candles casting yellow glances at the tented structure, with altarboys in black cassocks swinging their thurifiers and puffs of incense rising like smoke-signals to the domed roof, Dunnyboy began a low howl that could not be stilled. After prayers at the altar, Father Romiel came through the sanctuary gates, led by altar servers carrying cross and candles and followed by a little rascal bearing the brass urn of holy water. Old De Niese banged away at the Hammond organ and Pinky Markwick opened her mouth and bellowed 'Nearer my God to Thee' with such spirit that everybody turned their heads to look.

The prayers and blessing around the catafalque over, it was time to deliver a few words on Maudiegirl's earthly stewardship while Leah, Anna and Elsie clung to each other, sobbing, and Iris Holdenbottle, not to be outdone, gave a piercing shriek and fell to her knees and Totoboy in a state of near stupor rolled over her and caused a general confusion in the pew. Finally, with the cross and candles leading, the coffin was carried outside and the long, slow journey to the Kanatte cemetery began. Rickshaws trotted ahead, piled high with wreaths and cars inched behind the hearse and those on bicycles carried their wreaths on their handlebars and Cecilprins wore a black armband and the women wore black hats and veils and some rushed to the bus stop while others accosted Cecilprins with excuses. 'Cannot come, *anney*. If leave Doddy alone, you know, no?' and Cecilprins would nod and say, 'Enough you did, Lilly, thank you for coming to church. You go and see to Doddy. All have own troubles, no?'

The cemetery, being all of five miles away and the funeral procession at snail's pace with many of the young ones walking the distance, took its time. At the graveside a choir had been organised to sing the old traditionals and the sight of all the gravestones sobered Totoboy considerably. He teetered around, peering at monuments and granite angels and stone crosses and shook a bewildered head. 'Here lies, here lies,' he muttered, 'and resting only and sacred to the memory . . . my God, where they putting my mama? Nobody dead here I think,' he told Iris, 'All taking rest!' and rushing ahead he came to the open grave, the ropes in place to lower the coffin and the choir singing furiously. Staggering over the mound of earth he bent over: 'Mama, you are already in there?'

Sonnaboy tried to grab at him but it was too late. With a howl, Totoboy vanished. This, naturally, caused great consternation. At the bottom of the grave, covered with sand spitting mouthfuls of earth, Totoboy gave a series of banshee wails. Those on the outskirts who had not been privy to Totoboy's disappearing act, heard the hollow trumpeting and said, 'My God, men, what is that?'

'Someone screaming from inside grave.'

'What? Inside grave.'

'That's what. Must have buried alive, no?'

'What? What? A ghost?'

'Murie, you heard? Ghost inside grave. And screaming!'

Murie had no answer for such an ungodly situation. She fainted.

Attempts to pull Totoboy out tumbled more sand on to him and this caused sheer terror. 'Don't bury me!' he shrieked, 'My God, trying to bury me!'

Panic rose in a wave and a stampede for the gates began with wreaths flung helter-skelter and young bucks scaling the cemetery wall to get away. By the time Totoboy was hauled out and fiercely dragged away and Maudiegirl lowered, many of the mourners were headed for home,' convinced that murder had been done. Prayers were said and hymns sung and the earth piled back and the wreaths piled over the mound. Sadly, faces wan and drawn, the family turned for home. Old Simmons asked: 'How did it go?'

Cecilprins said: 'Okay. Totoboy fell into the grave.'

'Totoboy what?'

'Fell in. Into the grave.'

Simmons stared. Then he gave a whoop of laughter and suddenly it seemed mandatory that everybody laugh too . . . except Totoboy, that is, who didn't see the humour of it.

Simmons went 'hoo, hoo' and wiped his eyes, 'Should have buried the bugger also. Hoo, hoo, fell in, how did it happen?'

'Don't know,' Cecilprins roared, 'bending over and then phut! went inside.'

'Hoo, hoo, must have been pukka sight, no? Bella, you heard? Totoboy fell into the grave! Hoo, hoo.'

Laughing, arm in arm, they went indoors for a drink. A month later everyone in Dehiwela agreed that it was a good Burgher funeral and Totoboy was a hero and slapped on the back heartily wherever he went. But he didn't touch a drop for a week, and that, in itself, was a miracle of sorts.

Elsie discovered Eric's weakness a week before they were married. It all began with the rearrangement of the Station Lane home. Aggie's mauve flower-patterned sofaset had always upset Elsie who declared it to be the stuff of nightmares. 'But my dear one, that is my mama's, no? With her own two hands she put lining and stitched and told she broke her back doing it.'

Elsie said she didn't care how many backs Aggie broke. 'Don't come to dear one me,' she said, 'Get tailor fellow to put new covers. Getting sick when I see this.'

Eric muttering under his breath, went to the almirah.

'What did you say?' Elsie demanded, 'So already you're scolding me, no? Cursing me to yourself, no?'

Eric hadn't a chance. Elsie was upon him seized him by his neck, pushed his head into the almirah and rained a series of blows on his back and shoulders. With his face screwed into a shelf of clothes, Eric could scarcely breathe. He wriggled and squirmed, but was stuffed into the shelf and lay helpless, trying hard to breathe and feeling increasingly sick at the smell of mothballs. When released, he tottered to the bed and slumped gasping. Elsie stood over him, glowering. 'If you don't want to marry never mind,' she said defiantly, 'I'm going to tell Papa.'

Eric leaped up with a howl, sprang across to fall at her feet, clutch her ankles. 'How you must be loving me,' he croaked, 'beating me like this. Tomorrow we will put new cloth on chairs. Ah, you always are my dear one. Love you like anything now.'

So Elsie had her way and they had a quiet wedding and the wedding photograph recorded for posterity the satisfied smirk on her face.

George de Mello found a house in Wellawatte since he didn't favour the idea of taking Leah to Kandana. Papa de Mello was displeased. 'Why she cannot stay here with us,' he asked, 'Can help your mama also, no?'

'How to bring Leah here? Whole day walking about without elastic in your pajamas and shouting the whole time. And what is she going to do here? Just sit and listen to you talking about the cows?'

True as this was, George was anxious that Leah continue to work at the florist's in Dehiwela and the Wellawatte home was just a few cents bus fare away. Much better, he thought, than a jobless wife and he out in the port all day. The decision pleased Leah no end. She was touched that George could be so considerate. There had been long moments when she had entertained calling it all off but there were those other days when he would call at the florist's and slyly put his hand up her dress under cover of the counter and she would say: 'Don't, *anney*, suppose someone comes,' and press a little closer. All things in account, she classified George as some sort of necessary evil and the wedding took place in April and everyone said that Leah made a beautiful bride and Cecilprins, who was now ready to retire from public service, went to great pains to give her as good a wedding as any.

Things were not so straightforward for Totoboy and Sonnaboy. Indeed, the complications that set in were such that one wonders how such a tangled skein could be ever unravelled. The problem had many sides to it and should be highlighted as follows:

A. A Customs Officer, Bertie Carron, saw Elva da Brea and knew at last that this was the answer to the sweet mystery of life. He loved her to distraction.

B. Elva, determined to score one over her cocky younger sister, Beryl, was as set on marrying Sonnaboy as Bertie was on marrying her.

C. Mama da Brea who was determined to palm off Elva to the first comer, considered that Sonnaboy filled the bill perfectly. 'You marry Elva if you like,' she kept saying, 'My Beryl is too small. She is my Buiya (Florrie da Brea's pet name for Beryl) no?'

D. Sonnaboy, who began to call Beryl *'Buiya'* (a term Beryl deplored) said it was Beryl or nobody and this led to words. 'Don't come here again,' Florrie screeched.

E. Iris Holdenbottle, a seamstress, had sewn several dresses for Elva and casually informed Totoboy that she knew the da Brea girls, which information was relayed to Sonnaboy who decided to cultivate this situation.

F. Sonnaboy's fiancee, Elaine, was determined to hold on to her man.

G. Elaine's beefy brothers declared that nobody plays the fool with their sister and lives to talk of it.

Everything, happily, was sorted out in the end. Bertie claimed Elva, Sonnaboy married Beryl and Totoboy married Iris, but before this thrice-happy outcome, Iris and Totoboy suffered injury, Elva was forced to run, shrieking along the beach and Elaine's brothers had to make several visits to the Municipal Outdoor Patients Dispensary. Also, one must not forget Bertie's black eye which was a glory to behold.

It is the duty of the chronicler to now add fat and muscle to these bare bones. The visit of Cecilprins and Maudiegirl to the da Brea home—which has been alluded to in part one of this chronicle—was not a happy one. Even Maudiegirl had remarked later: 'No wonder, child, the poor boy always in a temper. Disappointed, no?'

Cecilprins did not agree. 'But hammering people left and right? Bottle man shout on road, going and hitting. You saw that Beryl, no? Child, men, a child. Only fifteen. What he thinking, I don't know. And what about Elaine? How many months now they are carrying on.'

'Not a small one, that Beryl,' Maudiegirl observed, 'Saw the way she was looking at Sonnaboy.'

Florrie da Brea had been firm. 'My Buiya is too small and studying also. Every night I think about this and praying to Saint Anthony also. If like he can marry my Elva. Can marry any time he wants and I will give this house and go and live in Maradana with my Juppie. Can send Beryl by rickshaw to school from there or even put in Kotahena Good Shepherd convent to study.'

Cecilprins had to agree that Florrie had her rights. Beryl was under age and there was nothing that could be done. Sonnaboy was furious.'Who wants to marry Elva? I love Beryl.'

Florrie gave Maudiegirl a pained look.'If so let wait for six years.'

'Six years!' Sonnaboy snorted.

'Yes. When my Buiya is twenty-one can marry if you like. Useless your looking at me like that. If coming here to argue and fight I will go and tell the police. All alone here with my girls and you coming to fight and in my house also.'

Cecilprins hastened to soothe the old lady. 'No, no, no need for all that, no? Didn't come to fight? Only came like decent people to meet you, no? So never mind, we'll go.'

Florrie was not mollified.'And what about my Elva?' she asked.

Sonnaboy rose. 'Come go,' he said darkly, 'Came to ask for Beryl and trying to push Elva on me. Who wants your Elva? Did I come to ask for Elva? You give Elva to anyone. Who cares? Give to the police. Best thing for her. But I'm going to marry Beryl!'

'We'll see,' said Florrie, the blood of the da Brea's warming up several degress, 'You come near my Beryl and I'll put entry in police station.'

Cecilprins tugged Sonnaboy away, 'For goodness sake come go,' he urged and for goodness and Beryl's sake, Sonnaboy went.

Things didn't go swimmingly at home either. Elaine Werkmeister had soured considerably over the eleven months of being Sonnaboy's fiancee. They had met, of all places, in the Dehiwela fish market and Sonnaboy had been fascinated by her severely bobbed hair and thin features. She swung her arms as she walked and her narrow shift brought out her boyish figure to good effect. Nothing very feminine about Elaine. Two hulking elder brothers, one in the Municipality Power Station and the other a supervisor in a Kawdana brickyard, had treated her as one of them since she was so high. They weren't the doting, protective brothers everyone thought they were. Elaine had to be one of the boys or nobody at all. The fact that she was a girl had been a disappointment to the two strapping lads who grew tall and matured fast. At thirteen, older brother Eustace had a few hairs in his armpits. He hadn't noticed until the younger Merril had remarked: 'You're getting hair like Papa.' It was even more interesting to discover later the soft down that had begun to discolour the skin over his penis. The brothers examined each other and Elaine was also made privy to this marvel of growing up. 'It's a secret,' Eustace told her, 'Swear you will not tell anybody else you saw.' Elaine promised and was never tired of this new game and they would creep into the garage to look upon each other. The boys would examine her vagina with deep interest and part her labia and touch the little pink button that throbbed visibly at their touch. 'Like a tiny birdie,' Eustace would say and Elaine would run her fingers along their hard little cocks and gently massage their testicles and push their foreskins back to look at what she called their 'pippie holes'.

When Sonnaboy came on the scene years later, Elaine was not surprised at his advances. And, she thought, Sonnaboy didn't ask for too much. All he wanted was that she cross her legs and stand still while he pushed his penis between her thighs. His effusion made if rather messy but if this was all her man wished of her, she was happy to oblige. She never dreamed that to Sonnaboy, she was just another boy and he was using her just the way he used the *hopper* boy and the young cleaner in the railway running shed and so many others. She was a woman, and Sonnaboy said he would marry her, and her father, too, had approved. But old Werkmeister was a surveyor and left nothing to chance. 'You send me a letter,' he told Sonnaboy, 'Write and say that you love my Elaine and want to marry her and promise to love and look after her always and then you can get engaged, right?'

So Sonnaboy went home and wrote a letter and old Werkmeister grunted in satisfaction. 'You see,' he said, 'this tells me you are a gentleman. You are not just playing about with Elaine, no? You have no ulterior business. Now I will also send you a letter saying that I am giving my consent and always you remember that this is the way gentlemen must be. Now anyone can say anything for when people ask me I can say proudly that you are a gentleman and my Elaine is marrying a gentleman and you have put it all down on paper.'

Sonnaboy was pleased. Nobody had called him a gentleman before. Also, he had a sneaking respect for Papa Werkmeister who was a clever man, educated, too, and doing very well. He even talked better. Sonnaboy sighed and thought it might be nice to be a cut above the rest and talk 'bookish', as Werkmeister did.

When Sonnaboy told Elaine that he had no intention of marrying her and that he had found another girl to so honour, he was ready for a scene. Elaine was unnerved, true, but she did not get hysterical. She had a shrewd mind and considered this very much in the line of convent friendships. Best friends suddenly cool towards each other and find new friends. There was a sort of circle in this business of being inseparables today, on nodding terms tomorrow and bosom pals again next week. She had noticed this with her brothers, too, like when Merril developed a crush on Mister de Jong next door. De Jong would give Merril books and help him make his catapults and teach him how to shoot with the Daisy air rifle. For months, Merril was full of Mr de Jong said this and Mr de Jong can do that and he would nip over the fence and seek out de Jong all the time. Then one day he came home and never went there again. Even when de Jong would pop his head over the fence and say, 'Hullo, Merril, haven't seen you for a long time,' Merril would go quite red and lower his eyes and mutter something about being busy. No one could fathom why, and even Papa Werkmeister would say: 'Such a nice chap, that de Jong. Very fond of children. Don't know why he doesn't think of getting married.'

Elaine told Sonnaboy: 'Anney, I don't know about all this. You promised to marry me, no? Everybody knows this, and you gave ring also—'

'That's all right. You can keep ring if you like. Only what I'm saying is that this Beryl is whom I want to marry.'

'But you said, no? that she is very young and her mama won't allow. All foolishness, I think. Having me and here I am doing everything you like and all these months you're coming and everybody knows that we will get married and all. Supposing you cannot marry this Beryl? Now you are promoted also. I thought we can get married soon. Instead of which you are telling something else.'

'But what to do, Elaine, this Beryl is—is—don't know, men, not like you at all. When I saw her I felt like something. You keep the ring, never mind. You can get any other fellow.'

Elaine considered him darkly. 'What other fellow? You think after getting engaged and all I can just go and find someone else? You're mad, I think. And you yourself telling that Beryl cannot even see you.'

'That's what they think. Every day I manage to see her somehow. Go to Retreat Road on the other side of the convent and she comes out from the side gate and we go to beach for a little and talk and nobody knows.'

'And you're doing that way to her also?' Elaine like to get things straight.

'You're mad, men, on the beach? With everyone looking?'

This made Elaine angry. 'Yes, but you can come here and do to me. Quietly going round the kitchen and whole time saying 'tighten your legs' and putting your stuff all over. But did I say I can't? And inside my thighs all red by your rubbing. And after all this now you say don't want to marry me even.'

'What can I do, men. You think I'm not sorry? But when I saw Beryl . . . .'

Elaine raised a hand. 'So you saw her. I know, I know, so you thought she is nice and must be nice to do to her also, no? Like doing to me. That is the way with men nowadays. You think I don't know how men think? Only one thing, when we marry no going all over the place putting between anyone else's!'

'But I'm telling you, no? I want to marry Beryl.'

Elaine sniffed. 'We'll see. You promised to marry me. Gave ring also. And we had a party also, no? If I tell Papa now what you're saying, think he will keep quiet?'

'So tell,' said Sonnaboy recklessly, 'You think I'm worried what he can do? What can he do? And what can you do? Think you can catch and force me to marry you?'

Elaine's reserve broke. She had tried, she told herself, to be understanding and treat this business in a dignified manner. It hadn't helped. She tossed an angry head and rose, 'All right, if that's the way you're thinking. I'll tell Papa whole story and you see, what he will do. If you don't marry me you're going to get it properly!'

These were the sort of fighting words Sonnaboy understood. He strode out, stood in the porch and bawled: 'You think I'm afraid of anybody? Tell them to come if they want—your papa and your brothers—all three I'll send to hospital!'

So Elaine went to old Werkmeister and he listened and nodded and said: 'Why did you go to argue with him? He has to marry you. I have his letter. If he won't we will go to courts and sue him. You don't worry.' Then a thought struck him. 'You didn't allow him to take liberties, miss?'

'Liberties?'

'You know, child, like meddling with you and doing unnecessary things.'

Elaine thought awhile. 'No, Papa.'

'Good, good, but if did anything can make bigger case and disgrace him. Never mind, I will write a letter.'

Elaine consulted her brothers. The latter half of the conversation had given rise to some doubts. She was not very sure if what Sonnaboy had been doing to her constituted 'liberties'. Eustace and Merril listened. 'Only putting between and going like a dog,' she explained and Merril unwittingly burst out: 'Like what that de Jong used to do,' and his brother and sister stared at him and he turned crimsom.

'What?' said Eustace, 'That old bugger did that to you? When?'

'Long time ago. 'Member I used go there to shoot with his gun and all? One day he standing behind and showing how to aim and telling this is foresight and must hold gun correct and then he slowly start feeling my bum and then he quietly unbutton my trousers and pull them down and made my one stand up with feeling it.'

'He also tell to cross the legs?' Elaine asked.

'No. He squeezing and saying have nice fat thighs and then from behind he suddenly put his one between and going backwards forwards. I don't know what to do. I'm with gun in my hands and he going on and panting also and suddenly he finish and give me a cloth and tell to wipe and put the trousers and asking me to come again. But I never went. How to go, men. The way he breathing and hugging me round the stomach . . . .'

Eustace patted him on the shoulder. 'Never mind, men. In school Father Theo did the same to me when I was small. And that is no harm, actually, for girls. If Sonnaboy doing the same thing to you then you are all right. If he start doing inside only must be carefully because he put the white in and you can get a baby.'

Elaine was relieved. 'No, he never try to go inside. Quite happy doing outside, and I allow him because he is going to marry me, no? I thought if I don't allow will start doing to some other girl. And now, after all this he is saying I can keep the ring and he doesn't want to marry me.'

The brothers thought this over. 'You told Papa?'

Elaine nodded. 'Papa said don't worry. Will go to court and make him marry me. *Anney,* I don't know now. If make him marry also he may just marry because he has to and then will hate me and won't even come near me.'

Merril was thinking. 'So why he saying to cross the legs?'

Elaine shrugged and did not wish to discuss the matter but the boys must have thought more on the subject for that night they crept over and later had to agree that Sonnaboy was right. Elaine had to cross her long, lean legs before giving them any satisfaction.

Meanwhile, despite Sonnaboy's claims to daily meetings with Beryl he found this particular romance hard going. His duty shifts were not always timed to Beryl's end-of-school hours and there were weeks when he never did have the opportunity to meet her. Also, he found to his dismay that he had a great deal to study. Apprenticed as an engine driver, he was not merely standing on the footplate of a steam locomotive, yanking on the regulator and hauling on the vacuum brake lever. There were handbooks to con over and diagrams to pore over and tables to memorise and the operation of all manner of gauges to keep in mind. All very fascinating, of course, if he hadn't Beryl to think about and spending a lot of his working moments scheming how he could be at Retreat Road, Babalapitiya by 3.30 p.m. But he had to admit that all his great love for the plump-cheeked schoolgirl would not get him far up the road. So, when Totoboy remarked one day, 'Funny thing, no? My Iris not in when I went yesterday and her mama said she gone to Bambalapitiya to take Elva's measurements. I asking what Elva? And she saying I don't know child, some friend. So I wait and talking to the mama and old lady, and I put a small brandy also, and then Iris come and I ask who this Elva you went to see and she said why, you didn't know, that is Sonnaboy's girlfriend's sister who is friend of mine and how she is sewing frocks for her for a long time. Funny no? How Iris knowing this Elva like that?'

Sonnaboy's head swam a little as it usually did when he had to listen to his brother. But he caught the gist of it. 'Iris knows Beryl also?'

'Don't know. I'll ask and see. Must be knowing, no? After all, going there and all.'

Iris did, of course, and Sonnaboy hatched a neat little egg. He could use Iris to get to Beryl. A made-to-order messenger. And he could concentrate on his job and get over a raft of difficulties. 'The thing is to keep in touch with Beryl,' he explained to Iris the next day, 'Now I'm in locomotive yard and have to do firing also and learning signals and shunting and points also. Must see all the diagrams. Get mad trying to follow them.' Therefore, he would like Iris to take his letters and the occasional gift to Beryl.

'If that you can do she will know I'm loving her and thinking about her and never mind then if I can't come and I can tell how much I'm working and learning and soon I will be shunting driver and next year I will be class three driver also. Imagine salary I will then get.'

Iris thought this over, 'Only thing is if start going there everyday, will wonder why I'm coming up and down.'

'Not everyday, men. How to write everyday? Maybe once-twice a week. Only thing tell that Beryl to hide letters. It her mama find them . . . .'

'Better if I tell to read and burn, no?'

Sonnaboy nodded with slight regret. He couldn't imagine his masterpieces consigned to the kitchen fire. Anyway, Iris agreed and actually unhooked her lower lip to smile, and Sonnaboy smiled and thought what a fine girl she was and how he had misjudged her. Also, as things developed—and they were bound to develop—he had his own problems to countenance.

Papa Werkmeister came calling and aired his grievance to a bemused Cecilprins who wondered if he could plead insanity or something in the face of the gathering storm. Sonnaboy was nonplussed. He imagined that his father would support him; but Werkmeister stood, as it were, on some lofty pillar of propriety. A private discussion with his sons on Elaine's predicament had let the cat out of the bag when Merril blurted: 'And that's not everything, no? Elaine told us that this Sonnaboy was doing dirty things to her also.'

'What!?'

Eustace nodded. 'Only don't tell her you know, Papa. Just come out of her mouth when she was talking to us.'

'So why didn't you tell me straight away? Fine children you are. But now he can't escape. I'm going to see his father today.'

Cecilprins had expected Joe Werkmeister ever since this Beryl business begun. He had no Maudiegirl to help him now, and he felt extremely guilty about the visit to the da Breas which, he felt, he should not have consented to. 'Should have washed the hands from the whole thing,' he muttered several times over, and now here was his old friend Joe looking very severe and not even saying 'How' when he said, 'How, Joe? come, come, come and sit.'

Werkmeister had that look. When he had said his piece, Cecilprins could only bleat, 'I know, men, don't think I'm trying to pull for Sonnaboy even if my own son and all. Very ugly, no? the way he behaving and won't think, men. That's the trouble nowadays. These young buggers won't think. Told him that he is very lucky to have girl like Elaine from such good family, but what's the use—'

'My Elaine is too good for him!' Werkmeister declared.

'Of course, of course. As if I don't know. My poor Maudiegirl turning for sure in her grave with all this. Really, I'm thanking God she not here now to see all this.'

Werkmeister was not interested in Maudiegirl's graveyard gyrations. 'You are the father. You must make the boy see sense. Tchah! If I have a son like this do you know what I will do?'

'What, what?'

'I'll kick the bugger out. What for keeping? Damn disgrace, no?'

Cecilprins had to concede that Sonnaboy was not doing anything for the family escutcheon.

'In the mud!' Werkmeister exclaimed, 'Dragging your name in the mud. And you know something . . . ' he looked around, leaned forward and muttered, and Cecilprins raised a hand to his mouth and said, 'No! You are sure? *Chee,* men, no respect for girl, no? Going every Sunday to church and all, and this is how he behave.'

'So what are you going to do?'

'Can talk to him. Good if he listen and start to think properly. Don't worry, Joe, when he come home I'll catch and give good lecture.'

Sonnaboy and lectures were as distant as—to quote a popular expression—a Moorman and pork. Cecilprins said, 'My friend Joe came to see how we are and not happy about you and Elaine. You giving letter also, no? What for doing the la-di-da with that Beryl after saying will marry Elaine, I don't know. And now you okay in the railway so why you not marry and bring Elaine to stay here. Can manage a small party even.'

'What did that old bugger say?' Sonnaboy demanded, 'I told that Elaine, no? I won't marry her. So that's all. Let them do anything they want.'

'But he telling me you ruin his daughter, no? You meddling with her and now spoilt her for other men and because of what you have done how she can get married to anybody else. You're not thinking. That's the whole trouble. If your poor mama here what she will say I don't know.'

'What will she say?' Sonnaboy growled, 'When Dunnyboy meddling with everybody here and showing to all the children in the lane what Mama say? If Elaine didn't like, why didn't she tell? When doing not a word. Now because I tell I'm not going to marry everything is bad. If so bad, then why she still want to marry me?'

'Again you're not thinking,' Cecilprins shouted, 'That's the trouble with you. Only if married that you can do anything, no? And she must have allowed also because you promised to marry, no?'

'I don't care. Let them say anything. I'm going to marry Beryl.'

'But you know, no? What her mother say. She not of age. How you can wait six years?'

'I don't care, I tell you. Old bugger coming here to complain. As if can't find 'nother chap for Elaine. If ask me I can bring twenty fellows from railway for her to choose.'

Cecilprins found the conversation getting nowhere, or rather, far out of reach. 'You're not thinking!' he shouted, 'You wait and see what will happen for your stubbornness. So go and do what you want, but don't you bring that Beryl here. Even if you marry you take and go somewhere else,' and with that, he went trembling to his room and refused to come out for dinner that evening.

Sonnaboy considered Werkmeister's visit was unwarranted. So he banged his bicycle against the latter's gate the next evening, strode in and declared that he had nothing more to do with Elaine, so there!

'Nothing more?' Werkmeister quivered, 'After you do too much already? What sort of gentleman are you?'

'So who said anything about gentlemen?' Sonnaboy gritted, 'You're the one, taking letters and starting all this gentleman business. What I'm saying is, useless your coming to say things to my papa. I'm not going to marry your daughter. Told her that, no? What, men, simple thing like this even you people cannot understand?'

'Oh, I understand,' said Werkmeister coldly, 'After promising and having fun with my girl, now you want to wriggle out. I should have known better.'

'So now you know, no? And what fun you're talking about? You think I have fun? Who told you that? Can have better fun with the *hopper* woman.'

'So that's the kind of person you are! But don't think you are going to get away with this. I will make you pay for this.'

'Pay? Why, you want money from me for not having fun? You can do what you want. Only came to tell you and don't you come to upset my papa again. Telling all sorts of things behind my back.'

'Lucky for you my boys aren't at home,' shouted Werkmeister, 'or they'll teach you a good lesson.'

'Lucky for them, I think,' said Sonnaboy, 'Tell them to come anytime.'

'Get out of my house!'

Sonnaboy grinned. 'You think I want to come here again? But if I catch you or that Merril or Eustace in Boteju Lane . . . .'

'What will you do?' Werkmeister hooted. 'You think you can come in here and threaten this family?'

'Not threatening. Only telling. Put a foot near our house to see,' Sonnaboy promised and stormed out. And that was Act One, Scene Four.

It can only be hazarded what Werkmeister told his children, but it is believed that a fierce before-dinner argument took place and Elaine received an even fiercer slap from her father and cried herself to sleep while the boys decided that with some luck, both of them could get the better of Sonnaboy, if they could take him by surprise. So they went to bed plotting in whispers, and then shelved the scheme the next morning, for the light of day mocked their plans and reminded them that even their combined muscle could not save them from all sorts of grief.

Sonnaboy was in a good mood. He was very satisfied with himself. He told his papa that he had reached a settlement with old Werkmeister and that the wedding with Elaine was off. Cecilprins tried to guess what might have happened but hadn't the imagination. 'Settlement' could mean anything as far as Sonnaboy was concerned. The last time he had reached a settlement with the Bocks boy, there was a bill for a set of upper dentures. He dared not probe further but was relieved to find that Joe and his sons were in good physical shape, although they would cross the road quickly on spying him. He was sad about this. He had lost a friend. He had to admit, of course, that Elaine never did appeal to him as a daughter-in-law. 'Too horsey and walks like a man,' he had thought. But that was all over. He shuddered instead at what lay ahead. A Sonnaboy, waiting six years was no pleasing prospect. Somehow he had to convince that da Brea woman to unbend.

Meanwhile Iris took a long love-letter and a small box of chocolates in a shopping bag and called over at Nimal Road and discussed the situation with Elva who regarded this new development as a way to put one over her sister.

'You give letter here, will you,' Elva said.

'But what about Beryl?'

'You don't worry. Here, you take the chocolates. What men, he paying you for doing this? No, no? Mama told him to marry me and telling to give me to police fellows. Damn cheek of him. And here I listening to Mama and won't go with anyone else because Mama says I can marry him anytime he like.'

Iris was puzzled. 'If so, then why he writing to Beryl?'

'How to know? Trying to take from cradle, that's what I think. But Mama won't allow, so all this letter business is useless. And now because can't meet Beryl that writing.'

'But what to tell him?' Iris asked, 'Sure to ask if gave letter. Might ask for Beryl to give reply also.'

Elva frowned. The thought that Iris may have to be a two-way messenger hadn't occurred to her. 'Let's see what he is writing,' and she ripped open the envelope. Nothing fascinates girls of today and yesterday—and, it is supposed, tomorrow—like other people's love letters. Elva and Iris were fascinated. After a vast discourse on the path of true love which Sonnaboy declared resembled a corkscrew, there were colourful allusions to Beryl's form and features with a lip-smacking definition of what her legs were to him. He also explained how he had to stay away in order to get through his railway examinations and how he was determined to better himself for her sake. Darlings and dearests were scattered like petals in May and when he described how he longed for her and ached all over below the waist, Elva and Iris pinched each other and giggled fit to burst. 'Write to me, darling,' Sonnaboy begged, 'Iris will bring your letter to me,' and there were more pages of how birds sang sweeter every time he thought of her and how he put his pillow between his legs at night and imagined it was her.

'So now what to do?' Iris asked, 'Asking to reply, no? Sure to ask as I go back.'

'Wait, will you, saying he cannot see her, no? So how to know if Beryl wrote or not?'

'What do you mean?'

'He wants reply, no? So I'll give reply.' And Elva wrote a long letter full of syrupy things about how the birds were singing arias in Nimal Road and how she wished she was a pillow and that he could stay away as long as it took because she was ever true and would wait for him till the cows came home.

'Don't forget the chocolates,' Iris chortled, and Elva nodded and gave thanks prettily and added that the side gate to Retreat Road was now locked and there was no way Sonnaboy could meet her and he had better not come any more because someone was sure to see him hanging around and what if some neighbour saw and told her mama and thus get her in trouble?

This, thought Elva, was a master stroke. Sonnaboy would have to be content with the letters and when Beryl found that he was no longer coming around she may think that he had cooled off and was no longer interested and that he had found someone else. Oh, Elva was devious. She liked her scheme. After some time she would herself drop the ardour in the letters and hint that Beryl was losing interest herself. Then she, Elva, would move in to offer her sympathy and let him know that as an alternative she was, like Barkis, very willing.

Sonnaboy was in transports of joy. Beryl's first letter was read a thousand times over. Iris was to him that rare creature who surely was Florence Nightingale, a Grace Darling, a Jeanned' Arc all rolled in one. He rushed to reply, spending hours over his letter which became a veritable tome crammed with all manner of quotations and extracts from Leah's old romantic magazines. Joanna Baillie, a tedious writer of the age appealed to him, for he found among her laboured writings such gems as:

Friendship is no plant of hasty growth,
Though planted in Esteem's deep-fixed soil,

The gradual culture of kind intercourse
Must bring it to perfection.

Sonnaboy didn't quite grasp what it all meant but the words did give a ring and he reasoned that there was something about the lines that should give Beryl food for thought—things like 'kind intercourse', for instance.

Iris would look at the bulky packet and say, 'That's a letter?' and Sonnaboy would grin and belabour her with questions about what Beryl said and how was she and is she sorry that he cannot meet her. Soon Elva began to make specific requests. Beryl could do with some biscuits (Sonnaboy would despatch a large tin of Almond Rings) or soap (Iris took away Pears Best Scented) or was longing to eat some cherry tarts. Sonnaboy was in his element. His Beryl asked . . . his Beryl received. Poor girl. Her mama must be starving her. But what did she want red currant jelly for, and bottled plums? He could understand lace and two yards of organdie and a brooch to match a yellow Sunday dress but his Beryl did ask for the strangest thing—like American cheese, nectarines, an egg-whisk, ivory napkin rings. She was a great one for ribbons, he thought as a demand arrived for three yard rolls in several colours. To Elva and Iris, this was mother-lode. They grew quite reckless and Elva found letter-writing a full-time job while Iris said: 'Feel like asking for a pair of shoes. Mine getting wasted by coming up and down like this.'

The game lasted all of six months and meanwhile, Bertie Carron of His Majesty's Customs Preventive Office who always wore white with white hose and white calf shoes, and had a very red face (like a side of mutton, Elva said) had seen Elva at St. Mary's church, Bambalapitiya, and decided that she was the sun, moon and stars of his existence. Bertie was weekending in Bambalapitiya and had been dragged to church by his hosts, the Bulners, who considered that Bertie needed some religion thrust on him. Bertie treated God with all due respect, true, but wanted no truck with priests who, he never tired of pointing out, were all overfed and mumbled in a sort of sacerdotal pig-Latin. Bertie had strong views on a lot of things. Also, he was a fine product of British education and would quote Addison and Cowper and had read Plutarch's *Lives* and knew enough Latin to have sailed through the London Matriculation. His views on church-Latin were thus not contested.

In introducing Bertie, the chronicler feels it incumbent to fix Burgher society of the 1930s in proper perspective. The reader may be inclined to dismiss all Burghers as a roistering, bawdy breed who spoke funny and were extremely Catholic in matters of sex. This is not absolutely true. The characters we have met so far do run true to form. Burgher boys and girls who were wont to marry young, had no formal sex education in those days and no parent to even hint at such things as the birds and the bees. The children learned, so to say, 'on the run', from childhood to puberty and had no pretensions about how they undertook their 'practicals'. These were, the chronicler may well call them, the 'lick and a quick polish Burghers'. They did everything to that finite degree of 'getting by' and were content.

This does not mean that all Burghers were remarkably heterosexual, singularly unambitious, unashamedly incestuous and given without reserve to booze, large families and the principle that tomorrow never comes. The tempora and the mora were an influencing factor. With the British in control, life was good and there was that general feeling of release from long years of Victorian morality and drawing-room ethics. It may be even mentioned in passing that this was also the time when King Edward VIII of merrie England was fanning the air with the great Windsor scandal and being pretty shameless with his American Wallis Simpson and really tipping over the royal applecart. The cost of living in old Ceylon was marvellously low (unbelievably low, in fact), and all the best and worst of British manufacture and make was available; and not just from Britain but from her other colonies too: Australia, the East Indies, Hong Kong, India, East and South Africa and wherever else the Raj held court. Oh, life was good in the 1930s. It was no wonder, then, that the Burghers—favourites of the white administrators, found little trouble in employment and in managing their lives and paying scant heed to what the future may hold. Boys grew up to be pushed out to tea and rubber plantations, or the railway, or the police.

While most Burghers were content to move in their small circles of workaday bureaucratic influence (and it is the British who made bureaucracy a fine art in the colonies) others took fullest advantage of British education and technical training to become scholars and academics and engineers and architects and excel in all manner of disciplines. Thus there was, at the time of introduction of Bertie Carron, a sort of Burgher social step-ladder. At the top were those who had risen to be physicians and professors and engineers and judges and civil servants and such like. Such had furthered study in England and returned with letters behind their names and were Fellows and Licentiates and Associates and excelled in their particular callings. These were the Burghers who had clawed their way up from the roistering, boisterous bottom-rung to study hard, tread the rainbow of academic achievement and look back on their beginnings with pure horror. Naturally, not every member of the normally over-large families of the age could make it to the top. It depended on the individual. The von Blosses, for example, had no superfatted aspirations. Cecilprins rose from counter supervisor to assistant postmaster and was more than content. After thirty years service and having raised thirteen children he retired and drew a monthly pension and mooched around the house, suitably appalled at his children's pyrotechnics. It never occurred to Cecilprins that he could, with some application, take the qualifying examination that would make him a postmaster or that, with some dedication, actually become a Grade I Postmaster in charge of his own post office. He was content, and, with many more of his ilk, proclaimed that contentment was all. As long as there was a regular pay packet and money enough to feed, clothe and house his family and throw a regular party and show the neighbourhood that the von Blosses were 'well off', what else could possibly matter?

But while the 'top' Burghers drove around in their cars and held sway in their offices and became educators and architects and scientists and legal luminaries, they could never shake off the reality of the 'common herd', especially when Aunty Mona would come to the Royal Academy and demand to see her Ralphie. Ralphie was a professor of English and a figure of great eminence. He was the proudest boast of the Meerwald family in their home in Kotahena. 'See that Ralphie,' Papa Meerwald would say, cuffing his son Spencer, 'If learn like him you also can be big man like him one day, no? Went to England and all and now can even teach English people to talk English.' The Meerwalds preened themselves and basked in the glory of professor Ralph Meerwald. 'Sister's son, men,' Papa Meerwald would say, 'and must just hear him talk. Like six books. And writing books also. One thing, our family all bright.'

Professor Ralph would blanch when told of Aunty Mona's arrival. The old woman had this jarring habit of screeching her greetings from a mile away. Why couldn't she stay on the bottom rung where she was so immensely popular? But Aunty Mona didn't see things this way. 'Going to see our Ralphie,' she would tell Sophia Gogerley, 'See, taking him a small bottle of my lime pickle.'

'Who, that profferso fellow?'

'Who else? All the time learning and reading and books, books everywhere, and sure he not even eating properly. Lucky for him his Aunty Mona there to think about him. When he was small, real one for currant cake. So yesterday baked small one for him.'

So Aunty Mona would trip the corridors of the Royal Academy and on spying her nepnew screech: 'My, just look at your state! Like a stick, no? Brought some currant cake. Now cut and eat a big piece at once. And here some lime pickle also. Real rice puller. Give you appetite.'

Professor Ralph would dearly love to curl up and die. He looked on Aunty Mona as one of those poor relations who should never be allowed to crawl out of the Kotahena woodwork. He was, after all, one of the elite. Aunty Mona was a downright embarrassment. And what—perish the thought—if the boys started to call him currant cake?

So Ceylon, and thereafter Sri Lanka, has its Burgher bowl of cherries and its Burgher pits. Great men and women emerged and are remembered to this day. They were eminent historians and antiquarians, anthropologists, great literary figures, educators and scientists. Also—and of undying interest—were the Burgher *hoi polloi*: the mechanics, the white-collar workers, the engine drivers and police officers, the foremen and storekeepers, the teachers and lighthouse keepers and tugboat masters and those in the armed forces where the old C.R.N.V.R. (Ceylon Royal Navy Volunteer Reserve) preceeded the R.Cy.N. (Royal Ceylon Navy) and the S.L.N. (Sri Lanka Navy) and there was a mushrooming Ceylon Army with the C.L.I. (Ceylon Light Infantry) and Ceylon Artillery and C.A.C. (Ceylon Armoured Corps). The Royal Ceylon Air Force began with one Sunderland and lots of types with pointed moustachios and grey-blue jackets, swagger sticks and flying goggles. It would be correct, then, to say that the 1930s saw a Burgher upper, middle and lower class. But, in fact, hardly any lower class for, as a rule, the Burghers themselves considered it comfortable to be labelled middle class with the fine distinctions of upper and lower middle, while only those who moved in exhalted circles with the British were regarded as upper and belonged to some sort of Burgher 'holy of holies'.

Bertie Carron, then, as a Customs Preventive Officer, was decidedly upper middle. It did not deter him from seeking Elva out in order to press his suit. He considered her lower middle and nice to look at from any angle, especially if he focussed on her lower middle. Bertie considered himself as a divine gift to any young lady and could not understand the stories he heard about how this Elva tossed off suitors the way a dog would diligently rid itself of fleas. Obviously, he told himself, Elva was selective. She wasn't going to commit herself to the first man who hove into view. What she needed, he told himself, was a 'good Burgher', not those *mikos* (a nondescript half-breed) who go about on bicycles and don't know to knot a tie. 'Class will tell,' he informed his mirror as he angled his peaked cap with the silver Customs badge. He would call on Elva in full regalia. He would tell Elva's parents of his intentions. He would be friendly and firm and display just the right amount of condescension to impress on them that they were in the presence of their better. It was a bit of a shock when Elva looked him over and asked him why his face was so red.

'Red? Oh, you mean my complexion?'

'Like boiled mutton,' she giggled, 'and see, over the collar also, very red your neck.'

Bertie frowned. 'It is impolite to make such personal remarks,' he said loftily.

Even Florrie, who was quite dazzled by this immaculate apparition, said, 'If wore khaki like prison guard then red won't show so much.' But she was pleased. Elva would do well to marry the fellow. Talked funny but that's what comes of learning too much. 'But no harm, no? to have gentleman like that in family?'

Despite herself, Elva was quite impressed by Bertie. For one thing, she told Iris, she liked to see him in his starched white shorts. 'Lots of hair on his legs, men, and when crossing the legs can see hair going up the thighs also.'

Iris said wisely, 'Ah, if have hairy legs, good, men. That type men very good when doing the job, they say.'

Elva giggled. 'Your Totoboy also got hair on the legs?'

'*Apoi* yes.'

'So?'

'So what?'

'So tell, will you, if true.'

'True? True about what?'

'True about doing it. Totoboy also very good?'

Iris gave this some thought. 'I don't know still, men. Getting drunk too much, that's the trouble. If can catch him after two-three drinks . . . . Trouble is he bringing bottle to the bed and when I get all ready and opening his trousers and all, he says one for the road and puts two more drinks and then fall on top and going to sleep.'

Anyway, Bertie was duly accepted and Beryl was relieved. Now that Mama had decided on Bertie, she obviously didn't entertain hopes of Sonnaboy marrying Elva. So maybe she may consent to Sonnaboy marrying her. She decided to test the temperature.

'Mama, why that Sonnaboy not coming now?'

Florrie glared. 'Butter won't melt in your mouth, no? the way you're asking. Let him try to come and see what I will do.'

'But Mama—yeeeeee! why you hitting? Only asking, no?'

So Beryl ran in to weep and wonder what had become of Sonnaboy. Months passed and she would nip out after school and dawdle on the road and no sign of the man. She told her pillow that her heart was breaking and her pillow, in its wisdom, lay silent. In the evenings she would wind up the gramophone and play 'Where's my wandering boy tonight' and wallow hugely in her misery.

Six months had seen a lot of changes in Sonnaboy's career. He was now a Class III driver and had been informed that he would soon receive his first real station transfer. Transportation Superintendent Aleric de Bruin said he would be posted to Kadugannawa where Sonnaboy would run the short haul trains to Kandy and back and Rambukkana and back. Also, lots of shunting and wagon movements in Rambukkana, Kadugannawa and Peradeniya and Kandy. 'You'll get a small bungalow if you are married,' de Bruin said, and Sonnaboy knew that he had 'arrived'. This news was too good to be conveyed to Beryl by mere letter. He decided to meet her, and met, instead, a cheeky-looking girl named Maxine Foenander who accosted him in Retreat Road and said, 'You're Beryl's boyfriend, no? I know because Beryl pointed you out to me one day.'

Sonnaboy nodded.

'My, I'm in Beryl's class. Fine one you are. Everyday she used to come here and you are not to be seen and sometimes she crying also because for how long you did not come.'

Sonnaboy stared. 'But I'm writing, no? And she is also writing and she knows I can't come because of my exams and all.'

Maxine wrinkled her eyes. 'I don't know about all that. If so what is she crying and waiting for you everyday? Last week only she said maybe you are not coming any more because you have somebody else and now she is going home by the main gate.'

Bewildered, Sonnaboy went home and there was Iris with a letter from Beryl and this confounded him even more. It also struck him as he read it that surely Beryl didn't need a spice-box or a pair of size four kid-gloves and garters with embroidered roses. Surely not.

Iris waited. Sonnaboy scowled.

'So any reply?' Iris asked.

'No men, no time to write now. You tell her I'll try to meet her.'

'Meet her?' Iris blinked.

Sonnaboy nodded. 'Now almost six months I not see her, no?

Never mind what anybody says. I'll go even to the school and meet her.'

This put Iris into a blue panic. 'But she telling me everyday please tell him not to come. If Mama find out then she put me in boarding or send to married sister's place or something. You only causing trouble for the girl, no?'

'Can't be helped. What happens let happen. Can't go on like this everyday, no?'

Iris decided to attack. 'And then what will happen to me? You go there and then everybody will know I taking the letters and all and Elva and I both get into trouble!' and Iris clapped a hand over her mouth and stared wildly as Sonnaboy said, 'Elva? What has Elva got to do?'

Giving a little hoot, Iris bolted and was through the gate in seconds flat while Sonnaboy, quite perplexed, tapped the letter on his palm and wished he knew what was going on. Something told him that there was a mystery here. But what? He went to his table and looked at the stack of letters in the drawer. So many, and so full of demands for this, that and the other. And what the devil did she want with garters with embroidered roses? He had gone along with her without demur. She wanted a wash-hand bowl. Fine. A kneeling mat? Of course. One kneeling mat coming up. Will my love care to kneel? And Sonnaboy thought . . . a fifteen-year-old needs ivory napkin rings? And a lemon squeezer? He shook his head. He had expected to send her schoolgirl things . . . like autograph albums and those little songbooks from Paivas and perhaps posies and chocolates, but Beryl wanted gloves and a butter-beater. Also, that Maxine Foenander made no sense at all. He had to see Beryl. He needed help and he thought and thought. Then he made up his mind and went to bed that night feeling easier.

The next morning he made a packet of all Beryl's letters, dressed neatly and went to the Holy Family Convent, Bambalapitiya where he stood at the visitor's parlour door and asked to see the Reverend Mother Superior. Old Mother Gonzaga, whose vinegary face was the dread of generations of schoolgirls, swept in and eyed the caller narrowly. 'Are you a parent?' she asked.

'No mother, not yet, I'm not even married, no? I came to see you about 'nother matter.'

'Oh, very well. But I have a class at ten-fifteen. What is it you wish to discuss?' and the reverend mother listened fascinated, as Sonnaboy related to her the whole story of his meeting with Beryl, his determination to marry her, his work, his promotion, the clandestine meetings with Beryl until he found somebody to carry his letters. Mother Gonzaga tapped a foot and listened and stared fiercely and clucked and shook a disapproving head and even crossed herself once, but she heard the man out. 'And here,' said Sonnaboy, 'have all Beryl's letters also. Only 'nother girl say that Beryl waiting for me everyday now stopping that also because I not coming to meet. But yesterday also letter coming. Then I think this is funny, no? On one side writing and asking all sorts of things. On the other side she is waiting for me on the road but she knows I'm not coming and that's why she's writing.'

'May I see the letters?'

Sonnaboy handed her the packet and Mother Gonzaga's eyes grew large as she read. 'My girls,' she said shakily, 'my girls can write such things . . . Beryl da Brea . . . hmmm . . . in Form Four, yes . . . but these . . . ' she shook her head, shook the letters and scowled. 'You know, young man, it is very wrong of you to upset schoolgirls like Beryl in this way. No wonder the poor child's grades are failing. Of course, you did right in seeing her mother and declaring your intentions and I know that girls of your community marry quite young, but,' and there was asperity in her voice like a ribbon of lightning. 'Beryl is my pupil and you will respect this institution and the girls in my charge!'

Sonnaboy made no reply. This old woman was formidable and her magpie habit awed him.

'Leave these letters with me,' Mother Gonzaga said, 'and come and see me tomorrow afternoon. Can you come?'

Sonnaboy shook his head. 'Can come in the morning,' he said.

'Then you should come at ten-thirty. I can give you a little time and advise you.' She shook her head, 'I suppose I have to thank you for coming to me with this. It never occurred to me that my girls could do such things. And there is more to this than meets the eye.'

'Can I—can I see Beryl?'

'What!'

Sonnaboy raised a placating hand. 'Going. Going, I am. I'll come tomorrow.'

The nun nodded severely then turned away and allowed herself a tiny smile. Impudent man, but quite a forthright fellow. Oh, she thought, what a tangled web we weave . . . . Now to take that Beryl by the ear and get the truth out of her. For Land's sake, what did the child want a spice box for? And three hatbands with artificial rosebuds?

When Sonnaboy learned that Beryl had not written a single letter and that he had lived for half a year in a sort of fool's paradise (not counting the small fortune he had spent on gifts), he was a man to be shunned. He was almost paralysed at the news. Mother Gonzaga was very firm, very convincing. Beryl, she said, had never received a letter from him or written him a line. And Mother Gonzaga was satisfied that none of her girls had practiced this cruel deception. He had to look elsewhere for the culprit. She was sorry she could do no more but she was going to visit Beryl's mother. Something had to be done about that girl.

Sonnaboy had one thought as he got over the shock. To find Iris and tear her limb from limb; but as he cycled past Nimal Road, the packet of letters stuffed into his shirts, he recklessly turned into the road and pitched his bicycle against the low boundary wall. He was in no mood to trifle with latches and hinges. With a mighty kick he made matchwood of the gate and swept in. Elva, running out, saw what she took to be the end of the world closing in on her. Sonnaboy was fishing out a stack of letters from inside his shirt and at the sight, Elva gave a high squeak of fright and turned to collide with Florrie who was rushing out with a flour-sprinkled apron and grey hair straggling down her forehead. With another yelp, Elva turned, skipped past Sonnaboy and leapt the debris of the broken gate like a gazelle. 'Where are you running!' Sonnaboy roared, 'I want to talk to you!'

Elva shifted into second gear.

'Come here, you!' the voice blasted, rattling windowpanes.

Mouth open and with a sound like a punctured piano accordion,

Elva fled. She didn't pause to consider what direction she should take when she reached the Galle Road. She simply swung left and kept going until the gates of the convent told her that here lay sanctuary.

Sonnaboy turned furiously on Florrie who was staring white-faced at the ruins of her gate. 'She must be the one!' he thundered,' Otherwise why ran like that. Bloody bitch, writing all these letters and putting Beryl, Beryl and taking everything!' Neighbours ventured to the wall and Mr Schokman asked what was going on. 'Bugger off!' Sonnaboy snarled, 'None of your bloody business!' and Schokman buggered off with military promptitude.

Florrie was one of those fighting Dutch (or Portuguese, or Irish, or whatever) and could give as well as she took, but even with the servant, Soma, creeping up behind her with the meat-cleaver she sensed that this Vesuvius of a man couldn't be met with a show of arms. But she had to know what all this cyclonic activity was about. 'Why you coming here and chasing Elva out of the house,' she cried,' not enough you upsetting my Beryl?'

'Elva!' Sonnaboy spat. 'Why she running unless she guilty and playing me out!'

'Elva? What did Elva do? She now going with 'nother boy, no? Nothing to do with you!'

Sonnaboy flung the letters at Florrie and turned to glare at more venturesome neighbours who retreated rapidly. Florrie contrived to flick through a page or two at random and croaked: 'Beryl writing all this? Wait till she come! Saying homework, homework, and this what she is doing.'

'Beryl? Beryl never wrote anything. This must be Elva's work:'

The old lady's head reeled. 'For what Elva write and put Beryl? She mad or what? And now God only knows where she went.'

Sonnaboy picked up some of the fallen letters. 'All these things I sending, see? Here, can see, no? what writing and asking. Now about six months. And where is all this? You think Beryl got? And fine one, you are. Don't know your children's handwriting even.'

Florrie felt sick. She was out of her depth and there was Soma with a large kitchen knife skulking in the corner of the hall. She turned her anger on the woman. 'Go and some tea make,' she stormed 'And why you not come inside and sit down, child. No need to be shouting like this, no? Can find out what happened.'

Still simmering, Sonnaboy strode in and sat at the large dining-table while Florrie fluttered around nervously and Sonnaboy told her the story. 'All your fault,' he said severely, 'When I come like gentleman you putting parts to me. So I told that Iris to bring letter to Beryl and—'

'Iris! That black creature who always coming and giggling with Elva? *Aiyo,* don't know where Elva is also. Soma! Soma! Bring the tea and go and see if Elva on the road. Ran without slippers even.'

'Let run,' Sonnaboy gritted, 'So Iris bring me these letters and telling they are from Beryl. And I believe, no? What else? Nicely replying me, so how to think otherwise? And saying send this and send this and everytime I buying what ask and Iris taking and next letter saying send me this and again Iris taking and giving.'

'My godfather,' breathed Florrie,' and all this Beryl asking and Elva writing?'

'No. Beryl not even knowing I'm writing. Beryl crying and thinking I'm not even coming to see her and even telling friends in school she is sure I am giving up and finding' nother girl, but I told, no? I loving only her and will marry her. All because of you, this. If have to wait six years you want me to marry her when I'm old man? And now that Elva play me out. Don't care if she is girl. If I catch her I'll break her bloody back!'

'You wait, will you. Here, drink your tea. I'll see in Elva's cupboard what have.'

Florrie dumbly discovered the makings of another demanding letter, a lemon squeezer, a thick notepad, a set of ivory table napkins, Pears soap, an egg-whisk and something bulky in a wrapping which proved to be a blue enamel wash-hand bowl. That Elva! My goodness! What disgrace she putting on her family and her poor dead papa's name! And writing some more! My darling darling Sonnaboy. I'll darling darling her. Florrie was deeply ashamed. That all this skulduggery could go on in her home and under her nose. And now everybody will come to know and snigger at her and point and whisper in church and who will come to marry the girls after all this? My godfather! If that Bertie knows will go and tell everybody how he have lucky escape and . . . and . . . and . . . . She was in a fever of agitation. She gazed imploring at the picture of Clarence and got no help at all. 'Just standing and staring,' she muttered,' After leaving me and going and I have to put up with everything.' She tried to spread the guilt: 'How to know if that Iris put idea into Elva. Told how many times not to encourage that Iris here. Not good Burgher like us, no?'

'But Elva writing, no? Both getting together to play me out. That Iris won't escape. Put all her teeth in her stomach, wait and see.' Sonnaboy then sprang another shock by relating now he went to the convent and of his meeting with the principal, and Florrie's hands trembled and fluttered nervously. 'My godfather! Now all the nuns know and damn shame in school also. Boys I have and never gave so much trouble.'

Soma came in breathlessly to report that Elva had seemingly disappeared off the face of Bambalapitiya. *'Aiyo,* nona, way that missie ran, now in the Fort must be. To police better if tell, otherwise to find how?' Florrie pushed her spectacles to her forehead.'And where, then, all the letters you wrote?'

'Must be somewhere. Or must have burnt. Feel like telling this whole thing to the parish priest here. Fine way your daughter behave, no? Bloody rogue, that's what she is. And you telling for me to marry her. Pukka woman to marry, no? That's why from start I say you give Beryl and I'll marry like a shot. You go now to Railway and ask. Now I am driver also. And in January going to Kadugannawa, transferred with own bungalow there.'

'Chut, child, you think I don't know you are good man? And you came anyway to see me with no hanky-panky. Only because Beryl so young I say no, no? And now all this nonsense. You can't go on the bicycle and see if can find Elva?'

'Can go, but if I catch her . . . .'

'No, no, never mind. If see you she run again.' Florrie wrung her hands, 'If jump in the sea also, don't know. As if devil chasing, the way she went.'

It was decided that the nearby Pollock's boy borrow Sonnaboy's bicycle and tour Bambalapitiya, hither and yon, and the pimpled fellow set off in high glee and when more tea was being consumed, in sailed Mother Gonzaga with a snivelling Elva who saw Sonnaboy and wailed and had to be held firmly by the nun and slapped hard by Mama who panted that, 'Good thing not with my slippers or will slipper you, madam,' and dragged her by the hair to the bedroom and shut the door on her.

Mother Gonzaga said that the poor girl had suffered enough and it was most reprehensible that all this should have happened. 'Oh, I understand how hard it must be for you,' she told Florrie, 'Girls of this age need a father's discipline too. But don't take this matter any further.'

Florrie sniffed. 'Now not like those days, no? When my Clarence alive he gave them everything. Now only pension and widows and orphans monthly something so have to cut with cloth that have, no? But to do disgraceful thing like this . . . and even him coming to the convent to tell everybody. Could have come here and told me, no? Bringing shame for all of us like this. And that Elva now with nice fellow in the Customs also.'

Mother Gonzaga tapped a foot. 'So you should see that Elva is married. The sooner the better, I think.'

'And I will marry Beryl.' Sonnaboy declared.

'I cannot say anything about that, nor do I approve,' the nun said, 'Beryl is a child.'

'That's what I'm also telling,' Florrie said,' but couldn't keep quiet. Went to write letters and now see what happened?'

'Well, I must go,' said Mother Gonzaga, rising, and Elva, listening at the bedroom door gave a wail of protest. *'Aiyo,* Mother, don't go. Leaving me alone. Will kill me for sure.'

'I think Mister von Bloss should also go,' the nun said.

Sonnaboy pointed out that without his bicycle he had no intention of going anywhere. 'Then you must promise me that you will leave Elva alone. Her mother will punish her for what she has done. You have been cheated by her but remember that by sending letters against Mrs Brea's wishes you acted wrongly too. I cannot advise on these matters, but Elva has done much wrong. Send her to confession and let her make her peace with God.'

With his bicycle back, Sonnaboy was also urged to leave. Florrie wished to sort out her domestic affairs in her own way. First, she needed to inflict on Elva a lot of torment which she decided would be character-forming and necessary for the girl's black soul. Then she had to assess what had to be done about Beryl. Then she had to get her gate repaired before street urchins took away the pieces for firewood. 'Problems,' she barked, hauling Elva out by an ear, 'problems, problems, problems. Not a hum from you, miss. Bring all those things from your cupboard, and where are all the other things he sent?'

'Iris also took,' Elva blubbed.

'Pair of rogues, both of you. Let that Iris come here again, will you . . . and where all his letters?'

'Here. Put under my clothes.'

Each request was accompanied by a rap on Elva's skull. 'Give all here,' (clunk!) ' and go and light a candle.' (clunk!)

So Florrie took her troubles to Saint Anthony and bent her grey head and asked to be shown a way out of 'this botheration' and Soma sobbed and shook her head and blew her nose on her sleeve and looked as draggled as a half-drowned cat.

Saint Anthony must have been in a mellow mood because he obviously came up with an answer. Florrie rose, put her spectacles into their snap-lid case and went to the dresser to put a comb to her hair. 'Now Beryl will also come,' she said, twisting Elva's ear, 'Go and tell Soma to make some tea and cut some bread for tiffin. And you go and wash and put on something else. Looking a sight you are. Serves you right for all your wickedness. You think God not looking, no? You heard what Mother said? In evening you go and tell all to Father Robert and make the penance he giving.'

'But Bertie will come,' Elva said in a small voice.

'So take him also. Go to church. Let him also kneel and wait until make your confession. Now go to bathroom before I take firewood stick from the kitchen!' Elva fled . . . and Beryl tiptoed in with eyes full of fear. Neighbours had told her of the rumpus and the broken gate and how Mother Gonzaga had bustled down the lane with Elva and about a huge man with arms like logs and the caterwauling that had gone on. Florrie hugged her and said,' Here, all these letters for you,' and there were tears in the old lady's eyes.

'Mama,' said Beryl, 'Why you are crying? People in the lane saying all sorts of things.'

'Never mind them. See, all this Sonnaboy writing. And I think when I read some he must be really loving my Buiya, no? And even Saint Anthony telling me that you must be old enough. So if you want to marry him you tell now and we will arrange.'

Mother and daughter looked at each other and there was a long silence . . . except, of course, in Florrie's heaven, where Saint Anthony must have been laughing his head off!

Everything else happened at hectic pace. Sonnaboy, calling the next morning, was informed of Florrie's consent. He had his transfer and, if he married, a bungalow to call his own in Kadugannawa. So he was rushed, very rushed, but he still found the time to waylay Iris and give her such a slap that old Simmons actually wrote a song about it and it became a party hit. Totoboy, rising to protest, was duly smitten and went to work with a belladonna plaster on the right side of his face. He got no sympathy from his fiancee. 'Your face? What about my face? For one week it benumbed and can't even eat.' She told Totoboy that they either get married right away and move out of range of his lunatic brother or he was never to look her in the eye again.

So Totoboy went, quite inebriated, to the altar and Sonnaboy scowled and said she already had enough wedding presents from him (referring, of course, to Iris' share of the loot) and Totoboy embraced him and said, 'That's all right and let bygones be bygones,' and drove away for a liquor-laden honeymoon singing 'Show me the way to go home', at the top of his voice.

Sonnaboy and Beryl planned an end-November wedding. They did not reckon on the obduracy of Father Romiel of St. Mary's, Dehiwela, and Father Robert of St. Mary's Bambalapitiya. The Werkmeister affair had been noised abroad and old Werkmeister was determined to haul Sonnaboy into courts. Attorney-at-law Bumpy Juriansz had opined that this was an open-and-shut breach of promise. The priests began to shilly at Dehiwela and shally at Bambalapitiya. Florrie stared accusingly at her intended son-in-low. 'Never said, no? about this other girl thing?'

So Sonnaboy went to All Saints Church, Borella and when Eustace and Merril Werkmeister got wind of the wedding, they rounded up a gang of Sinhalese thugs from Kawdana and went to the church. It was the 26th of November. Father Bernard Coelho was startled to find his church doors guarded by burly railway men, each wielding a heavy stick. The bride arrived with her mother, brothers and sisters to be surrounded by Kawdana roughnecks who suddenly raised their sarongs and fled as the railway moved in with well-directed cudgels. So Sonnaboy and Beryl were married behind closed doors and emerged into the sunshine to find Eustace and Merril at the gates mouthing obscenities and making threatening gestures. Sonnaboy needed no bidding. He had, he roared, had enough; and married life began in spectacular fashion as the bridegroom fared forth to give the Werkmeister brothers the drubbing of their young lives. Never had such a crowd gathered outside All Saints. It was reported that even the guards from the nearby Welikada prison trotted up to watch the fun. With his wedding suit in tatters, Sonnaboy continued to pound the Werkmeisters to a pulp-like consistency, all the while hampered by people who tried to drag him away and drape his head with ribbon and bits of bouquet. It was a glorious morning. Having tipped both brothers into the roadside storm drain, he dusted his suit, sucked at his knuckles and grinned hugely.

At the Nimal Road residence, Beryl dabbed iodine on his bruises while guests ate and drank hugely, and Cecilprins rose to wish them all happiness, and Florrie kissed Beryl, and Elva cried and Bertie, uncommonly drunk said, 'Just a moment, I have a small score to settle.' And hadn't Sonnaboy threatened his Elva and wasn't an apology in order? Sonnaboy smiled and said yes, he had threatened Elva but that was all over and Bertie was welcome to his sister-in-law. Bertie said it was a matter of principle. 'I demand ana 'pology. Elvash going—going to marry me. Nobody can threaten her, d'yer hear?' So Sonnaboy nodded and went up to Bertie and poked a large fist into the man's eye and the poor idiot fell back into his chair, rocked over and went to the floor with a crack and lay there until dragged away to a bed where his puffed and purpling eye was covered with a slice of raw meat. Florrie laughed herself into stitches, cackling, 'Come and look, will you, mutton face with beef in the eye,' and everybody gathered to look and drink a toast to Bertie.

Totoboy, as expected, struck form quickly and went into one of his music hall routines:

Mama's gone dancing, baby don't you cry,
Mama's down at the Savoy—oh boy!
Mama's gone dancing, baby don't you cry.
Mama's gone and Papa
Wouldn't ever dare to stop 'er . . .

He sat on the floor with an old doll of Beryl's and pretended to rock the baby while he sang and in the merriment, Elsie with a big stomach and Leah and Anna, still showing no signs of pregnancy, were telling a fascinated Beryl about this brother of theirs she had had the misfortune to marry; and Elva sat stony-faced and Iris drank her seventh whiskey and smiled a benediction on everybody although she had reached the stage where she had to close one eye to bring a face into focus. Even Dunnyboy found the revels to his liking for he mooched over to the kitchen and was able to corner Soma in a corner between kitchen and garage where it was an instant's work to raise the woman's cloth to her hips and perform in his singularly deft manner while Soma urged him to 'quickly finish before somebody comes' and then asked for a rupee which he said he did not have. Soma was disappointed. She decided that there was no use in allowing these gentlemen to get between her thighs. In future she would adopt a more mercenary attitude, like payment in advance.

So Sonnaboy and Beryl went away to a hill-station called Brookside, off Bandarawela with second-class railway warrants courtesy of the Ceylon Government Railway and Cecilprins warned that if he met Viva, 'Don't go to hammer.' Beryl found that the sleeping berth on the night mail to Badulla was a most uncomfortable marriage bed. She had thought that her husband would operate along the lines of that old man in Lauries Lane who used to fondle her and give her sweets and small coin. This was a rampage. Crammed, stark naked into the narrow berth with the thrumming of the train and the whistle of the engine piercing the night, she was penetrated with scant ceremony and bit her lip in pain as a huge shaft seemed to drive in and out and the weight of her husband made her gasp and want to cry halt. The pain stayed and throbbed even when he spent himself and lay over her and stroked her hair and did not see, in the faint light, the tear that trickled down her face. Bending his head and climbing out of the lower berth, he stood, penis streaked with her blood and said, 'You want to clean?' and dumbly watched as he wet a cloth in the tiny washbasin and wiped her vagina and rubbed at the blood on the boiled cloth sheet. 'It's paining, *anney*,' she whispered and he bent to kiss her and squeeze her small breasts and say, 'That's the way first time. Have to break, no? And your hole also small. Thought I couldn't put right in. See, have blood on my hair, also. I'll wash and come.'

Beryl was trying to rise when he came out of the toilet and he was erect and he pushed her down and took her again and this time she put her arms around him and opened wide and it was long and slow and she felt the excruciating tickle of his public hair on her clitoris and she began to arch her back as he rode her. Then there was no more pain and only wave upon wave of sensation that stormed through her and she shuddered in earthy ecstacy. She had never known anything like this before. And so they lay and loved as the train climbed and raped each tunnel on its way into the mountains and Sonnaboy later said that no train in no railway on earth could boast of such a bout of lovemaking. They finally pulled apart when the berth attendant tapped and said, 'Tea or coffee, sir,' and realised that their station was not far up the line. Shivering in the mountain cold, they dressed and Sonnaboy changed the stained lower bunk sheet for the upper and both slipped into warm coats and readied their luggage. 'Only four days we have,' he said, nuzzling her, and she giggled and said, 'I'm Mrs von Bloss now,' and he pulled her on his lap and stroked her breasts and said, 'You like to fuck, no? About twelve times I think we did last night. How the feeling?' Beryl blushed like a ripe apple. If this was being married, she thought, why, play on. She buried her face in his shoulder and held him tight and he thought that all the birds in Heaven were in full-throated song. Who would have dared to tell him that when he was fifty, she would be thirty . . . and then the shame and the heartaches would begin . . . .

PART THREE

Bearing Fruit

Elsie brought a girl into the world, and Eric was pleased. He would look at the pink bundle and say: 'I did that?' until Elsie scowled and told him to go to the devil. Eric never thought he could do it, having been quite clueless about the matter. It had been a problem, this business of procreation. Elsie finally took charge and practically drilled the poor fellow in matters of procedure. 'Keep moving, you fool,' she would blare, 'If want to have baby you think you can just put in and keep? Everything I have to tell?' So, with Elsie barking the orders like some physical training instructor, he would juggle and joggle and succeeded in impregnating her despite his awe at her fat outspread thighs and a vagina that seemed to threaten him.

Poor Eric lived in fear of Elsie all his life. She even decided when he should sleep with her. 'Because I know you men want that I'm allowing,' she would say sternly, 'You think this is fun for me?' And she never admitted to an orgasm. Many years and many children later she told Anna: 'That Eric useless, men. After so long, still don't know to do properly. Everything have to tell. Only thinking of race paper and putting doubles and trebles. What for, I don't know, got married to him. Even after I grab by the bum and shout and make to go up and down, he crying and saying can I get up now. If don't put a clout nothing will he do.' A strange relationship, to be sure. The fact is that Elsie, after marriage, discovered her true self. She was a sadist. Bashing Eric was her way of masturbating.

Eric never realised how much satisfaction his wife derived in ill-treating him. He took her slaps, her buffets, her viciousness in bed as an outpouring of love and she in turn experienced deep sexual pleasure in watching him squirm. Each time she beat him she would begin to breathe hard and then cross her legs very tight and bend and stretch until the paroxysm came and passed. She would then release him and rush to the bathroom to squat and slap water between her legs.

Nevertheless, here was Noella, the first of a new generation. The baby was hailed by Cecilprins as the wonder of the age and he insisted on all the family being present for the christening and a grand party. 'Now I'm grandfather, no?' he said to everybody in

Boteju Lane. 'And now my other children all uncles and aunties also.'

The baby had, in truth, a surfeit of uncles and aunts and while on this subject the chronicler feels that it might be a revelation of sorts to detail the manner in which the family kept branching out. Like one of those hardy, unstoppable jam fruit trees!

A. CECILPRINS HANS VON BLOSS of Kotahena married MAUDIEGIRL ESTHER KIMBALL of Colombo
They produced:
1. DUNNYBOY PRINS who did not marry which was considered a great mercy.
2. ELSIE MAUD who married ERIC HENRY son of HENRY WORTHINGTON DE MELLO and AGATHA JOSEPHINE DE WITT.
3. ANNA CONSTANCE who married DIONYSIUS RICHARD, son of DIONYSIUS RATNAYAKE COLONTOTA and SISILIANA GODAMUNARALAGE SEETIN AKKA.
4. TERRY ANDERS who married BERTHA ROSE, daughter of ANTHONY WILHELM McHEYZER and CLAUDIA RUTH VANCUYLENBERG.
5. VIVA RICHARDSON BONIFACE who married OPEL SARAH, illegitimate daughter of JAMES WITHERSPOON LUDWICK and MISSIENONA MORAES.
6. TOTOBOY DAVIDSON BRENNAN who married IRIS ELIZABETH, daughter of GEORGE GREGORY HOLDENBOTTLE and MAVIS JOHANNA FRUGHTNEIT (or so it said in the birth certificate which did not explain how Iris became so black).
7. MARLA MONIQUE who left home and no record of her subsequent movements exist.
8. RUTHIE RAMONA who eloped with ANTHONY FERNANDEZ, a Goanese cook who served in the Royal Navy.
9. PATTY FRANCISCUS who died early.
10. FRITZY STANISLAUS who also died.

11. LEAH BERNADETTE who married GEORGE GLADSTONE, son of MAXWORTH DE MELLO and MATHILDA HONORIA MUSPRATT.
12. VINTO GRATIEN PRINS who died early.
13. SONNABOY DUNCAN CLARENCE who married BERYL HYACINTH, daughter of CLARENCE FENNIMORE DA BREA and FLORRIE MARIA TODD.

With this point of reference, as it were, the number of relatives Elsie's daughter was inflicted with was legion. And what of the goodly ranks of in-laws and those on the 'mother's side' and 'father's side'? Indeed, any Burgher celebration always saw the strangest claims to those ties that bind. Perfect strangers would roll up and say: 'Why, men, I am Ivy's third cousin, no? Kelaniya Mullers, men. What? You never knew? And this is my cousin Eardley. He also connected. His sister marry your uncle Bunno's cousin on mother's side. So how about a drink?' To continue . . .

B. <u>HENRY WORTHINGTON DE MELLO of Chilaw married AGATHA JOSEPHINE DE WITT of Mutwal.</u>
They produced:
1. MADELINE ROSE who became a nun.
2. PARKER RUDOLFUS who married MARY VIOLET, daughter of TENNYSON PHOEBUS and MARION DELICA VANDERWERT.
3. <u>ERIC HENRY who married ELSIE MAUD, daughter of CECILPRINS HANS VON BLOSS and MAUDIEGIRL ESTHER KIMBALL.</u>
C. <u>DIONYSIUS RATNAYAKE COLONTOTA of Gampaha married SISILIANA GODAMUNARALAGE SEETIN AKKA of Gangodawila.</u>
They produced:
1. DIONYSIUS RATNAYAKE SOLOMON who went to Moneragala to view a prospective wife and never came back.

2. <u>DIONYSIUS RICHARD who married ANNA CONSTANCE, daughter of CECILPRINS HANS VON BLOSS and MAUDIEGIRL ESTHER KIMBALL.</u>
3. SUMAMA RATNAYAKE who married BARKIS SINGHO POLONWITA who was not really certain who his parents were.

D. <u>ANTHONY WILHELM McHEYZER of Colombo married CLAUDIA RUTH VANCUYLENBERG of Mount Lavinia.</u>

They produced:
1. JOHN BLOOMFIELD who married CARMEL MARIA, daughter of DICKYBOY GONSAL and PETUNIA BAKELMAN and was cut off without a penny!
2. MORRIS DENVER who married NAOMI JANE, daughter of ALEX VANDERSTRAATEN and ZOE CAROLINE PRINGLE.
3. <u>BERTHA ROSE who married TERRY ANDERS, son of CECILPRINS VON BLOSS and MAUDIEGIRL ESTHER KIMBALL.</u>
4. MARTHA PATRICIA who married Captain JOHN DERRICK, son of Regimental Sergeant Major MAXWELL WALES MARTENSZ and YVETTE GWENDOLINE OHLMUS.
5. KENNETH PICKERING who married THOMASINA HARRIET daughter of GEOFFERY 'BUNTY' SPITTEL and JEAN OLIVIA MARS.
6. ADRIAN WAVELL who married MELANIE MARGARET daughter of JOHN SPENSER BARTHOLOMEUSZ and CLARICE BUBSY FERREIRA.

E. <u>JAMES WITHERSPOON LUDWICK of Bambalapitiya took to bed MISSIE NONA MORAES of Bambalapitiya.</u>

This illicit union resulted in:
1. <u>OPEL SARAH who married VIVA RICHARDSON BONIFACE, son of CECILPRINS HANS VON BLOSS and MAUDIEGIRL ESTHER KIMBALL.</u>

Missie Nona Moraes is reported to have taken off when Opel was five, having told Ludwick that 'it not good to having bastards and if not going to get married I going to live with my people in Chekku Street.' She kept her word. Papa Ludwick, much shattered, took his woes to a bunch of itinerant Pentecostalists who tracked down Missie and persuaded her to come back whereupon, in celebration, Ludwick promptly made her pregnant. Missie was distraught. She told her sorrows to the vegetable woman who recommended papaya milk and gin for an early abortion. So Missie collected the milk of the papaya tree—half a tumbler, mind—topped it with Rawlings gin and sent the concoction down the hatch. What happened inside her could best be described in hushed tones by an obstetrician. She was carried out of the house, stiff as a board, haemorrhaging madly and shuffled off the mortal coil in the small hours.

F. GEORGE GREGORY HOLDENBOTTLE of Dehiwela married MAVIS JOANNA FRUGHTNEIT of Dehiwela.

They produced:

1. SAM DUNSTAN who died.
2. ROLLO SYLVESTER who ran away with the girl who came with the dhoby woman. Further details are shrouded in mystery.
3. ERIC WINSTON who married ANNIEGIRL EMILY, daughter of WINSTON BAAS, a Sinhalese carpenter, and MENIKE. (Or so it is claimed although there is little evidence to indicate that any form of marriage took place).
4. IRIS ELIZABETH married TOTOBOY DAVIDSON BRENNAN, son of CECILPRINS HANSVON BLOSS and MAUDIEGIRL ESTHER KIMBALL.
5. MARVIN PUTHA—raised and reared in Borupane, Ratmalana by DAISY AKKA, a woman of easy virtue who swore that George Gregory Holdenbottle was the boy's father. The fact that she received eight rupees a month from George lent credence to her claims.

6. BARDO BABY—mothered by MATTIE NONA of Kollupitiya in a hovel at the bottom of Station Lane until he was brought to the Holdenbottle residence one day by an irate Mattie Nona who insisted that she could not bring up George's son on love and fresh air and insisted that Bardo Baby be cared for by the father. It is recorded that Mrs Mavis Holdenbottle beat her husband senseless that day and had to be locked up until she was in a better frame of mind.

G. MAXWORTH DE MELLO of Kandana married MATHILDA HONORIA MUSPRATT of Ragama.
They produced:
1. BARBARA FIONA who married 'JUNIOR' JIMBO son of JIMBO HOLSINGER and LAURA MAY LEEMBRUGGEN.
2. MARTIN EXCALIBUR married DULCIE, daughter of THOMAS WENTWORTH DAVIDSON and DUCKYGIRL THOMASZ.
3. DOLORES married MARLO MEREDITH, son of JOSEPH MORGAN JACKSON and MAVIS PRISCILLA VAN TWEST.
4. GEORGE GLADSTONE. who married LEAH BERNADETTE, daughter of CECILPRINS HANS VON BLOSS and MAUDIEGIRL ESTHER KIMBALL.
5. DUNCAN DANNISTER who married SYLVIE, daughter of JINORIS RATNAYAKE and PATTIE FONSEKA.

H. CLARENCE FENNIMORE DA BREA married FLORRIE MARIA TODD (both of Mutwal)
They produced:
1. CHARLES WHITECHAPEL who married HAZEL MARJORIE, daughter of BILLYBOY PETERSON and EUNICE GABRIELLA HERFT.
2. MARION PRIMROSE who married HUBERT LINCOLN, son of LIONEL 'BULL' BERTUS and GWENDOLINE VERA BROHIER.
3. LILIAN NORA who married 'BUNNY' PETER, son of

PATRICK BRIAN TOUSSAINT and DEBORAH RAUX.
4. MURIEL EMMALINE who married VICTOR LAWRENCE, son of EUSTACE VANDERWALL and EVANGELINE NICHOLAS.
5. MARYANNE DAISY who died at birth.
6. ELSPETH 'JUPPIE' IRENE who married RONALD GEORGE, son of DORIC LOOS and ABIGAIL BLOSSOM FOENANDER.
7. ROSEMARY MAY, who died.
8. HENRY LIVINGSTONE who married DULCIMER, daughter of ERIC WINDSOR DUCKWORTH and FRANCINE ODILE CAMILLUS.
9. MILLICENT JUNE, spinster.
10. KATHLEEN MARGARET who married CHARLES RODERICK, son of JEREMIAH DE LA ZILVA and SONIA CRYSTAL FORSYTHE.
11. ERNIE 'BIRDIEBOY' who married IRIS CLODAGH, daughter of JOHN JAMIESON HEPPONSTALL and MARIA RABOT.
12. ELVA COLUMBINE who married BERTIE PUGWASH, son of JOSEPH DREADNOUGHT CARRON and NELLIE 'KONDAY' RULACH.
13. <u>BERYL HYACINTH who married SONNABOY DUNCAN CLARENCE, son of CECILPRINS HANS VON BLOSS and MAUDIEGIRL ESTHER KIMBALL.</u>

The reader might find it an eminently time-consuming, albeit absorbing exercise to figure out the number of immediate relations who could lay claim, through ties of blood (and water), to two-day-old Noella Marietta de Mello, who slept all day and howled all night and made mother Elsie as mad as a hornet. In the grand uncle and grand aunt circle there were de Witts, Colontotas, Godamunaralas, McHeyzers, Vancuylenbergs, Ludwicks, Moraeses, Holdenbottles, Frughtneits, blighters in Goa and the Lord knows where else in India, Muspratts, da Breas, Todds, Phoebuses, Vanderwerts, some village types in Moneragala, others called Polgasowitas, Gonsaals, Bakelmans, Vanderstraatens,

Pringles, Maartenszes, Ohlmuses, Spittels, Marses, Bartholomeuszes, Ferreiras, a few from a dhoby clan in Bambalapitiya, some members of a Sinhalese carpenter's family, a shady lady from Borupana, a streetwalker from Kollupitiya, the Holsingers, Leembruggens, Davidsons, Thomaszes, Rauxes, Vanderwalls, Jacksons, Van Twests, Ratnayakes, Looses and Foenanders, Fonsekas, Petersons, Herfts, Bertuses, Brohiers, Toussaints, Nicholases, Duckworths and Camilluses, de la Zilvas, Forsythes, Hepponstalls, Rabots, Carrons and Rulachs. And the infant still had two grandfathers and a grandmother and was blissfully unaware of the hordes of cousins that would await her, besides brothers and sisters.

The chronicler maintains that the foregoing has been recorded to illustrate how well the jam fruit tree spreads its branches. Naturally, of this tribe, some gave themselves airs and tried to ignore the others, but that is silly thing to do. You cannot cling to one branch without a thought about the others that also rise to the sky. The celebrated Jack, it is recalled, just had the one beanstalk, and as the story goes, he had to cut it down in the end! But who would take an axe to a jam fruit tree and imagine that once cut down it would stay down? It gives you the raspberry and shoots up again!

Leah, too, found life in her, after George had covered her nightly for three months and constantly expressed his chagrin that his seminal fluid kept faring forth from the lips of his wife's vagina. 'What, men, putting right inside, no? Then why it all coming out again?'

Leah, who left it all to George and admitted to but a general working knowledge of 'these caddish things' just lay back and hummed a hymn to Mary. In truth, George was new to the game despite his worldly airs with a lot of theory and no practice whatsoever. A book on sex by an Indian maniac had told him all he needed to know. All he had to do was translate this wisdom into deed. He began to reason with Leah, bringing in a bottle of Parker Quink blue ink and fountain-pen filler. 'Now look, will you, when put the filler and squeeze the top it takes in the ink, no?'

Leah would watch interestedly.

'Now see, filler full with ink. Now put filler inside and squeeze on top and all the ink going. See the filler now. No ink. And where the ink? In the bottle. And won't come out.'

Leah would nod. She always admired George when he got scientific.

'So if my cock is filler and I put it in and all the stuff comes then like going into your bottle, no? Then why it coming pouring out?'

'*Anney*, I don't know. Must be you're putting too much inside and it overflowing.'

George considered this and was pleased. 'You mean too much in my filler? Must be that cow's milk I drinking when at home. Then must be having enough inside, no?'

'So that's all right then?' Leah would say, trying to rise, 'must go and wash.'

'Wait a little. Think have some more in the filler,' and he would straddle her again and Leah would wish he'd get the business over with. Like any full-blooded Burgher girl, she had thought long and lustily about sex. She and George had not kept their hands to themselves and the pre-marital fondling had been tremendously exciting. Quite unnerving at times, in fact. But the sameness of the business, night after night was becoming, to Leah, a bore. And George, too, was a bore. He did not make love. He practiced technique. He was quite exhilarated about having a woman all to himself. Leah grew tired of his sexual posturings, yet, her own appetite needed to be met and so she made the best of these nightly encounters and felt that, on the whole, her marriage was secure and theirs was a mutually satisfying relationship. (If only the bugger would stop strutting around the bedroom and saying: 'See my cock. Bigger than this where will you get?' Pooh! Dunnyboy has twice that size!)

Leah didn't know it at the time, but she was nurturing in her womb a perfect genius of a child. Perhaps there is something to be said about extraneous impressions that are registered on the mother and are imparted in some mysterious manner on the foetus. Leah could never understand later how it could have happened. And George, at his best, made a rather negative impression—nothing to excite any foetus. Only one thing could be considered and attributed: Leah's collectomania that grew to fanatic proportions after marriage. Two things contributed to this totally indisciplined process of what could be called, self-education. First, there was a visiting bookman. This patient little individual would come over once a week with a pyramid of books and magazines on his head. A sort of perambulating lending library. The type no longer exists in the Sri Lanka of today. Leah had her favourite whose name was Daniel.

Daniel was quite a knowledgeable lender of books. Blessed with no literary tastes, he would pick up anything that consisted of covers and pages. Old Royal Society journals, poetry, penny dreadfuls, novels, Sexton Blake series, old Strand magazines, pulp romances, children's readers, hymnals, Bible stories, fairy tales, engineering and agricultural pamphlets and medical gazettes. The pyramid was always tied up in a large white diaper, and when he came calling, Leah would help him lower the load and watch breathlessly as he untied the bundle and display enough books to fill a goodish veranda. Daniel was a patient man. He did not mind that Leah would wallow in his books for half a morning. She would leaf through the entire stock and select many she would try to read. She had no decided tastes but took what appealed to her and what would give her hours of pleasure in selecting and writing out excerpts and passages. Daniel would note what she chose and quote: 'These three, good novels five cents each, and those women's magazines—how many lady took? Five? That is ten cents for all, and those two books ten cents each, so altogether forty-five cents.' Leah would clutch at her breast and imitate a dying swan. 'So give forty cents,' Daniel would concede and Leah would revive immediately and say, 'You're mad? old books like this? How to know how many pages gone, also? Then never mind. You take and go.' Daniel would smack his forehead and wail: 'Carrying on this head all day, no, lady? And see the time to take out and put back again. Thirty-five cents.'

'Other people take only one book. See how many I'm taking. And when you come next week even if I haven't finished reading you will take and go. Here, twenty-five cents. Only one week, no?'

And this was the first part of Leah's cultural 'induction'.

Secondly, she had all the time in the world and a goodly collection of very large Port of Colombo ledgers which George had snaffled one day and stored on the top of his almirah. George had this kleptomaniac conviction that anything he snaffled would always come in useful some day. The handsome, leather-bound ledgers each with 200 stout pages were bound to be of use some day. It was no real effort to get them out of the port—all twelve of them—although it is not known what effect their loss could have had on such sections of the port as Administration, Audit, Stores or the Custom's Long Room where such ledgers were normally used.

Leah had never been great shakes as a student. She would add laboriously and calculate with a total disregard for every mathematical principal. She had no head for geography, abhorred history, and was the despair of Reverend Sister Theresa who took singing and was of the opinion that Leah's octave C sounded like a Mississippi tug boat. But Leah was fascinated by words—pretty quotes and descriptive language. The Burgher patois which surrounded her in her everyday life may be as colourful and as vibrant as a toucan in a baobab tree, but she discovered, quite early in life that people like Shakespeare and Donne and even Disraeli and Voltaire used 'proper' English and found a priggish satisfaction in poring over all manner of little literary offerings which she would encounter in her school literature texts, the family Bible, the newspapers and even the cheap romantic magazines and other pulp she would avidly collect. That she rarely understood did not deter her. She felt that she was gathering together masterpieces of a rare order. Soon this became an impulse that could not be quelled. She had biscuit tins stuffed with clippings and the bright verses of Christmas cards.

When she found the ledgers she was more than delighted. Now all her 'gems' could be neatly glued in . . . and they were. Each ledger held quite a hotch-potch, to be sure, but they did become comprehensive albums of a rare literary beauty.

There was, for example, a sober directive on the engaging of servants:

Every portion of work which the servant will have to do should be plainly stated by the mistress, and understood by the servant. If this plan is not carefully adhered to, an unseemly contention is almost certain to ensue, and this may not be easily settled; so that a change of servants, which is so much to be deprecated, is continually occurring.'

Commonsense, certainly, for the ages!

And these curious words of Ben Jonson on the effects of a formal dinner on men:

Before dinner men meet with great inequality of understanding, and those who are conscious of their inferiority have the modesty not to talk. When they have drunk wine, every man feels himself happy, and loses that modesty, and grows impudent and vociferous; but he is not improved, he is only not sensible of his defects.

And a couplet from Campbell;

The world was sad! The garden was a wild!
And man the hermit sigh'd, till woman smiled.

Little verses were collected from everywhere and many were not even attributed. Like this verse on the virtues of being a good housewife:

The woman the name of the housewife doth win
By keeping her house and of doings therein;
And she that with husband will quietly dwell
Must think on this lesson, and follow it well.

and Jeremy Taylor's stirring lines on what a good wife will always be:

A good wife is Heaven's last best gift to man; his angel
and minister of graces innumerable; his gem of many

virtues; his casket of jewels. Her voice is sweet music; her smiles his brightest day; her kiss the guardian of his innocence; her arms the pale of his safety, the balm of his health, the balsam of his life; her industry his surest wealth; her economy his safest steward; her lips his faithful counsellors; her bosom the softest pillow of his cares; and her prayers the ablest advocates of Heaven's blessings on his head.'

There were even some old lines from Tusser, written, believe it or not, in 1557:

THE PRAISE OF HUSWIFRY

I serve for a day, for a week, for a year,
For lifetime, for ever, while men dwelleth here;
For richer, for poorer, from north to the south;
For honest, for hard-head, for dainty of mouth;
For wed and unwedded, in sickness and health;
For all that well liveth in good commonwealth;
For city, for country, for court and for cart,
To quiet the head and comfort the heart.'

There were 'Advice to Cooks', various recipes, Shakespeare, Disraeli, Rules for Choosing Good Meat, Macbeth's 'Let good digestion wait on appetite, And health on both', lines from Ralph Hodgson, Pope, Herrick and Shelley.

What Leah could not clip out and paste in, she laboriously copied, and in her large flowing hand she would record Tennyson's *The Beggar Maid* and James Hogg's famous *The Boy's Song* and even Robert Louis Stevenson's *Requiem*. All manner of proverbs, sayings, *bon mots*, extracts from after-dinner speeches went into the pot, stirred briskly with typical autograph album offerings, the dying words of Anne Boleyn and the words of Toplady's immortal *Rock of Ages*. It was certain that some lines had been copied out from cemetery headstones for there lay, between a passage from Goldsmith and some words of Cardinal Wolsey:

Born into beauty
And born into bloom
Victor immortal
O'er death and the tomb

With her first child in her womb, Leah would spend long lazy hours of each day with her ledgers. She was on a sort of literary safari. She would even take little poems and sing them to the tune of popular songs and hymns, making the potted ferns in the veranda stand on end. And so her nine months passed pleasantly enough and she brought forth a girl who was named Marlene Christina and Cecilprins grumbled long and loud because all he was getting, he said, were granddaughters and, 'With all these buggers married, nobody getting a son.'

He would go to 'High Street bottom' to regard Anna with a jaundiced eye. Anna, who had taken to wearing voluminous house coats and moved around like a three-masted schooner in full sail, showed no sign of an abdominal dilation. 'Tchach!' Cecilprins would say, 'What you buggers doing, men? Elsie, Leah, both get daughters and still you sitting here making *mallung* and cooking fish and no baby coming yet?'

Anna would roll her eyes and say piously: 'Must wait, no, Papa, until God give.'

Cecilprins would snort. 'God give? Then what is husband doing?'

Anna would sigh gustily. Her papa did have a point but Colontota was convinced that, whereas he had performed with textbook thoroughness, it was Anna who was to blame. His parents, too, were disappointed and when several clinical examinations confirmed that Anna was incapable of ovulation, they were naturally huffed. 'Parents must have known and not a word said,' old Colontota remarked while his wife nodded. But the woman was too fond of her Burgher daughter-in-law and would not allow her husband to say too much.

'So never mind,' she would say firmly, 'Still she is good girl even if getting fat too much. And not like other Burgher girls going dancing and parties and all; and putting red stuff on the mouth and cutting off the eyebrows and putting black lines with pencil. Sometimes I think, like village girl, only going to the church and once in a way to sisters' house and that's all.'

But old Colontota felt that it had all been a ghastly mistake. Should have married a strong girl from the village. He could have arranged a match with some good coconut land as dowry.

Meanwhile, in Bandarawela where Viva had secured a small house close to the railway station, Opel went about her slatternly way, quite enchanted at the thought that in this crisp mountain climate she would never need to take a bath. In fact, Opel found life in the hills quite welcome. For one thing she was free of that abrasive father of hers who, she thought, was getting quite strange in his ways of late. Papa Ludwick would sit with his Bible in his lap and roll his eyes and mutter bits of Scripture. Then his eyes would fix unintelligently on her knees and he would lose himself in some blissful reverie, then suddenly leap up, shout 'Alleluia!' and rush to the lavatory. Most disconcerting.

Viva, his disciple, was no better, actually, but she could put up with his peccadillos. They had found the little two-roomed bungalow which his company had provided, quite suitable. There was a pear tree in the small garden and quite a lot of peach trees too. Chrysanthemums straggled about ill-kempt beds and the previous tenants had done big things with barbetan daisies. There was an outhouse lavatory (presumably for an emergency or for servants) and a large piping system that brought in water from somewhere up the mountain behind the house, crystal clear spring water that flowed all day and night into a large trough, large enough to conduct a naval exercise in. In the backyard, cabbages and leeks grew in well-ordered beds and Viva felt that a coolie could be pressed into service to tend the yard and grow more vegetables. 'Can have some carrots and radish,' he said.

What was most acceptable was the company van. It was parked under the tiny porch at nights and Viva would set off in it each day. A chauffeur would pop in each morning at seven, wearing a big blue Burberry coat (Royal Navy surplus, to be sure) and with a thick cloth swathing his head and ears. He would check the van and then sit on the front step until Opel brought him a cup of tea and he would grin and regard the buttons of her housecoat wishfully.

The day began, Viva insisted, with a prayer. He would stand beside the van and begin with a strident 'O Holy Father!' and proceed to remind God that it was He who delivered the Israelites from bondage and sent an angel to Daniel's fiery furnace and gave Moses the Ten Commandments and put a hex on a fellow named Uzzo who had tried to get too familiar with the Tabernacle. Having recounted all this (in case God had forgotten) he proceeded to ask for a great many things which he felt he was entitled to as a chosen one and for being such a good and faithful servant. 'Bless the driver,' he hooted, 'and the road also, and grant, O Lord, that the van stays on it otherwise we go down the precipice for sure . . . Bless the van, O Lord God, and the steering-wheel and don't forget the tyres, Lord, because you know these roads, God, all curves and hairpin bends and going round and sometimes feel as if the tail-light is touching the head-light also. Praise the Lord and proclaim His mercy . . . Alleluia! Alleluia!'

Then, having kissed the top of Opel's head he would climb in and go away, beetling around the mountains, browbeating shopkeepers to stock more milkfood and distributing samples in tea estate homes and telling everyone he encountered about God and stopping to harangue estate workers and tea pluckers and urge them to magnify the name of the Lord and dwell forever in His mercy. His sales itinerary took him far afield, and while husbands would groan and say, 'Omigod! here comes that bloody lunatic with his Bible!' wives gave him welcome, and old ladies would pray with him and collect large tears in handkerchiefs, and Viva would urge them to take their sins to the Lord.

He would insist that they 'testify', which was usually done in company, and old Mrs Ludekens would stand up to say in a quavering voice that she had almost become a secret drinker, having found that her husband's whisky was just the ticket for the cold nights and now she knew how wrong she had been after brother Viva brought her the message of Jesus. Listeners would tremble deliciously and sing-song 'Amen, amen' and Viva would cry: 'God will keep you warm henceforth, sister! How great is the power of the Lord, Alleluia!' and Mrs Ludekens would raise her eyes to glory and declare, 'But now I leave Jimmy's whisky alone and I tell that he must not drink also, because whisky drinking is the work of the devil.' Jimmy, of course, had told her to go to the devil because he did not fancy going on the wagon to please anyone, but Mrs Ludekens wisely made no mention of this. Then Viva would place a hand on her head and ask for a special blessing and declare that he would pray for poor Jimmy who was surely in Satan's coils and would urge everyone to also pray for the poor sinner.

Opel meanwhile would mooch around the home and scratch her head and wonder what to do with herself. At times she would step out to walk the tiny town and buy glass bangles for her wrists and blush each time the booking clerk in the railway station winked at her. She knew that Viva would never approve of the bangles. The trouble with these Pentecosts, she thought, was that they never approved of anything. Even going to bed with her man was tiresome. He had to first kneel and carry on a long conversation with God and then get under the covers to tell her all about the sanctity of marriage and the good angels who did sentry-go at the head of the bed and all sorts of other nonsense until she would say in exasperation: 'You want to do the job or just talk the whole night? Not enough whole day you're talking?'

This would dampen whatever ardour Viva had and he would sulk and protest that children of God required a divine stamp of approval and Opel would bang a fist into her pillow, turn away and pretend to sleep, making sure that her back was arched enough to press her big buttocks firmly against him. This would bring Viva to the realization that the world and the flesh could not be denied and he would spring up with a glad shout: 'Behold, the handmaid of the Lord!' and mount her. Opel was not happy with these performances. She felt, as she later confided to the railway station booking clerk: 'Like God fucking, men, not Vivi,' and the clerk, a strong, black-haired fellow named Morrell, would laugh and tumble her in bed and show that when it came to sex, he could give God a handicap any day, any time.

Opel had found Morrell good company when she occasionally strolled around town. The booking clerk, a strapping twenty-year-old had considered her aimless to's and fro's, and determined that here was a young woman who could use some diversion. True, she had scarcely the looks that evoked passionate ecstacy but, as a punter would study form, he was satisfied that 'this was a nice hunk of flesh'. Opel, with no friends in Bandarawela was flattered at the way the booking clerk would wink and smile and say, 'How are you,' and observe that she must be new in town. Opel would go home humming and when Morrell came to the gate one day ('just passing, men, didn't know you lived so close') she hummed even louder and invited him in for tea and confirmed that she was alone most of the day and was very glad to know somebody 'from hereabout'.

It is believed that while Viva prayed, Morrell got to first base, although this had never been established, and Opel declared that she was in the family way, giving Viva occassion to assail God all night in delirious thanksgiving.

And so, Patricia Naomi was born—a third granddaughter for Cecilprins, who, when informed of the blessed event by Papa Ludwick, was fit to be tied. 'What! A girl? What the hell is this, men? Everytime girl, girl, girl!' Papa Ludwick tried to preach, of course, and was crisply invited to go to hell. Cecilprins was inconsolable. He had three granddaughters now. It wasn't fair!

Iris, finding it increasingly difficult to sit at her sewing-machine as her stomach began to balloon, told her mother: 'You wait and see. Another drunkard for sure.' Mrs Holdenbottle, who went around Dehiwela with an expression of permanent shock, was indignant. 'How you can talk like that of innocent infant, I don't know. One thing, you girls nowadays are too much!'

Iris sniffed. 'Everyday coming drunk, no? Must see the state when coming to bed.'

Totoboy, like most happily inebriated husbands, imagined that the wife waited in breathless anticipation, and all he had to do was get the buttons of his trousers undone. To Totoboy in his cups, this was as complicated as a Rubick's cube. Iris complained of getting dizzy just watching him.

But in good time she too was taken to the lying-in home and was delivered of a bonny baby girl. Totoboy passed out and had to be wheeled away on a ward trolley to the waiting area where he lay on a couch and snored and went 'snnrrkk' until Cecilprins trotted in and swatted him across the head. Iris said: 'Lucky to get a girl,' and promptly decided to name the baby Fortune Ira. Cecilprins went home crestfallen. Only a month ago Terry had cabled the happy news that wife Bertha had had a girl and the baby had been named Bubsy. It was a conspiracy! 'If that Beryl also putting girl,' he told neighbour Simmons darkly, 'that is last straw. Last straw! That's what!'

The old man was finding it quite wearying maintaining the Boteju Lane home. Anna, with no babies anywhere on the horizon, was the only regular visitor, and he was lonely. He thought long and hard and decided to go visiting. There were the von Blosses of Kotahena who would be happy to see him, even have him. Indeed, they were, although Constance Koelmeyer, who had married his brother and considered herself too up-market to hob-nob with her in-laws, was in two minds about receiving Cecilprins as a house guest.

The chronicler has avoided mention of this branch of the family since it is felt that things have got complicated enough as it is. Cecilprins had twelve brothers and seven sisters. Maudiegirl had nine brothers and four sisters. To keep track of them all would require a well-staffed and equipped Department of Home Affairs! They had created little enclaves of Gerryns and Koelmeyers and Plunketts and Beckmeyers and Lisks in Kotahena and Modera, Kelaniya and Jambugasmulla, Nawinna and Battaramulla and even as far away as Badulla and Nawalapitiya.

There was an old reprobate whom the Boteju Lane von Blosses knew as 'Uncle Boy' who would suddenly turn up, requisition the lounger and go to sleep. He insisted on bread and butter and Bovril for breakfast and pork chops for dinner. Once in the lounger it took a couple of weeks to dislodge him.

There was also Aunty Nellie who was as thin as a garden lizard and had a face like a badly-dented saucepan. Her arrival would set off a storm of giggles for Cecilprins would smack his head and say:

'My God! Look, will you, who's coming. Aunty Nellie! Take to the back veranda and give that old chair to sit.'

The girls would run to the gate to welcome Nellie and slyly pinch each other and titter and say, 'How, Aunty Nellie, after a long time, no?' Nellie would shake her umbrella at them and say, 'Where's your Papa? Tell to give rickshaw-man ten cents. Head is turning coming in this sun.'

Cecilprins, affecting pleasure, would come to the step. 'Hullo, hullo, what brought you?'

'Why? Now must tell why I coming also? See to that rickshaw-man, where is Maudiegirl? In the backside, I suppose,' and stalk in to accost Maudiegirl and complain that it was impossible to come earlier. 'What, child, chillie grinding, back washing, such a lot to do, no? before can think of getting out.'

Maudiegirl would wave her to a chair. Nellie would tuck up the back of her skirt, sit and say: 'Hot, men, what sort of sun this is I don't know. So how are you? Cooking, cooking, with all these devils to feed, no? Don't know why you went and had so many.'

She accepts the cup of tea and naturally stays for a meal, shredding the air with her criticisms. The children enjoy her visit hugely. Nellie has much to say about her 'good-for-nothing Hiram' who is drinking himself to his grave. Hiram's exploits are legion. 'Just imagine, child, sleeping on the Lord Nelson Hotel steps. Police had to carry to the station and put in the lock up and coming home in the morning to tell to come and take.'

But the real fun began when she had picked up her umbrella and trotted off with a bag in which she had asked and received a bottle of *seeni-sambol* (a hot relish of onions, Maldive fish, chillie, garlic and tamarind, fried and sweetened to taste), a tin of condensed milk, a loaf of bread, some yellow thread and a small tin of cheese. Cecilprins would wrinkle his nose. 'Put that chair in the garden and pour some boiling water. Bloody woman has no shame. Going all over the place without her knickers.'

It was an established fact, vouched for by everyone in the family. Nellie never wore knickers, and she would pull up the back of her dress quite unashamedly wherever she sat and to blazes with present company. This was not because of some peculiar quirk of character. Nellie, all the family knew, had a notoriously weak bladder. She had only to laugh, or grimace, or register any sort of emotion and the faucet started to drip. Which was why the poor woman never wore knickers and which also explained the need to get her skirts out of the way wherever she sat. It was a family ritual to wash chairs and mop floors and sprinkle Jeyes Fluid after Nellie had been and gone. As Cecilprins was wont to say, with relations like this who needed friends or enemies? Many were best off in the closet, but they insisted on circulating.

Yet, there was no question of ostracizing even the worst of the litter. There has always been an amazing tolerance among the Burghers which has been their strongest survival factor. Even as these words are written in this year 1991, the Burghers in Sri Lanka could number a mere 0.8 per cent of total population. But their overabiding sense of 'living together' has made then merge and meld with the fabric of the island in a manner that is wondrously enlightening to know and behold. One could well say that the Sri Lankan Burgher is as native as the most strident Sinhala native. They may still be, in the main, the 'eat, drink and be merry' men of their particular Sherwood Forest, but they are all Sinhala-educated today, mix with enthusiasm, intermarry with almost boisterious abandon and remain an object lesson of how a tiny minority can live in absolute freedom and security and be accepted by the majority without bais, envy, malice, of any of those other miserable attitudes that are the harbingers of ethnic rivalry, intolerance and strife. This is why, wherever the Burghers live in Sri Lanka, one could well hear them say with pride: 'What the hell, men, if I can live in this country and work and support my family and educate my children and be reasonably comfortable, what's wrong with these other guys who are going around throwing bombs and demanding separate states? We are Sri Lankans, no?'

This, in the chronicler's mind, is what has made the Burghers unique. They knew how to fit in, to belong. They accepted, centuries ago, that Sri Lanka was their land. There was never any thought that they could, if things got bad, pack and hie back to Holland or to wherever they could trace back to. They were at home, and where else could they 'put a party' and enjoy life as much as at home?

Later in this book the chronicler will need to record a diaspora of sorts. The Burghers did leave to find new homes in Australia, England, Canada in the main. Let us, however, come to that distressing situation twenty years hence. We will instead learn how Cecilprins, having struck a deal with his brother Claude, gave up a lifetime of living in Boteju Lane, Dehiwela, and moved to Kotahena where he found life of a singularly even tenor and, diplomatically, stayed out of the way of sister-in-law Constance as much as he could.

Naturally, the children didn't like it. Kotahena was too far away and they never did like their Aunty Constance who wore her hair in a bun and seemed to have been born with a fierce frown which her husband, in lighter moments, said was because of the doctor's forceps.

Anna was pained. 'But why you want to go there? Can come and stay with us, no?' And Cecilprins in his wisdom would shake his head. 'You want your husband's people to say that I am now living on him? And why I must burden—that's right, burden, my children when having so many brothers and sisters? And another thing, Kotahena close to even go for the pension.'

So Cecilprins moved to Kotahena and made the best of all worlds, descending on Leah, Anna, Elsie whenever he had a mind to and staying for a week or two when the charms of Kotahena palled. Thus, the von Bloss family quit Dehiwela and thus, too, was Cecilprins quite unaware of how far Joe Werkmeister had progressed in his efforts to extract a pound of flesh from the errant Sonnaboy. Elaine was made to give a signed deposition, outlining as best as she could, what Sonnaboy had done and not done to her on the pretended promise of marriage. Lawyer Bumpy Juriansz was in his element. 'Sha!' he said, 'Cut and dried case. Not only can we hold him to his letter but can drag his name in the mud in court. All this will influence the verdict, you wait and see. I will ask for the maximum. Two thousand five hundred rupees. Judge is sure to award.'

'So he will get summons?'

'Oh yes. Let him find a lawyer to defend. But we have him nicely. He doesn't have a leg to stand on.'

Werkmeister was pleased. He would have been more pleased if Sonnaboy really hadn't a leg to stand on and was pained to think that Eustace and Merril had not broken Sonnaboy's legs. He had lost considerable faith in his sons who spent all of that fateful wedding day moaning and groaning and then making several visits to the Municipal Dispensary to have their bruises, contusions, bumps and lumps medicated. They were a pathetic sight indeed, and even Werkmeister failed to understand how two hulking men could have been pounded so thoroughly by one man—and in a wedding suit at that.

Meanwhile Sonnaboy and Beryl went to Kadugannawa where the pregnant Beryl found the little bungalow a nightmare of sorts. It was small, and built slap between two sets of railway tracks, about one hundred yards west of the station. The track that ran past the front door and the tiny, box-like veranda was the main Colombo-Kandy line and the trains would roar past, an engine in front and another at the rear pulling and pushing up the steep Kadugannawa incline. The track behind the house was a shunt line and all manner of locomotives and carriages and wagons and what is generally termed railway rolling stock kept shuttling to and fro at the most ungodly hours. As Sonnaboy told Beryl, 'Good thing we not sleeping too much in the night anyway,' for the roar of the railroad traffic could not be stilled.

And then the summons came and the Transportation Superintendent was displeased. 'Leave, leave, leave,' he said despairingly, 'That's all you buggers come for. And what, pray, is this summons? Going to courts for what?'

'Breach of promise,' Sonnaboy said.

'What? But you are newly-married, no? And your wife, young thing, no? and already getting a bundy. Only yesterday my wife was saying damn sin to marry so young. Should be in school instead of washing your overalls and cooking and getting pregnant. Anyway, that's not our business. What is all this breach of promise business?'

Sonnaboy explained and the Trans was fascinated. 'You're a bloody fool, men. Sure to sue for a big amount and how are you going to pay? And if you don't pay you may be arrested and sent to jail. And what about your wife then? You young fellows must think a little. After this station you could get an increment and promotion also, and now everything will get fucked up if you have to serve time. If you have money to pay up and come away then the railway will not worry, but if you get into jail you're in big trouble. Get the sack also.' He scribbled approval on the leave chit, 'Here, you go to Colombo and do something. Try to borrow some money and what about a lawyer? You have a lawyer?'

Sonnaboy shook his head.

'Get a lawyer. Judge will not like if you have no lawyer. My God, your poor wife. What a time for her to have all this worry. I'll tell my wife to keep an eye on her. You go to Colombo and do something. My best advice is to find some money and try to settle out of court. Your family can help, no?'

The family tried, but all that could be scraped together was a thousand rupees which, in 1935, was a small fortune. Totoboy, as a funding source, was a total loss. Anna wrung her hands and said Colontota would never unbend and Leah said much the same. Didn't Sonnaboy remember how he had beaten up their respective husbands? They were not going to give him money with cries of gladness. Cecilprins said that he had nothing. He was giving the bulk of his pension to Constance who waited for him on pension day with her hand outstretched.

So, with a thousand rupees in his pocket, Sonnaboy went to court and declared that he had no lawyer to plead his defence and that he was married with a wife who was expecting a first child in October, and put himself at the mercy of the bench, having denied vigorously that he had any carnal knowledge of Elaine who sat like a statue of the Virgin of the Seven Dolors while Bumpy Juriansz painted him black and blue and said he was a monster of infidelity and avarice who had blighted the life of his poor, trusting, innocent client, plighting his troth to her while arranging to marry another woman.

The court lapped all this up and the judge, who was decked in a new white wig and looked like Robespierre of the French Revolution leaned forward to study Sonnaboy as though he was inspecting some alien life-form.

'Does the defendant admit to the promise of marriage,' the judge asked.

Sonnaboy stifled a yawn.

Bumpy Juriansz tabled the famous letter which was taken to the bench by a red-sashed court sergeant. This was studied.

'This letter is addressed to the plaintiff's father?'

'As the natural guardian, my Lord,' said Juriansz, 'It is a binding promise to marry my client.'

'And this was accepted?'

Juriansz said, yes, my Lord. His client's father wrote a letter of acceptance, a copy of which is also exhibited.

Sonnaboy was shown his letter and grudgingly confirmed that he had written it: 'Because he said to write, no? Said I must write because that's the way with gentlemen.'

'I see,' said the judge, 'and are you a gentleman, Mr von Bloss?'

'I am an engine driver.'

This raised titters of laughter which were quickly quelled by the court sergeant.

'I see. I was not aware that present society makes distinction between engine drivers and gentlemen. You do admit you wrote this letter?' Sonnaboy nodded.

'And you did promise to marry the plaintiff?'

No answer.

'The defendant will please answer the bench.'

'Yes. I said I will marry her. But that was before . . . .'

'Before?'

'Before I met Buiya.'

The judge frowned. He decided it wiser not to pursue this line of examination. Who or what a Buiya was he didn't wish to know. Crude fellow, this. Seemed to think he could just waltz into court—his court—with no legal representation and not a clue about how he should conduct himself. He rapped his gavel.

'Does the defendant admit liability to a promise of marriage and a solemn engagement and to having given in token of such promise, a ring to the plaintiff?'

Sonnaboy had to concede that Elaine still had his ring which had cost him thirty-six rupees and that it was generally accepted that he and Elaine were to marry. He also had to admit that as result of this contract, Elaine had eschewed the attentions of other suitors, 'But nobody else come for half a mile near as long as I'm there,' he grinned, and that, as would be expected, sealed his fate.

It was taken, naturally, that Sonnaboy intimidated the 'competition' (which was very true, though considering Elaine's mannish, impudent manner, was not of any considerable size), made plans to marry her, then ditched her most unceremoniously and in midstream, mind, to marry another. This cavalier attitude and conduct merited judicial censure and, as Bumpy Juriansz prayed (legally, that is) the plaintiff was awarded the princely sum of two thousand rupees and Sonnaboy was also informed that costs would run to another 125 rupees. He said he had a thousand and asked for time, whereupon he was given a month to make good the balance and so he emerged into the sunshine of Hulftsdorp a thousand rupees in debt and with thirty days to find more money.

Sonnaboy was, by nature, a most unconcerned man. There are, it is supposed, many like this. Thirty days was a long time away. He pushed aside his need for 1125 rupees and returned to Kadugannawa where, back at work and with Beryl to care for, he put the whole unpleasant business out of his mind for the next twenty-four days. Then he began to worry and took to pacing the tiny veranda and scowling at the passing trains and generally giving his fireman a hard time. Beryl was in her seventh month. He would need money for her confinement and all the things a baby would need. He mentally consigned the entire judiciary of the island to the Kalahari. Elaine, too, could go there.

So he didn't appear in court and the judge was most annoyed. A writ was issued. Seize, the law decreed, the wordly goods of Sonnaboy Duncan Clarence von Bloss, Esquire; the said worldly goods and possessions would then be auctioned by the court and the sum of Rupees 1125 owing to the plaintiff and the Crown so recovered. The defendant, by his failure to appear in court and discharge his obligations is hereby called upon to pay a further sum of Rupees twenty being in the nature of a fine for wasting His Lordship's time and giving him a headache which he certainly did not have when setting out that particular morning.

Cecilprins, who had come to court to see how his son fared, took the afternoon train to Kandy, arriving in Kadugannawa at dinner time, wringing his hands and slumping into a chair with impending doom writ large on his face.

Sonnaboy was astonished. 'Came alone all the way?' he marvelled, 'And how you found the house?'

'Never mind,' Cecilprins panted, 'stationmaster told. Why you didn't come to court? Even if hadn't the money should have come, no? And if I didn't go how to come here and tell what they are going to do? That Juriansz fellow hell of a chap. Talking in court as if you promised to marry *him*! Going my lord, my lord, and crying through the nose. But I got good tip from old Bocks. You know that Bocks, no? Living in Wellawatte? He is lawyer also and met him in court, no, actually outside court when I coming out. I told how that judge said to send fiscal fellows to take everything. Everything, you hear? Even this chair I'm now sitting.'

Sonnaboy gaped. He couldn't make head of tail of this rigmarole and had to get the old man sorted out. Eventually, after several false starts the story became more intelligible. And advocate Cecil Bocks had given them a fine legal point of great interest. The seizers could only enter a premises through the front door. The worldly possessions they were expected to seize and carry away had to be in the premises upon their making entry and these worldly goods had to be carried out through the mode of entry, viz., the front door. If said front door remained closed, the seizers must wait opportunity when the door was opened to march in and take possession. They had no licence to force their way in or act in any manner that could be interpreted in the loosest sense as illegal, high-handed, injudicious, obstreperous or just plain ungentlemanly. Any attempt at breaking and entering was to be abhorred as highly illegal. And only the front door, mind. There was no other legal way into the house.

Sonnaboy thought this over and saw the light. 'You are sure that is what Bocks said?'

Cecilprins nodded. 'But how to know for sure. Have a lawyer here to ask?'

143

Sonnaboy thought this over too. 'Have in Kandy. Fine thing you come to tell, and this time in the night also. Now Beryl also looking worried. Bad time, no? to get upset. Bought cot also for the baby. She making all the things in pink.'

'Pink!' shouted Cecilprins, horrified, 'What is this pink business? She also wanting a girl? My God, don't know what's the matter with all of you!'

Beryl pouted. 'So my baby, no? I told I want a girl.'

'Told? Whom to tell? So what's the harm, child, if have a boy?'

'But I like a girl. Can dress her and put ringlets and bows in the hair and all.'

Cecilprins glowered. Ringlets and bows indeed. 'Vain I came,' he said hollowly, 'All the others having girls. Like measles, getting girls, girls, girls all over the place. Anyway, never mind that for now. What you going to do about this other thing? If come tomorrow or even tonight?'

'Don't open the door. Go from round and see who and if say to open the door I'll put a clout with the *molgaha* (the mortar).'

Nobody came, not the next day either, which gave Sonnaboy the opportunity to consult Josh Bevan, a Kandy lawyer who said that old Bocks was right. It was only through the front door that the law could serve itself, satiate its appetite. The back door, windows, side doors could all be left open quite invitingly. Cheered, Sonnaboy returned, banged at his front door, remembered and went round the house. Cecilprins said: 'So how?'

'It's right. Close the front, open the back. And if we want to move the furniture out for safety can move all out from the back door and they cannot do anything.'

Kadugannawa hadn't seen anything like it. The affair was talked about for months. The western railway yard, where Sonnaboy's bungalow was situated, became a stage where all the men and women (and a fair sprinkling of pariah dogs) became merely players. First came a dirty blue fiscal lorry that wheezed and panted up the road, nearly dying of apoplexy near Dawson's Tower. It struggled up the rise with a great clashing of gears and then coasted down to the station with a sigh that must only be reserved for the long-suffering.

From this contraption issued four men, an official type in a khaki pith hat who held a file of papers and three burly workmen who had obviously been press ganged in order to march in at the crook of a finger and seize and carry away Sonnaboy's movable possessions. Two station porters, doubtless instructed to keep their eyes open for such a development, immediately alerted stationmaster Thilainathan, a fussy little Tamil whose cap covered his ears. The Divisional Inspector of Mechanics, Vere Cook, was also informed. A linesman named Swaris was sent at the double to sonnaboy's bungalow. That worthy, whose mouth was always full of chewing betel leaf, jogged up, spat a stream of betel juice on a pile of sleepers and told Sonnaboy: 'There they coming. S.M. told to tell the front door close and our boys ready.'

Meanwhile the eager writ-servers were in earnest conversation with Thilainathan. Apparently there was a problem. Pith Hat said he needed to take his lorry to the bungalow and Thilainathan said that, as Pith Hat could plainly see, that was an impossibility. 'Look around,' he invited, 'Where's the road? The house is between the railway lines.'

Pith Hat puffed. 'We have to take everything in the house. I have court order.'

Thilainathan smiled. 'I know, I know. But you cannot take the lorry to the house. So you tell your men to carry all the things here.'

This, too, was not satisfactory. 'My God, men, that will take the whole day. See how far they will have to go, up and down. And only three men.'

'That,' said Thilainathan, 'is your problem.'

Pith Hat suggested that the lorry could be manoeuvred along the path beside the main line to a point directly opposite the bungalow and Thilainathan told him to perish the thought.

'Why? Can go that way. What's the harm?'

'Harm? Railway Ordinance. That's the harm. Standing Orders. That's the harm. If I allow every Tom, Dick and Harry to come into my yard and drive vehicles all over the place what do you think will happen? This is railway property. Not a thoroughfare for lorries and buses and carts and rickshaws. You are trying to set a precedent? Next time kerosene oil man will came and say he want to take his bull-and-cart.'

145

'But this is judicial matter,' Pith Hat bawled, 'You cannot obstruct. You have to co-operate. I have court order.'

Vere Cook, who was enjoying the conversation immensely, told Pith Hat what he could do with his court order and another stormy session erupted. From the east end of the platform came Alex Raymond, the Way and Works Inspector, to join the party. Also striding up was 'Jowls' St. John, the Mechanical Engineer, whose red nose blazed in the morning sun. Pith Hat was outgunned. Then Foreman Plate Layer Salgado reminded him that all railway property was, in a sense, private property. People paid for user's privilege. The public, for whose purpose the railway ran, could not enter a station or board a train without a ticket. To trespass on the railway track was a punishable offence. Pith Hat conceded that this was correct.

'Then where's your platform ticket?'

'Eh?'

'You people are trespassing. First thing is to buy platform tickets. So you go and do that.'

'But—'

'No but business. I can give you in charge of Railway Security. You are trespassing.'

'This is official government business,' Pith Hat bawled.

'Then where is the official government letter addressed to me requesting that you and your crew be permitted to walk all over railway property? Where?'

Pith Hat waved the writ. Thilainathan waved it away. Vere Cook told him once again where he could put his writ. Meanwhile this platform summit had attracted all manner of people—a few interested passengers, porters and coolies, the gatekeeper and the cabinman who, like Swaris, shot a blob of betel juice close to Pith Hat's foot and said: 'What, gentleman, you're saying? First ticket get and come, otherwise will chase from platform.'

Pith Hat pointed out, shakily, that the intention was to go to Sonnaboy's bungalow and not to dally on platforms or catch trains.

'Then what for here coming?'

'Because there's no other road,' Pith Hat hooted.

He was advised to take his lorry and his cretins, park beside the embankment on the main road facing the bungalow and make his way down a tiny footpath. That is the way. Not this way.'

'Ho! And the people in the bungalow also go up and down that hill? Even a goat cannot climb that.'

'They come through the station.'

'Ho!'

'But they are railway employees. Other people who want to go there go on the footpath.'

Pith Hat raised a point. 'How they bring their furniture to the bungalow, then? They carried their things down the bank?'

Thilainathan smiled. 'Their furniture all came by goods wagon. The wagon was shunted to the back door and unloaded. You should have come in a wagon like wagon goods with a goods shed ticket.' Roars of laughter greeted the look on Pith Hat's face.

'Oi!' said the cabinman who deplored long-winded arguments, 'Your lorry take and go. From main road go to the house.'

'You will hear about this!' Pith Hat bellowed.

'I think,' Vere Cook told the stationmaster, 'this constitutes a public nuisance. What do you think? Shall we hand them over to the police?'

The porters crowded in. Passengers pushed into the tightening circle to stare at these 'Colombo Fellows' who had come with some crazy 'Colombo ideas.'

'What they trying to do?'

'Mad devils, on the railway, lorry trying to take.'

A couple of mongrels who hung around the platform canteen and never needed to buy platform tickets also nosed in to sniff at ankles and bristle and bare teeth at each other. Eventually the fiscal team retreated to a round of cheers, hoots, jeers, whistles and clapping, while Vere Cook went to Sonnaboy's, picking his way along the tracks while the fiscal lorry backed out, turned and rattled to a halt beside a fifty-foot cutting which was directly above the bungalow. The moving men were visibly moved. How, they wished to know, could anything be lugged up such a precipice. In easier circumstances Pith Hat would have entertained such objections as more than reasonable, but he was as mad as a hornet and determined that justice would be served. Once in, he would strip that bungalow clean. 'We will go in and take everything,'he shrilled.

'Everything?'

'Yes! Beds, cupboards, almirahs, stoves, tables, chairs, everything.'

'And bring to lorry?'

'Yes.'

'How? Up and down this?'

'Yes!'

'Gentleman is mad or what?'

'That is what we came for! We have a job to do!'

Mutters and scowls and the blackest of looks accompanied them as they warily stepped out to the steep footpath that necessitated single file descent. Then Pith Hat froze. The damp, tall undergrowth was thick with leeches. Some had already swung aboard and latched on to elbows, and gone exploring under trouser legs and inside socks.

Meanwhile it seemed that all of Kadugannawa, alerted to what promised to be a merry morning's entertainment, had begun to make tracks to Sonnaboy's bungalow. The postmaster, some off-duty policemen, Joronis who operated a sleazy tea kiosk, a Public Works Department overseer and his men who left off inspecting the road, the resthouse keeper, a gang of carters and all manner of citizens who considered it their lawful duty to gather round and watch. A fruit seller who rejoiced in the name of Sarnelis brought along a bag of avocado pears. He thought it was a party of sorts and being a considerate soul, felt that a contribution would be in order.

Sonnaboy sat on a shunt track and watched the road and the tall blade grass of the embankment nod this way and that as the swearing, slapping, panting fiscal men plunged through, now with a long slither, now with a gravelly slide on a path that was ideally suited for the nocturnal ramblings of a porcupine. Eventually they broke through to the main line amidst a wave of encouraging cheers from the assembled Kadugannawans although many were holding their bellies and laughing like a chorus line of hyenas. Old

Jossie Nona, who supplied *hoppers* to the platform canteen cackled like one of Macbeth's witches. 'Hee, hee, hee, look will you those lunatics. Ammo, leeches eating for sure.'

Limping slightly, Pith Hat crossed the tracks to the veranda and tried the front door. Locked. He peered through the window. Not bad, the furniture. 'Hoy!' he called, 'Open this door.' Nobody did. Pith Hat banged angrily, and Beryl said she suddenly felt ill and had cramp in her legs and swayed through the back door to flop down in the little hall. Sonnaboy called in two railway types. They carried up the chair with Beryl in it and went out. Pith Hat, at the window, fumed. 'Hoy! Where are you taking that chair? You bring it back, do you hear! And open this bloody door!' A porter who came in to grin, made a rude gesture with a half-closed fist and a finger which told Pith Hat that he was pitted against men with imagination. He nearly choked in fury and went back to assaulting the door. His crew, meanwhile, sat on the front steps and picked off leeches which had shown grim tenacity and the urge to explore all manner of unmentionable places.

Carrying Beryl out gave Sonnaboy an idea. He would carry out all the furniture and, hopefully, drive Pith Hat mad. One fiscal officer going back to Colombo in a strait jacket would show that judge what he was up against. The crowd was delighted. They trooped in *en masse* to quickly empty the house before Pith Hat's popping eyes.

As has been said, Kadugannawa had never seen such a sight. Even as this is being recorded, well-known Sri Lankan poet and writer, Jean Arasanayagam of Kandy says how, when she was a little girl in Kadugannawa in 1935 she remembers how she saw a pregnant lady being carried along the railway lines in a chair by two men. Well . . . this sort of confirmation is only to be expected. Jean Arasanayagam was, in 1935, Jean Solomons—a sweet-faced tot of four or five years and daughter of railway guard Solomons who lived in a railway bungalow close to the yard. This chronicle, I must remind readers, is 'faction'—the new word that has been coined to describe a work of fiction that sails very close to fact. Another famous Sri Lankan singer, Lylie Godridge recalls the day, long, long ago, when he was a choirboy and had to sing at a funeral . . . and somebody who was quite drunk, fell into the grave! The hullaballoo, Lylie says, was quite extraordinary . . . and this 'fact' became 'faction' in Part Two of this chronicle. But, it is maintained, that this is a work of 'fictional-fact' or 'factual-fiction', or whatever else it could be called. The fact of the fiction must be recorded . . . and the fact suitably fictionalised. I hope the reader understands, because I cannot get the real grasp of it all myself!

Well . . . Kadugannawa was vastly entertained. The highlight of the morning's events was the sight of Beryl, big with child, being borne in a chair along the tracks to the station, where she was deposited in the First Class Waiting Room and given iced orange barley water. Jossie Nona tripped alongside, fanning Beryl with an old newspaper and small boys and dogs got into the way of others who formed a motley procession. The fiscal crew, now divested of leeches, stared, fascinated.

'What is that?' asked one.

'*Perahera* (a religious procession),' said another.

Pith Hat strode the narrow veranda like Shakespeare's colossus, a picture of frustration and rage. His vocal chords had apparently thrown in the towel, for he kept opening his mouth and the veins of his neck bulged but not a whinny came forth. All manner of people kept coming in from the rear of the house and helping themselves to all manner of wordly possessions and arranging them according to their peculiar fancies, all over the railway yard. Three big louts in khaki shorts had taken the settee and two chairs and a small table to the side of the water column. There, the louts sat and engrossed themselves in some deep scientific discussion. They were obviously enjoying themselves. An almirah was carried off by four men to a clearing near the signals cabin. It was placed there, its polished wood blinking in the sun, while a wash-basin and stand were placed beside it and the basin carefully filled with all manner of household odds and ends. The effect pleased Vere Cook who couldn't know at the time that he was giving Kadugannawa its first surrealist 'happening'. He told Sonnaboy: 'You go and see to your wife. If she is feeling bad, take her to my place and get a doctor. I will look after all this and see that nothing is damaged. Lucky it's a nice day.'

The overview, the whole scene, studied from any direction, was something to wonder at. The railway yard had begun to look quite homely. The sidings were festooned with pictures, piles of magazines and copies *of Girl's Own* (Beryl's). A line of empty goods wagons were given an honour guard of kitchen utensils—mortar and pestle, grinding stone, pots and pans, cane bags and boxes holding bottles and tins and all manner of gadgetry plus brushes and chopping knife that was big enough to decapitate a middling elephant. A hat-stand rubbed shoulders with dressing-table near the goods-shed and a glass cabinet, a writing desk and a dinner wagon had been spaced along the main line at ten-yard intervals to the admiration of all and sundry. Nothing remained in the bungalow. Only a small crucifix which everyone forgot about and which hung over the front door and went unnoticed by Pith Hat.

One of the fiscal crew said: 'If we go, good. Nothing can take, no? Now in house haven't anything.'

Pith Hat seemed to be wrestling with unseen demons. Never, in all his years in service had he encountered such a situation. Just when he was considering retreat there was a small thud and a click and the front door was opened. Vere Cook, with the straightest face he could muster, said: 'Good morning. You knocked?'

So, after another tangle with the leeches and a mighty struggle to climb the embankment, the fiscal men reached their lorry where they were surrounded by a bunch of roughnecks who patiently outlined what could be done the next time they were seen, heard or smelt in Kadugannawa. The very air seemed to smoke and grow purple. Solemn pledges were made that Pith Hat's liver—of all things—would be clawed out of him and duly consumed; that his intestines would be used as skippings ropes; that his mother would be subjected to a series of intimate encounters of the worst kind; that his face—and especially his ears—would be split like squishy oranges; that he would be taken apart, limb by limb and scattered in so methodical a manner that it would take a team of forensic experts a very long time to get him together again after all the kings horses and all the king's men had failed in their endeavours. The crew, wishing to disassociate themselves from their leader, leaped into the lorry and cowered ingloriously while the driver blanched and fumbled with the ignition and actually rolled in reverse for a full thirty yards until he dazedly clumped on the brake pedal and shouted 'Sancta Maria! All are mad here! Come go, come go!'

And they went . . . and Beryl said she was all right and the whiteness had left her lips and she smiled sweetly at everyone who had clustered around to see how she was. Mrs Cook wrapped a shawl around her shoulders and said: 'Don't worry about anything. Will put everything back and arrange the house nicely. Can you walk? Then come go home and you rest awhile. Can have some lunch with us today.'

Cecilprins, who strode the platform like a Nelson on the fo'c's'le was happy. Jossie Nona said: 'Boy for sure. See, will you, how the stomach is so low. If girl getting, stomach is high. Sure to get baby boy.' The old man quivered with pleasure. At last, he felt, one of his children would deliver the goods!

In Colombo, the court of His Lordship Bryant Ridgeway, J.,K.C., was not in the best of humour. The obvious step was taken. A warrant was issued. Sonnaboy was to be arrested and produced in court where it would make His Lordship graciously pleased to have the miscreant confined for a period that His Lordship would determine. He declared that justice would not be mocked at. Also, with Sonnaboy locked up for his sins, there would be no need to listen any more to the anguished bleatings of Bumpy Juriansz who was getting on His Lordship's nerves.

Stationmaster Thilainathan, too, had words with Sonnaboy. 'What, I say, all you have to do is pay the court. So what's the problem? Apply for a loan. I'll tell you what? Take leave and go to head office in Maradana and see the G.M.R. He's a pukka chap. Tell everything and say you want a loan to pay the court. Don't ask for the money. Just tell the railway can send the money to court in your name. Railway can make monthly deductions from your salary. All this nonsense you did, brother, when could have got the loan and paid and finished this business long ago.'

The General Manager of Railways was a stout, fussy man with a ball-of-cheese face . . . you know . . . round, with nothing of real prominence, not even the nose. He wore white and hung a dark blue tie around his neck, and liked to wear flannels and a blazer on

Saturdays and whenever he took his swanky rail car to go on a tour of inspection. He was a very important member (so he claimed) of the British Club in Colombo and was (others claimed) a great one for the ladies. He was Lyons—Alexander Lyons Jr. to be exact—and his favourite claim was that he was Lyons by name and a lion by nature, which impressed nobody save himself. Oh, he affected a great shock of yellow hair that curled at the neck and was leonine enough, but he would go home to a perpetually cranky wife and say yes dear, no dear, of course dear, and was strangely subdued when with her in public.

Sonnaboy was led to his sanctum where large, framed photographs showed Lyons in a running shed, examining the piston rings of a venemously dirty steam locomotive and another with his beefy leg cocked up on a cowcatcher, pith hat on head, below-the-knee length shorts and dark hose and posing like a big game hunter who has just shot his first railway engine.

Lyons was in a sunny mood. His wife was sailing for England on the 'Orcades' that evening. He had' just popped into office to 'show his face' and then go back home to listen to her litany of admonitions and instructions and the usual interminable things wives go on and on about when they are leaving their hubbies for three months. Lyons would have to go on board and listen to the woman until the klaxon sounded for visitors to proceed ashore, and then, as the Peninsular & Orient royal mail vessel upped anchor, he would board the Mackinnons launch and crane his neck to wave dutifully. He was looking forward to the moment when the 'Orcades' would begin its push out of harbour. He'd like to shake the master of the tug 'Hercules' by the hand and send a token of his deep appreciation to the Senior Pilot, Captain Edward Tucker. Three months of bliss! And here, before him stood a grey-eyed Sonnaboy looking, for all the world, like a dressed-up Gargantua who had come seeking money!

Lyons listened and adopted a frown. This would not do. His engine drivers couldn't be allowed to go around marrying willy-nilly and having fiscal men trampling all over railway property. There were three funds, of course, to which personnel had recourse: the P.S.M.P.A. (Public Servants Mutual Provident

Association); the G.O.B.A. (Government Officers Benefit Association) and the Lady Lochore Fund. This Lady Lochore must have been quite a woman. Lyons was hazy about the whole thing but it seemed that the good Lady had instituted a fund to help public servants in distress. 'Your only hope,' Lyons said, 'is the Lady Lochore, but I never heard of such a thing. You think Lady Lochore will pay for breach of promise. What on earth possesses you fellows to get into such scrapes?'

Sonnaboy shrugged. 'When meeting Beryl I knew she much better. Elaine all right, sir, but can't keep the mouth closed. You know, whole time going on do this, must do that, not so young as Beryl also. When I saw Beryl I thinking My God, if get married to Elaine she get old suddenly and just sit and talk talk talk the whole time and I'll go mad or something.'

Lyons listened and nodded sympathetically. Great God, he thought, the man could be talking of his own Margaret . . . 'Yes, I see what you mean. Anyway, I have very little time today. My wife is sailing for England and I have great deal to do. But I will recommend your loan . . . .' He rang the bell on his desk and asked that the Chief Clerk be summoned. This worthy was instructed to take Sonnaboy away and file a loan application. The C.G.R. would also make official representation to the Courts, accepting to pay and that in these circumstances, the writ on Sonnaboy's person may be withdrawn. 'Bring me the forms for my signature and recommendation and get the details sorted out for payment to Courts. Find out how this can be done. Well, my man,' to Sonnaboy, 'You're lucky I was in today. You have to agree on what deductions will have to be made. Settle that with Mr Velu, here. He will check your Pay and Records file.'

Sonnaboy was fervent in his thanks and Lyons grinned from ear to ear when the door closed behind them. Poor bugger. He'll be in debt to the Lady Lochore for years. But he liked the man. And that Elaine was too close to home. Brrr. Talk, talk, the whole time. Didn't he know it? Should have done the same thing, and left his Margaret holding the bag. Thank heavens she would be gone for three months. Three whole months! Great pity these P & O liners did not even indicate a propensity to sink occasionally. Yet, he felt that he had cause to celebrate. He really felt like doing a little jig.

Chief Clerk Velu looked Sonnaboy up and down and sniffed. 'Lucky devil, you are. Caught him in the right mood. And case like this! Never in all my service. And how? Personally recommended also.'

Having signed innumerable papers and after a great and minute checking through files, Velu said morosely: 'All extra work for me. Now have to call the courts and send forms in triplicate and get the warrant recalled and I don't know what else. These legal matters are a real bloody nuisance.'

Eventually, after two forays to the small canteen for tea, Velu came to the all-important question. 'Now deductions. We have to pay the courts 1200 rupees with two fines also. Let me see . . . that's 1248 rupees with the interest. Have four percent interest also . . . .'

'Interest,' Sonnaboy exclaimed, 'Have to pay Lady Lochore interest also?'

'Then what do you think? You think just giving money to anybody who comes and asks? How do you think the fund can be maintained? If you don't like then go and ask an Afghan.'

Sonnaboy sighed.

'Anyway, have to make monthly repayment. How much can you pay back every month?'

'How about five rupees?'

'Five rupees!' Velu shrieked, 'You're mad, men? For how many years are you going to pay? Twenty years? No, even longer than that!'

'But how to pay like that? Buiya is going to have a baby also. Now only two months more.'

Velu glowered. 'All this extra work,' he moaned, pulling Sonnaboy's file to him, 'Let's see . . . when is your next increment due . . . my God, that's in August next year. By that time you may decide to marry somebody else. I'll tell you, you sign for fifteen rupees a month deduction. That will be . . . let's see . . . about seven years.'

Sonnaboy shook his head. 'Can do about ten rupees, but even that is very difficult, men. I'll tell you, I'll go and tell the G.M.R. and say how hard it is to manage.'

Velu jerked up. 'No, no. He will only call and shout and ask why I cannot settle this.'

Finally it was agreed that a sum of Rs 12.48 per month be deducted for a period of eight years and four months and Sonnaboy said that was more like it. 'Fine thing,' Velu said bitterly, 'Lady Lochore will turn in her grave.'

So everything was satisfactorily settled and Beryl was delivered of a son, Carloboy Prins von Bloss, on an October full moon night at the Kandy Nursing Home—a lusty, bawling infant whom Beryl hated on sight. Sonnaboy and Cecilprins got very drunk the next evening and weaved up and down the Kadugannawa station platform lighting crackers and shanghaied Vere Cook and his wife to be godparents. The new generation was well on its way and the island of Ceylon surely held its breath. Here was new life in a new time. King Edward VIII abdicated in due course. In 1937 George VI was crowned king of England. A new age beckoned.

PART FOUR

The Ripening

Now these are the generations of Esau . . .

Oops! Sorry about that. When the chronicler thinks of the cherry-laden jam fruit tree, the mind strays to the Book of Genesis . . . .

Before we get on to this new generation of middling Burghers who turned their own trick or two, it would be convenient to record, for all time, the order of their coming into their earthly inheritance:

A. ERIC HENRY DE MELLO married ELSIE MAUD VON BLOSS.

They produced:
1. NOELLA MARIETTA
2. DORCAS MATHILDA
3. BEULAH CATHERINE
4. IAN STANFORD ERIC
5. THELMA MARILYN
6. CAROLINE DAISY

B. DIONYSIUS RICHARD COLONTOTA married ANNA CONSTANCE VON BLOSS.

They adopted:
SUNIL HENAGODA, son of SUMANA AKKA, the perfectly foul-looking servant woman who worked in the Colontota household. The boy Sunil's father was claimed to be a rickshaw man who operated out of Kirillapone slum, but this was open to debate.

C. TERRY ANDERS VON BLOSS married BERTHA ROSE McHEYZER.

They produced:
1. BUBSYGIRL EMMALINE
2. MORRIS GERALD

D. VIVA RICHARDSON VON BLOSS married OPEL SARAH LUDWICK.

They produced:
1. PATRICIA NAOMI

2. CLAUDE PETER.
3. WINSTON PAUL
4. JOHN JACOB
5. A girl who was only known as KUKKU, who was fat, very vicious and most unpleasant. It was assumed that Opel had borne her in a fit of pique while Viva, quite shattered, prayed for weeks for divine patience to endure the shame of it all. It was only when KUKKU was an ugly young woman and causing a great deal of family concern that Viva is reported to have snapped: 'How long have I got to put up with this! Not enough I gave that coolie's daughter my name and my home!'

E. <u>TOTOBOY   DAVIDSON   BRENNAN   VON   BLOSS married IRIS ELIZABETH HOLDENBOTTLE.</u>
They produced:
1. FORTUNE IRA.
2. BRENNAN MAURICE ROUNDTABLE
3. WINSTON VERNON ALBERT
4. CYRIL DAVID VICTOR

Iris is credited with saying, later, that Totoboy was in no condition to give her any more children which, she added, was a great mercy.

F. <u>GEORGE   GLADSTONE   DE   MELLO   married   LEAH BERNADETTE VON BLOSS.</u>
They produced:
1. MARLENE CHRISTINA
2. IVOR RUDOLPH WILHELM

G. SONNABOY   DUNCAN   CLARENCE   VON   BLOSS married BERYL HYACINTH DA BREA.
They produced:
1. CARLOBOY PRINS
2. DIANA EVELYN
3. MARIE ESTHER MAUD
4. HEATHER EVADNE MARYSE

5.   DAVID STEFAN LANCE
6.   MICHAEL GRANTON DUKE
7.   BEVERLEY ANNETTE
8.   A baby girl who died at birth.
9.   Another baby girl who was born dead. This was the result
     of some decoction Beryl had taken on the advice of a
     neighbour, Gwennie Pereira. There was this dire need to
     get rid of the baby which was certainly not Sonnaboy's.
10   DORIAN PERCIVAL
11. SHANE ROGER MEREDITH
12. MARY ANN THERESE
They also adopted:
     BONIFACE HU CHO CHIN, illegitimate child of a
     Chinese shopkeeper in Wellawatte and Dorinda Ebert
     who worked as a salesgirl in the shop. After Dorinda had
     inspected the Chinaman's etchings, she was kicked out of
     home by an irate father. The Chinaman then sent her to
     Mannar in the north of the island, where she gave birth
     to a male child, promptly abandoned it and sneaked out
     of the hospital and back to Colombo where the Chinaman
     welcomed her with glad cries and reinstalled her in his
     shop. The baby was baptised and named Boniface by the
     church in Mannar and despatched to Our Lady of
     Victories convent in Moratuwa. Sonnaboy and Beryl went
     to the convent to obtain, if possible, a servant girl from
     among the many orphans the convent cared for. They saw
     the infant Boniface and decided to formally adopt him.

So, as this chapter opens, we have a great many lives to
consider—all first cousins and moving in an ever-widening circle
of more cousins and aunts and uncles galore. Keeping track of them
all is a formidable task, but rewarding, for this was, indeed, a brave
new age.

   Education had spread throughout the island at breakneck speed.
Now was a stupendous levelling. Big Catholic and Methodist
institutions, Buddhist and Muslim colleges arose to spew forth the
finest men and women of all races that the island ever knew. This
was the age of scintillating literati who grew and matured in the

161

finest British tradition. Big schools and colleges for boys and girls still stand, harking back to that golden age. In and around Colombo were St. Joseph's College, St. Peter's College, St. Thomas' College, St. Benedict's College, the Royal College (once the Royal Academy), Wesley College, Ananda College, Nalanda College, Zahira College, St. Mary's College, St. John's College, Ladies College, the Pembroke Academy, St. Bridget's Convent, Holy Family Convents, Good Shepherd Convents, St. Clare's Convent School, St. Lawrence's School, Thurston College and so many, many more. Other beacons of education stood elsewhere: Trinity College, St. Anthony's College and St. Sylvester's as well as Kingwood College in Kandy: De Mazenod College in Kandana, St. John Bosco's College and Technical Institute in Hatton, St. Xavier's College in Nuwara Eliya, where another Good Shepherd Convent also operated; Our Lady of Victories Convent in Moratuwa; St. Aloysius College, Galle; St. Patrick's College, Jaffna, the Sacred Heart Convent, Galle, ad infinitum. It would be impossible to list every school, academy and yes, university—two were instituted in Colombo and Peradeniya—that each contributed to fine-tuning students, sent them for further research and study in England and made them of unique bent and calling in a host of scholarly disciplines. The brightness sprang up everywhere. No longer, then, were the Burghers the 'preferred' lot. In the ranks of professionals were the Sinhalese, Tamils and Malays and Muslims as well and the competition for slices of the cake grew fierce. It became an unfamiliar world to the old-time Burgher parents. 'My God, child,' Leah would exclaim, 'Our children nowadays learning things we never even heard of. So how to see what they are doing in the school?' Carloboy would sit with a Latin Grammar and grin hugely and say aloud: 'Faceo, Facere, Feci, Factum,' and Beryl would stop stock-still on the way to the kitchen. 'What is all that you are saying? Now learning all the filthy words at school and coming? You wait, I'll tell your father when he comes home.' Latin, for Beryl, was definitely not on.

Elsie's Noella was a little beauty. Long, black hair that waved naturally over her shoulders and quite classic features. Leah's Marlene, with her shock of black curly hair and dancing eyes and rich, full lips was a power to be reckoned with. Even Iris' Fortune, with her long lashes and high cheekbones was too attractive to be true. When she dimpled into a smile, she was totally devastating. Nobody in the family could tell how Terry's Bubsygirl fared, for when Terry retired and returned home to settle in Bandarawela, he chose a remote spot on the Welimada road, far from town and, he hoped, from his brother Viva whom he declared was a fruitcake. Bubsygirl must have had her moments, for she found a Royal Air Force flight lieutenant named Gerry Cowan who said he loved her madly and that it was very good for his glands—he got under her skirts regularly. Opel's Patricia, too, was pleasant enough, even if she had bow legs and spent all her time smoothing down the front of her dress so that her young breasts would be taken note of.

For many years the families did not see much of each other. Sonnaboy left Kadugannawa, on transfer to Chilaw, where Diana Evelyn was born. Then, when stationed in Colombo, he rented a house in 34th Lane, Wellawatte. Beryl was pleased. This was more to her liking. She had never liked being too far away from Nimal Road; but was most upset when she learned that her mother had moved into her sister's in Maradana and Elsie, of all people, had moved into her old home and had given birth to Dorcas Mathilda and Beulah Catherine and had become a downright dragon of a woman.

Elsie's three girls could never understand their mother's perpetual tantrums and black moods. While Noella came out bouncy and beautiful, Dorcas was a thin, awkward child who had to wear spectacles early in life and who stuttered when she spoke and buried her head in her books. Beulah was positively plain and devoid of any feminine characteristics. She developed a hunch, walked with her elbows stuck out, wore dresses that would have looked better on a camel and adopted a forbidding expression which is a characteristic of many a wretched woman who knows full well that no man would attempt to probe even with the proverbial barge pole. She was also a simpleton, and Elsie marched into the Holy Family Convent one morning, inquired after Beulah's progress and was told that while the child was growing fast and more awful with each passing day, was devoid of everyday Standard I intelligence.

'You mean she is a damn fool,' Elsie said.

The teacher was shocked.

'No, no. She understands what is said. But she cannot learn. No powers of retention. She knows her alphabet up to P only. And she can't join in any class activities. Won't sing or recite, can't count to more than fifteen . . . and she beats the other children.'

Elsie had heard enough. She took Beulah by the ear, hauled her out of the classroom and out of the school. Beulah squealed like a stuck pig, but there was no one to stop her being dragged home and slapped and pushed into the kitchen. 'No more school,' Elsie yapped, 'Sit in the house and work!'

Noella and Dorcas, on the other hand, were quite brilliant, and while Dorcas grew tall and gawky and looked quite stork-like with her long, unmuscled legs, Noella got by with long flashes of intelligence, clever fudging and her teachers always giving her top marks since they couldn't be sure if the girl knew nothing or too much of any particular subject Then Elsie, after resorting to a new and most savage way of reducing Eric to tears, became pregnant again. Eric would moan softly, but the fiery pain actually made him hard and goaded him to display more initiative than he had ever shown before. Elsie discovered this in those cruel moments when she beat him. Lately, she had resorted to the cane. Her daughters would watch with large, fearful eyes.

Elsie would leap up at the sound of the gate while Eric stepped in as though walking on eggshells. His face, like a trampled doughnut, would crease into an uncertain smile.

'You brought the beef like I told?'

Eric hung his head. 'When I went, all finished.'

'Finished? How to finish like that? All the beef markets in Borella and no beef? Here have no servants to go for beef. If went straight after work like I told, can easily buy. What, men, useless, no? If can't even buy the beef. So where were you all this time, then?'

Noella would edge out of the dining-room to the kitchen where Beulah was peeling onions. 'You can hear?' she would hiss, 'Sure to give a whacking today.'

Beulah would shudder. Dorcas, at the dining-table, would hunch over her school books and bite her lower lip.

'So where the beef money?' Elsie would grate.

'Here, dear.'

'This is two-fifty. I gave three rupees, no, for five pounds beef. Went and put an all-on, I suppose. If have horses running, enough for you. I must think of everything in the house. Small thing tell to do and that also say no beef and take fifty cents. Went to bucket shop first, that's why got late to go to the market.'

'But, my dear—'

'Don't you come to my dear me! Coming here to tell lies, in front of the children also. You wait, I'll give you!' and Elsie would take the long rattan cane from the top of the whatnot and Eric would give an alarmed squeak and run to the bedroom where Elsie would seize him and push his face into the bed and stripe him across the buttocks. Then, panting excitedly, she would slam shut the door and drag down his trousers and thrusting her hand between his thighs from behind, seize his testicles and tug at them while Eric screamed thinly. His saliva would wet the bed and Elsie would growl and tug and his back would burn where the cane had bitten him and the wrenching agony of that fierce grip would make his penis grow hard and throb in great thrusting jerks.

And that was how the seed that was Ian Stanford Eric was planted and the boy was born to be another Eric—a plodder without a will of his own, beaten into submission by his mother.

Elsie bore two more girls—Thelma Marilyn and Caroline Daisy, and for Ian, the only boy, it was a threatening world where only Dorcas gave him a pitying look, Thelma scorned him, Caroline looked at him witheringly and Noella did not hide her contempt and looked at him as though he was far beneath her. Beulah, too, had scarce the time for him, so he would creep, mouse-like into Dunnyboy's little room where the old man would pull him in by the hand and stroke his head and tell him that everything was all right. So Ian grew up a sad, befuddled boy. He liked to draw and was happiest with sketchbook and pencil and his line drawings were very, very good. But his young life held too many nightmares. Dunnyboy abused his body with impunity but there was no real pain in that . . . not the way his mother abused him; not the mind-pain his sisters gave him. And so he grew . . . and drew . . . and allowed Dunnyboy to do whatever he wished, and developed a stammer and a nervous tic under his left eye and the muscle of his left shoulder and withdrew into himself and masturbated incessantly. Even St. Peter's College held no charms for Ian where he was bullied and caned by priests and considered a strange, ill-assorted boy with a sullenness that sat very deep.

Cast in a happier mould Carloboy who was taken by Beryl to old Mrs Poulier's small private school in Wellawatte. Two Pouliers, actually—the old lady who was fat and pink and wore long dresses with lots of lace and kept her grey hair in a net; and her spinster daughter who wore black stockings and court shoes, carried a parasol and looked quite severe in dresses of beige and charcoal. Poulier's school was a Wellawatte landmark. Excellent grounding for the tiny tots who would stand around the old lady and recite nursery rhymes and 'I'm a little teapot' Carloboy was sent to the Lower Kindergarten with a 'Radiant Way' reader and was told to read, 'Sing, mother, sing, mother can sing,' which even at five years of age, was too, 'childish' for him. He had learnt many words and knew to read a lot more than the 'Radiant Way' could offer. For one thing, the tiny 34th Lane house in Wellawatte was full of Beryl's *Girl's Own* paperbacks; and those *Girl's Crystal* illustrated strips which cost fifteen cents each and which Sonnaboy bought for her. The comic book form captivated Carloboy who was soon caught up with the Hollywood and American heroes of the time—Gene Autry and Roy Rogers, Tom Mix and Gabby Hayes. Those were the 'cowboys' of the time, along with such gaudy characters as Torch and Toro, the Submariner and Captain Marvel and later, the Lone Ranger. So, while Leah's Marlene found her mother's scrapbooks a heady fuel to inflame her love of language, Carloboy discovered the wonder of words with each beat-up copy of Marvel Comics, the exploits of Dick Tracy, the adventures of Rupert the Bear and the many battered books he begged for each time the bookman came to the door—*Alice In Wonderland,* Edgar Rice Burrough's *Tarzan* and the exploits of the warlord of Mars, the pirates of Stevenson's *Treasure Island* and Conan Doyle's marvellous tales of mystery. All this made Carloboy quite the dreamer. He found his sister, Diana, an infinite pain in the neck.

She was as thin as a rail, sharp-featured, always ailing, and he disliked her. As a companion, Diana was most unsavoury. Beryl was blunt. She couldn't abide Carloboy who, she told the neighbour, was a perfect little monster as a baby, but she loathed Diana, who she said was like a smelly crow. Ivy Ratnayake lived next door, and Ivy was, through some complicated process, a relation. Wasn't Ivy's uncle Dr Elmo da Brea? And hadn't Beryl, at some time or another, seen this same Dr Elmo come to Nimal Road to be welcomed by her mother? If this Uncle Elmo was Ivy's uncle as well, there had to be some hook-up.

'Funny thing, no?' she told Sonnaboy, That Ivy is my cousin or something.'

'What do you mean or something?' Sonnaboy would growl, 'Not enough the relations we're having?'

'But she is a Todd, no? My mother is also Todd. And Uncle Elmo came there yesterday and you must see how she is going on because have a doctor in the family.'

'Who the devil is Uncle Elmo?'

'My uncle. Used to come to Nimal Road when we were living there. Anyway, I told to see about Diana.'

Seeing about Diana was quite a family preoccupation. 'Another Auntie Nellie,' Sonnaboy had said gloomily when it was known that the girl had an unbreakable bed-wetting habit. In fact, Diana's bed-wetting persisted well past her thirteenth year. She would rise each morning, reeking of urine and would howl the house down when driven into the bathroom to bathe. It didn't help any when Carloboy stood outside the door and hissed: 'Pisspot, you're a pisspot!'

At other times, too, he was quiet explicit. 'Pooh,' holding his nose. 'Pippie smell near you,' and Diana would bawl and run to Beryl who would swat her and drive her to the bathroom. Also, the family discovered, she had no stomach for travel. She was the only child, Beryl declared, who would vomit in a train. 'Damn wretch is deliberately doing it,' she would storm, 'If go in a bus, vomiting; sending to school in a rickshaw, vomiting; so all right, rickshaw must be jerking and in bus even other children also get sick. But when in the train how to vomit? And just listen to the way she's breathing, will you. Hoosh, hoosh, hoosh, hoosh, like something stuck in the drainage. Uncle Elmo said she is asthmatic or having esson ophelia or something. Never heard of such a thing. Will take now for blood tests and all.'

Sonnaboy was not particularly interested. He had worked a train to Polgahawela and back, and cycled all the way from Dematagoda. He was tired. Yet, he had refused the offer of a railway bungalow in Mount Mary. The rent allowance did not cover the rent he was paying true, but he reasoned that by staying in private quarters, he was his own man and well out of the railway's clutches.

'For one thing, no bloody call boy to come and disturb,' he said. It seemed that drivers and guards who lived in railway bungalows were 'on call' if the railway suddenly needed a driver or guard in an emergency. The call boy would come, bang at the gate at two a.m. and shout 'Cooolle Boooy! In the house, who is?'

Driver Samson's wife, who had just left a tumbled bed to wash would say: 'There, call boy is shouting. Get up and go and see.'

Samson, who is dozing off, deliciously tired after the previous hour's exertions, is not pleased. He goes to the hall window, hitching up his pajamas. 'What the devil, men, shouting like this. To sleep even won't allow.'

'Cole Booy, sir. Told to tell you have to work five-twenty down.'

'Fuck off!'

'Galle goods train, sir. Come to shed three o'clock.'

'Fuck off!'

The next-door bungalow lights come on. Driver Ben Godlieb is annoyed. 'Don't you buggers know the time?' he yells.

Samson spreads himself. He tells Godlieb to fuck off.

Godlieb insists that people are entitled to some sleep at night and it was all very well for Samson to say whatever came to his brainless head, and if it were not for the iron-rail fence that divided their properties, he would dearly love to dismember Samson and scatter his limbs over Baseline Road.

Samson listens interestedly and heaves a flower-pot at Godlieb.

The call boy, meanwhile, is yawning hugely. These small hour missions to Mount Mary are most unpredictable. Why, only last night he had been scared out of his wits by something white and indeterminate that had flapped at him in the moonlight from the top of a fence. Daring all, he had cycled closer and lo, it was a pair of knickers! He had puckered his forehead and tried to imagine under what circumstances these *'nona's jungies'*(*ladies* undies) could have found their way into the spiked rail of a fence. The wind could not have carried them off a clothes line for they had been carefully tied to the tip of the spike. Like a trophy of sorts. Pukka buggers these railway town people!

In the opposite bungalow, guard 'Tintack' Mack tells his wife: 'Mabel, those buggers are shouting again.'

'Who? That Samson?'

'Who else? There . . . what was that?'

'What, what?'

'Glass-breaking sound. See, men, if rogues are trying to get inside.'

Mabel covers her head. 'So you go and see, will you.'

Actually, that was Godlieb, who having received Samson's flower-pot, had returned the compliment by heaving a potted begonia through Samson's parlour window. More lights come on. More drivers and guards enter the fray. Samson's wife screams at him from the upstairs balcony: 'For God's sake dress and go. This the time to break all the flower-pots?'

So Samson clumps in, gets into regulation khaki overalls and goes to Galle, driving a line of goods wagons with a great deal of coupling and uncoupling and shunting boxes into sidings all along the way. Plenty of overtime on a job like this and that cheers him up marvellously.

The next morning his wife drapes herself over the balcony and sings out to Godlieb's wife: 'Hullo, Prinsy, how?'

Prinsy beams. 'Your devil went to work?'

'My God, yes. Come and take your begonia. Had to clean the mess in the hall.'

Prinsy nods. 'And your calladium all over the veranda, men. I'll tell to come and put a board in your window.'

'No, never mind. Can tell the buildings fellow to put a new glass. Your devil is still sleeping?'

'What to sleep. There he is in the back garden, shouting at somebody. Working in the afternoon. Now won't give peace the whole morning.'

By living in Wellawatte Sonnaboy did not have all the overtime opportunities that came the way of railway town drivers who had call boys to press them into extra work, but he was happy. He knew his 'turn' and all he had to do was report to the Dematagoda Running Shed, couple engine on train and take off. Beryl, naturally, was pregnant again and once more making a layette in pink. This was too quick, she thought. A third child at nineteen was most discouraging. She asked Dr Raeffel in Wellawatte about this baby business and that cheery soul had said she could go on filling the world with von Blosses until she was fifty if she had a mind to. It appalled her. At the going rate, she could have another fifteen at least. But greater, more dramatic things were to occupy her mind. Sonnaboy came home one day with a 'call up'; and on the May morning that Marie Esther Maud was born he cycled home in the full uniform of an Army lance corporal of the Railway Volunteer Reserve. It seemed that in Bavaria, another little corporal was shaking the world. A weasely little fellow with a Chaplin moustache and the frilly name of Schirkgruber or something. Only, he had taken hold of Germany and called himself Adolf Hitler and invented the goose-step . . . .

So Heather Evadne Maryse von Bloss could be called a 'war baby' and Sonnaboy, seeing this third girl was vastly disappionted. Even Cecilprins, who spent most of his time in the lounger in Kotahena, was upset at the news. Sonnaboy had started well. But to have three girls after Carloboy was a bit too much. Of course there was grandson Ian de Mello, but that Ian was hard to classify. The Bandarawela children had also been busy. Opel had two sons—Claude and Winston—and was once more in the family way. Terry had a boy too—Morris—but they were all in the hills and Cecilprins could not visit them. He fervently hoped that Leah would come up trumps second time around.

Cecilprins had been overjoyed when Totoboy announced the birth of his first son. He rode a richshaw all the way to Wellawatte to gloat over this new grandson . . . and was rudely shocked.

'My God, men, from where you went and got a black bugger like that?'

Totoboy frowned.'Is he black? Didn't notice.'

'Like *chatti* pot!' Cecilprins bawled, 'Even the mother not so black, no? How she getting such a black bugger?'

Totoboy squinted. 'Have, no, some black fellows in her family. Must be in the blood.'

'In the blood? Fine thing to say after putting negro von Bloss. Whole trouble is you're drunk and how to know who is coming and going here?'

Iris, listening, was enraged. 'What do you mean who is coming? You think anyone else is coming here. If baby is dark what to do? God is my witness, no? *Chee*! the way you are talking and old man also. Why you won't say what your son is up to? Now drinking arrack . . . everyday coming drunk and the time I have with him. See, will you, even Fortune. She is dark, no?'

It did seem that Iris would continue to produce a line of very dark-skinned von Blosses. Cecilprins, screwing up his eyes, had to admit that Fortune, too, was pretty dark-skinned. Funny, he hadn't noticed it before, but then, he never took much notice of the granddaughters. 'And now she's pregnant again,' he told Totoboy. ' 'Nother black bugger for sure. Never listened to your mama and me, no? Told not to get married to that woman.'

And Totoboy sent his father home and drank long and deep and told Mr Dole next door that he was very miserable.

Leah, however, came up roses. She brought forth Ivor Rudoph Wilhelm, a beautiful peaches and cream baby with a dusting of fair hair that hinted at gold. Everybody in the family was pleased while Cecilprins danced a little jig and was sent to bed early because he was quite breathless. Sonnaboy, who was quite taken aback at all the fuss around Leah and her son, decided to take Carloboy 'in hand'. 'You study,' he would yell at the boy, 'and be a big man and let everybody know who you are!'

Carloboy didn't take much notice. He had found E. Nesbit's *The House of Arden* a keen contender to *Alice in Wonderland* and loved the way the author had twisted familiar verse to his convenience.

He rose in class one day to declaim:

> *The Mouldiwarp of Arden*
> *By the nine gods he swore*
> *That Elfrida of Arden*
> *Should be shut up no more.*
> *By the nine gods he swore it*
> *And named a convenient time, no doubt,*
> *And bade its messengers ride forth,*
> *East and west, south and north,*
> *To let Elfrida out.*

Father Theodore, who took English and played a great deal of tennis, was not amused. That was at St. Peter's College, Bambalapitiya, where Carloboy was schooled after his term with the Pouliers. The priest considered the whole poem a sacrilege. To keep the bridge, as Horatius did, was a historic epic, and not to be punned on or distorted even by as popular an author as Nesbit.

This may be as good a time as any to mull over the 'British education' that made every student in the island more familiar with the glory of being British and the British culture, arts and letters than of what Ceylon held for him or her. Scant heed was paid to the island's history, its heroes, customs and traditions. In the Royal College were such stalwarts as Reid, Hartely, Harward, Marsh and Boake. In the many Catholic institutions, Irish nuns, French and Italian priests, Franciscans, Benedictines, Dominicans pounded out the Western and European values. Anglican and Methodist ministers also pitched in. Warden Stone held in his hands, the destiny of thousands who attended St. Thomas' College. In St. Joseph's College it was the sainted Father Le Goc. The Reverend W.S. Senior became the great literary figure of Trinity College and the hill country.

It was a peculiar situation. The most ludicrous sights were to amaze one . . . a Sinhalese affecting the grab of the white master to the extent of white topee, dark coat, shirt and tie, and a large belt to hold up . . . his sarong! He would also carry an umbrella and look, for all the world, like one of those 'Punch' caricatures!

Colombo's roads were named by the British for and after the British. So were the tea estates, the parks, the gardens, the public squares. The newspapers carried British cartoons by 'Phiz' and little descriptive articles about the Rev. J.C. Brown who was a missionary at the Cape of Good Hope, and the talent of Inigo Jones. Thus were the people of Ceylon steeped in all things British and, most regretfully, began to slowly but surely shed the colourful Burgher patios which this chronicle has faithfully followed. There was no getting away from the British influence. Sonnaboy would go to the Manning place market to buy beef; or go to Davidson Road to see his friend De Niese; or stop at MacHeyzer Road to watch a game of rugby football or go to Maitland Crescent to take in a few overs of a cricket match. Carloboy, at eight, knew that Sir Alfred Jones had been the President of the Liverpool Chamber of Commerce and never bothered to ask why this thrilling bit of information had been thrust upon him. He also knew that the most gallant British sea dog of the days of timbered ships was Admiral L.T. Jones . . . but he did not know how many rivers flowed to the sea in Ceylon and the distance from Colombo to Jaffna.

Oh, there were a great many books on Ceylon, written by Englishmen and some Burghers and Sinhalese too. Some locals even wrote things like the History of Ceylon and others attempted to give students the story of their own country in the form of 'popular tales' but none of these were encouraged classroom reading. Rather, students were called upon to give their opinions on whether or not Kaiser Wilhelm II, German Emperor and King of Prussia was a warmonger and general intriguer. School texts were *Tom Brown's Schooldays, The Mill on the Floss,* Shakespeare, of course, and a great deal of poetry from Chaucer to John Masefield. It was a period of the swift nurturing of the 'brown sahib', and yet, the chronicler maintains, some of old Ceylon's truly great and scholarly men and women were produced in this period, even if they thought and acted British and always maintained that the sun would never set on the long and heady days of empire. A paper, written by Dr Bernard Hollander and delivered before the Ethological Society sparked great interest and brought in its wake many learned letters in the *Ceylon Observer.* Hollander supported the view that criminals could be cured by surgery, and advanced the thought that moral defects could be righted by trepanation. Indeed, letters to the Editor (something compulsively British) were of such great charm and abiding interest that men like pensioner Johnny Foenander made of the exercise a real hobby and an enterprise. His letters would appear in print daily on every conceivable topic. His was the stilted, old-world English so admired in those times and one letter, on the evils of over-education, merits reproduction:

It is all very well to cultivate learning (which is not knowledge, by any means) but healthy bodies ought to be maintained at a health-standard as a primary duty, and evening lessons of the preparatory kind, by artificial light too (and in cities, God help us!), when the young wood of the young bow ought to be relaxed, are all wrong—and utterly wrong, believe me. I am not afraid of a race of fools; I am afraid of a race of rickety human encyclopaediettes, who are a nuisance to everyone and a health-drawback. I have children brought to me who go to bed supersaturated with what are called evening lessons, and who chatter in their sleep, and wake from bad scholastic dreams to begin again the weary Sisyphaean task of education. A nice set of neurotics we are breeding and rearing, to be sure!

Leah would always find space in her scrapbooks for such letters to the editor. This Foenander fellow must be a genius. Writing such marvellous letters. And the words . . . encyclopaediettes! Sisyphaean! Supersaturated! Marlene, inordinately interested in her mother's ledger-scrapbooks, wished to have her own albums. Leah said: 'Having here twelve big books, no? So anything you want to paste or copy just put in these books. All this for you to read and learn, no?'

None of the children of that age could escape the 'British connection'. Ian could be found, frowning over John Hare's *Reminiscences and Recollections* and Dorcas poring over the

Rt. Hon. Winston Spencer Churchill's *My African Journey.* Carloboy, quite indisciplined in literary taste would flit from anything to everything—cheap Sexton Blake library paperbacks to *Ivanhoe, Kidnapped,* the knights of the Round Table and the exploits of Hercules.

Everything took on an unmistakably British air. One could move around and there would be roads named Vaverset Place, Pennycuick Lane, Hampden Lane, Manning Place, Chatham Street, Vauxhall Street, MacCallum Road, Torrington Square, Maitland Crescent, Dickman's Road, Ward place, etc. etc. etc. In the hill country—the tea country—the estates and tea gardens were fondly named by their British and Scottish owners: Glenloch, Abercrombie, MacLaughlin, Brookside, Hatton (after Hatton Gardens), Great Western, Glenfinnan, Doone. Also, in perpetuating the old, staid and proper way of British life, British households maintained (and quite cheaply, too) Sinhalese and Tamil domestics who were schooled in the duties of house-stewards, butlers, nannies, grooms, valets, cooks, head and under gardeners, serving boys, maids and many poor, but blossoming village girls who were taken in to be kitchen, scullery and laundry maids and become fair game for the beefy sons of the house with their white duck trousers and tennis racquets and cricket bats and very eager to see how these native wenches fared under their cloths.

Before we move on, the chronicler recalls one Colombo road which stubbornly clung to its native name—Timbirigasyaya (the plain of the Timbiri trees), which must have sounded quite intriguing and exotic to the British, who decided to keep it. It was related how the Government Agent of the Western Province, a Britisher named Cummings, tried to frame his mouth on the word and gave up the struggle. 'Devil take it!' he said, 'It looks like timber, gas and somebody's bloody ayah!' and so the British called it Timber-gas road, leaving out the ayah which was the local equivalent of the Indian amah or nanny.

It is hoped that the reader has got, however hazily, a picture of the times. This was truly a period of transition. The easy days of plenty were petering away and with war clouds spreading over

Europe and the Far East, things began to look rather bleak. Christmas 1940 saw Sonnaboy and Beryl move to 18th Lane, Bambalapitiya. Heather was an infant, and the move was to facilitate Carloboy's access to St. Peter's College. Actually, that institution had been split, with a section housed behind St. Mary's Church, Dehiwela, and another in the large Catholic Seminary grounds in Bambalapitiya. St. Peter's too, was a war victim, for the actual college beside the Dutch canal at Wellawatte had been commandeered by the army and where troops marched around all day and ginger-moustachioed sergeants blew whistles and screamed till they were very red in the face.

Oh, the von Blosses, like all else, were not badly off, but things were getting 'pricey', as Beryl reminded. A loaf of bread was now twenty-five cents and duck eggs (imported from India) twenty-five cents each. Distinctions arose even in the buying of beef. The Muslim butchers offered 'beef without bones' for seventy-five cents a pound. If, however, you were prepared to take a chance, you could buy beef 'with bones' for sixty cents where you get a sort of 'lucky dip'—offcuts with a lot of skin and gristle, an assortment of knuckles and other scraps. Offal, however, remained twenty-five cents a pound and Carloboy was pressed into service each time Beryl brought home mile-lengths of tripe which had to be cleaned and washed many times over. Nothing was standing still. Prices were slowly, inexorably rising, and suddenly came another calamity—shortages! What? No beef? And what the hell, men, have to queue at Elephant House now for New Zealand lamb and Australian mutton. What about the local beef? Sonnaboy would ask and he would be told by municipality inspectors that the beef was going to the Armed Forces camps and trucks were rushing cattle to Trincomalee where they were slaughtered and distributed to the cold rooms of ships of the Royal Navy East Indies fleet. This is no time to grumble. This is the time for some sacrifice. We are at war! And there is enough dehydrated beef available!

War—even though the action seemed to be in northern and central Europe and soldiers were exhorted 'to hang out their washing on the Siegfried Line'— had the salutary effect of taking everybody's minds away from the lean times they were experiencing. The bulletins, the newspapers, the B.B.C. and the rumour mills kept everybody's mind on Montgomery and Rommel, the German Messerschmitt Me109 and the Vicker's Supermarine Spitfire. War comics became the new craze and stage shows had patriotic skits and the walls of Government buildings carried bold black slogans: 'Careless talk costs lives' and 'Help the war effort. Save paper, bottles and tins'. War songs became the in-thing. Totoboy, characteristically, became a veritable fount of such patter. He would stagger into the White Horse Inn, Chatham Street, or Brown's Bar in Canal Row, waving a tiny Union Jack and roaring:

Kiss me goodnight, sergeant major,
Tuck me in my little wooden bed,
We all love you, sergeant major,
When we hear you call, we show a leg.
Don't forget to wake me in the morning
And bring me a nice hot cup of tea,
So kiss me goodnight, sergeant major,
Sergeant major be a mother to me!

Everybody would flock to the cinemas to see the RKO and Pathe news bulletins and stand at attention for the National Anthem which was 'God Save the King' and had nothing to do with Ceylon!

The family will always remember Christmas 1940. Everybody came to visit at 18th Lane because Cecilprins came to spend Christmas there and, 'Must go and wish Papa, no?' It was goodly company indeed. George and Leah with Marlene and Ivor; Totoboy and Iris with Fortune and Brennan and baby Winston ('Named after Winston Churchill,' Totoboy said proudly while Cecilprins raised himself in the lounger, took a quick look and said that that was a real flight of fancy. 'Churchill is white and fat,' he said, 'and what is this? Never mind black, but like a well-sucked mango seed, no?'); Anna and Mr Colontota, Elsie and Eric with Noella, Dorcas, Beulah (who was shoved into the kitchen to help Beryl) Ian and toddler Thelma; and there was Sonnaboy's brood: Carloboy, Diana, Marie and baby Heather who, everyone said, was too sweet to be true. Cecilprins had hoped that Viva and Terry would come and he actually insisted that, 'Can wait a little, no? without eating so early. Can't say if Viva and Terry will also come. I wrote and told, also.'

Sonnaboy was outraged. 'What? You wrote to come? Fine thing, no, and without even telling us.'

Cecilprins ignored the black look. 'Today Christmas, no?'

To be sure it was. Most of the family had gathered at St. Mary's Bambalapitiya for midnight mass (Leah and George went to St. Lawrence's Church, Wellawatte, and so did Anna) and they were all decked out fit to kill. There had been the many usual rounds of Christmas shopping and Sonnaboy would buy two bottles of Black and White and tell Beryl: 'Keep in kitchen safe. Must put a stock in for Christmas.'

By evening he would decide that it would be nice to 'put a small shot' and in order to do so, needed company. So he would put a head over the back garden fence and bawl: 'Oy, Hatch, come for a small drink.'

Norman Hatch would trundle out, grinning. 'I was also just thinking must get a bottle today.'

'So come will you. Put a shirt and slippers.'

'Fine way of buying for Christmas,' Beryl would sniff, 'Now finish the bottle and go and buy again.' Beryl was right, of course. Drinks for Christmas were always bought early, finished long before the day and stocks were constantly replenished.

Totoboy popped in just before the family were ready to leave for midnight mass. He demanded a stiff one.

'But, Uncle, if you drink how are you going to receive?' Carloboy asked.

'Receive? Receive? Who giving me, men, to receive?' He took a big glass of whisky, 'Ah, pukka. You know that Father Robert's sermons, no? How to sit and listen without a drink?'

'But what about communion?' Carloboy persisted, 'You won't receive communion?'

Totoboy shuddered. 'My God, men, he told Sonnaboy, 'the things you're teaching these buggers. Now I need another one.'

Three drinks later, Totoboy joins the family for the 11 p.m. walk to St. Mary's after a hazy explanation that Iris and the children are at her uncle's in Havelock Road and will come to the church. There, he falls asleep and snores loud and long while everyone tries to drown him with spirited renderings of 'Adeste Fideles' and 'Joy to the World'. But he wakes up when it is all over to stumble out and join in the waves of wishes and kisses and embraces outside the church and singing out 'Happy Christmas' to everyone who swims into view.

This is what the children enjoy most. Knots of small boys are lighting crackers and Roman candles and sparklers and the girls are admiring each others Christmas dresses and everyone is grinning and yawning and saying 'same to you, same to you' and boyfriends are stealing swift kisses in the long shadows of the trees in Lauries Lane.

Elsie had herded her family in and out of church like a female warden from Belsen camp. Noella, who sat next to the Speldewinde boy, was hauled out of her seat and pushed between Ian and Dorcas while the boy, treated to Elsie's 'look', paled, rose, trod on Mrs Misso's new shoes, and scuttled off. Finally, with Beryl carrying a sleeping Heather and Sonnaboy carrying Diana, the family returned to 18th Lane and on the way there was a road-up sign where some sort of water mains repair was in progress. Totoboy was entranced by the red Municipal lanterns that hung around the makeshift barrier around the excavation. He was, as he explained later, in a Christmassy mood. He had insisted, in a nasal B flat, that the shepherds washed their socks by night and decided that these lanterns were Heaven's gift to midnight revellers. He took one and urged other pedestrians to help themselves. So six jolly men with six road lanterns wobbled bravely on, shouting 'We Wish you a Merry Christmas'. Iris and the children followed for they would all see Christmas morning in at Sonnaboy's it being 'out of the question, men, to go to Dehiwela at this time, no?' So it was wine and rich cake and Peak Freans crackers and cheese and everybody bedded wherever it suited them and slept like babes until the police pounded on the door at eight o'clock.

The law was not pleased. It seemed that other revellers in infinitely worse condition than Totoboy, had ignored the road-up sign which they had regarded as the Colombo Municipality's impediment to progress, and fallen into the excavation. That, in itself was regarded as one of the hazards of a silent night, holy night, but when it was discovered that the bottom of the pit contained a batter-like mixture of mud and water, their howls had been pitiful to hear. Inspector Leembruggen of the Bambalapitiya police, who superintended the rescue, wanted to know where the red lanterns were. 'Find those lanterns,' he snarled, 'and tell this lot to go home and bathe. God! the sight of you. And mud inside your socks also. All drunk, I suppose.'

'So Christmas, no?' one mud-streaked moron said.

'So Joseph also putting a drink in the manger and chasing the cattle? Go home or I'll lock all you buggers up.'

Some inquiry was necessary and a stroll down 18th Lane, and there, on the garden wall, where Totoboy & Co. had deposited them, were the lanterns.

Sonnaboy opened the door and looked at the constables interestedly. 'Happy Christmas,' he said.

'Where from on your wall came these lanterns?'

'Lanterns?'

'These lanterns. On your wall had.'

'Come, come and sit. Somebody must have kept and gone. Street boys work, must be. Last time took my flower-pots and put in the next door garden.'

The policemen nodded at each other. Boys, they agreed, will be boys.

Sonnaboy warmed to his theme. 'Why, you remember when there was a board advertising that some land was to be sold?'

'Where, here in Bambalapitiya?'

'No, in Dehiwela. Had a board. Land in Campbell place going to cut in parts and sell. Telling people to come and book their piece of land early.'

One policeman nodded wisely. 'Ah yes, have like that boards in lot of places.'

'So somebody take the board in the night and put outside the cemetery.'

The policemen stared, then began to cackle. 'Hee, hee, that is fine thing. *Maru* (expressive Sinhala word that could hazily mean 'tophole' or 'super') devils, these fellows. So anyway you did not see anything last night?'

'No, men. All went to church and came two-three o'clock and still sleeping. What about a cake piece. Sit, sit, I'll bring and come.'

Inside, Carloboy informed that Uncle Totoboy had seen the police and dived for cover.

'Where?'

'In the room. Under the bed.'

Sonnaboy grinned. 'Go and tell not to come out. Say police came to take him to the station for taking lanterns and are waiting to catch him.'

After double helpings of Christmas cake and biscuits the policemen left and Totoboy, doubled up under the bed and groaning that he had cramps on his cramps, was encouraged to stay put because quite extraordinarily, the police knew that he was the culprit and were anxious to ask him why. So Totoboy crouched and groaned for a full hour and the children began to bounce on the mattress to his added discomfiture and had him wailing: 'Stop that, my God you bloody buggers, jumping on my bloody spine, no? You wait, I'll Christmas you.' When he was told to come out, he did so with a barrage of oohs and aahs and needed two large drinks to put him right.

The chronicler has taken his readers through a Burgher wedding and a Burgher funeral. So why not a Burgher Christmas? Here, too, the seat of operations is the kitchen, and the most important item of all—the Christmas cake—is made in early November so that all the brandy and arrack that is liberally mixed in has time to take hold and give it the body it must possess. The making of the Christmas cake is an occassion where everybody needs to stick an oar in. Leah would run into Elsie. 'So how? When are you making your cake?'

'Thought of next Sunday, child. You can come, no?'

'*Anney*, I also thought to make mine next Sunday.'

'But Anna also coming. How about if you make this Sunday? I'll tell Anna and Beryl also to come. Can ask Iris also but that wretch has got piles of sewing to do for Christmas. Must be making enough money, men. Must see the amount of people coming for Christmas sewing.'

'Yes, men. I also told to do my dress. Charging seven rupees. One thing, she is pukka dressmaker but won't put a stitch without the money. You heard what happened to Sophie?'

'Sophie? Sophie who?'

'Sophie Juriansz, men, in Hampden Lane. Gave Iris cloth to make a dress. Iris said eight rupees. Full flared skirt and all with lining and big bow in the back and brought crinoline lady cutwork pieces and told to put round the skirt. Gave Iris two rupees and said will pay balance when fit on.'

'So, so?'

'So Iris make the dress and Sophie go for fit on and saying this is not right and this is crooked and the yoke is cut wrong and all sorts of things and then telling never mind, now that it is finished I'll take and go but how to wear when it is not done properly and then tried to take dress without paying the six rupees.'

Elsie laughed. 'That Sophie to pay? I know, no. Always hard up. So Iris gave the dress?'

'Just the Iris to give like that. Said, if don't pay, no dress. Then Sophie began screaming and saying Iris is hopeless tailor and in vain her cloth and all.' Leah paused to wipe her eyes and Elsie said: 'Wonder Iris kept quiet.'

Leah hooted. 'What to keep quiet? You know Iris, no? Took the dress to the kitchen and put it in the fireplace.'

'No!'

'Yes, men. Into the fireplace!'

'My Jesus! So what did Sophie do?'

'What to do? Started crying and ran on the road and shouting that Iris robbed her and Iris go to the gate and shouting what for you are screaming, you bloody bitch, who is your bloody mother? You know who your bloody mother is? And then she also get on the road and should have seen the way Sophie ran and should have heard the way Iris shouting. My God, men, the dirty words. I'm thinking how Totoboy has to put up with all this.'

So with all the delicious tittle and tattle, Sunday becomes cake-making day at Leah's and Marlene and Ivor are in their element as all manner of delicious things are being chopped up: seedless raisins, sultanas, mixed glace fruit which usually consists of pineapple, apricot and quince; preserved ginger and chow chow; mixed peel and glace cherries; blanched almonds and cashew nuts and lemon rind. Elsie has this talent for the chopping and the cutting and sets to work with an awesome concentration. She keeps up a steady stream of gossip as she chops up the raisins and sultanas, cuts the glace fruit into tiny squares and having drained the syrup from the ginger and chow chow, subjects them, too, to a click-clack treatment on the chopping board, and then to the nuts and the halving of the cherries. Beulah is told to beat eggs, which she does with a most mournful look.

When all this is done, the fruits and nuts are put into a huge bowl and Leah (the expert in the lacing of the mixture) is summoned with her pint of arrack and flask of brandy to decide on just how much of each should be poured in. It's an art, of course, and in goes the arrack . . . just so . . . and the brandy is dashed in with care. Holy water could not be sprinkled with such loving precision and care. 'Now, cover and keep,' Leah says and the bowl is placed between two large clay pots of cold water, 'The arrack and brandy will soak in much faster,' Leah explains, although nobody knows why this is so.

Anna is the grater and grinder. She sets to work on lemon rind and cardamoms, cinnamon, nutmeg and cloves and doles out careful measures of vanilla, almond and rose essences, honey, semolina, butter and sugar. Elsie, meanwhile sits back with a large mug of tea and says: 'Every year this dance, no? And see the amount of work. Next year feel like buying a Elephant House cake and serving.'

Anna says: 'Yes, child, but won't have everything like what we make, no? And you know, no, how our devils go and talk. Stretch the hand and take, and then go and say cake is hopeless and must have put *poonac* (cattle cake mixture).'

'Hah! As if I don't. Damn cheek. Last year that Mrs Toussaint came and my God, the way she ate. No shame, men, asking and eating. My, your cake is nice, I think I'll have another piece—as sweet as you please. What, child, if gobbling like that how to keep to serve everybody who comes?'

Leah nods. 'And not enough the people we have. That Beryl's children are another lot. Carloboy especially. Taking cake and giving the dog, men. Felt like giving him a thundering slap last year. See, will you, the price of things now.'

Anna says dolefully: 'Other people's cake everybody wants to eat. But when go to visit they say my, why you waited so long to come? Now even the cake is finished.'

They get together over the cake mixture, creaming butter and sugar and adding egg yolk and Beulah is pinched and told to 'beat, men, beat'. Anna adds the rind and spices, the flavourings and essences and honey and Beulah goes on stirring and stirring until she begins to sniffle and Elsie drags her away. 'Bloody useless lump. Now cry into the cake if you can,' and takes the wooden ladle and stirs with a great huffing and puffing and swirling blobs of the mixture to the floor where the cat waits, doubtless for this manna from Heaven. When the semolina is added, Leah takes over and Beulah is told to whip up some white of egg 'or you'll get this whole pan on your head, miss!'

The trick is in the stirring, for this perpetual motion needs to go on until Leah decrees that the fruit, steeped in liquor, is now ready to be mixed in. This is now Leah's operation, after she has washed her hands thoroughly and scrubbed them dry on a clean towel. Carloboy had been appalled to see Aunty Leah at work last year (when the in-laws had gathered to make Beryl's cake) and the sight must have prompted him to give his cake to the dog. There was this vision of Aunty Leah, both hands in the cake mixture up to her elbows, squeezing and squishing great gobs of chopped fruit into the gooey mess.

'Nothing like putting the hands for this,' Leah would say. Fingers could scrunch the fruit into the cake mixture best and it was much easier than using a spoon. In fact, the chronicler learns that to this day professional pastry cooks DO use their hands—both hands—but to Carloboy it didn't seem right at all. He told Diana: '*Chee*, see what she is doing. When she goes to the lavatory, washing the back with the left hand; and now putting it into our cake.' Diana looked positively ill at this information and urinated . . . naturally.

As would be imagined, it had to be a very big cake and the mixing was done in a great-grandfather of a pan. After Leah had done her damndest, scraping each finger against the side of the pan so that nothing, but nothing, went waste, stiff-beaten egg white is folded into the mixture and the large cake trays are brought out and lined with grease-proof paper and the mixture poured in.

The men are then assembled, for no home oven could accommodate such cakes which have spread to two and even three oversized trays, each like a goodish-sized drawer. This used to make a pretty picture, and usually at dusk, when, from many Burgher homes, men and boys would fare forth, laden cake trays borne carefully on their heads, to the nearest bakery where the trays are accepted, labelled and a collection time given. There, the cakes are baked and then carried back to be checked carefully and the women are satisfied that the cakes are rich and moist and not over-browned. Inspection over, each cake is then doused with more brandy and readied for the finishing touch, the almond paste icing. Children are now pressed into service—to cut squares of foil and coloured cellophane, serrating the edges to make pleasing cake wrappers . . . and this, too, is a traditional necessity, for each piece of cake must be individually wrapped.

While the men folk take away and later, bring back the trays of cake, Leah and Anna have ground almonds, sifted icing sugar and Beulah has been forced to beat more eggs. It's quite a mix: ground almonds, icing sugar, eggs, brandy, sherry and almond essence. Kneaded until stiff, it is then rolled out and ready. The cake is then brushed over with white of egg and the paste pressed on with the lightest pressure of a rolling pin. There! That's done, and now to get it all cut to pieces and wrapped. Anna takes over because she seems to know exactly how to cut that cake to give pieces that are not too big or too small. Elsie watches like a hawk. 'Keep an eye on these small devils,' she says, 'When not looking will stuff the mouth.'

The 'small devils' have been waiting for this moment. They have already had a whale of a time licking clean the mixing bowls and generally getting in everyone's way; and try as Elsie might, she just cannot have her eyes everywhere. Sonnaboy pops in. 'How the cake? Sha! Looks good, no?'

'You leave alone, will you. How to wrap cake when coming and taking pieces like this?'

'So what harm if put a taste? Carried and came all the way also.' Takes a piece.'Mmmm not bad. Should have put more brandy.'

And that, you would think, is that. But hold. Christmas in a Burgher home is lot more than Christmas cake. Mustard must be ground and potted and salt beef prepared. What's Christmas lunch without salt beef and mustard? And there must be the *breudher* for breakfast which is the rich Dutch yeast cake.

Making a real Dutch *breudher* is another art Maudiegirl excelled in and passed on to her daughters (who were also shown how to make excellent love cake and that intrinsically Portuguese sweet—the many layered cake which was a Burgher speciality: the *bola folhado* (pronounced Fi-a-dho). It is like a very rich Danish pastry and also, when Maudiegirl had a mind to, she would produce such marvellous things as the true Dutch Lampries (from the Dutch word 'Lomprijst—rice cooked in stock and baked in a wrapping of banana leaf); fish koftas, fried squid in what was known as a *'bedun'* (a thick gravy sauce) and that sneaky wonder, the *tara padre* curry which was curried duck but cooked with ghee, sugar, coconut milk and—hold your breath—half a cup of whisky!

'So why, Mama, you call it *tara padre?'* Leah would ask.

Maudiegirl (God rest her soul) would shush her daughter and say: 'So duck curry, no? Sinhalese people say *tara* for duck, no?'

'Then padre?'

'Padre is priest, child. What, I don't know, you learning in that convent. Today sending meal to Father Romiel and for him always I make *tara padre*. Good for him. Poor man. Cannot drink because priest and all. But who going to see if put the whisky in the curry?'

Christmas lunch called for the Dutch *frikkadels*—the forcemeat balls which were deep-fried and delicious; and a prawn blachan and the pungent *kalu pol sambol* where coconut meat is roasted dark brown in the ashes of the fireplace and then ground with onions, lime, salt and Maldive fish.

After the bread dough has been brought from the bakery, the *breudher* mixture is prepared. Ten egg yolks, mind, and the men are commandeered because the *breudher* needs a strong beating arm.

A special marble slab was placed on the kitchen table. Sonnaboy was the obvious choice, for the dough had to be hurled onto the slab for well over an hour while an egg yolk is added, one at a time and Sonnaboy says: 'Ten eggs putting? My God, men, how long will have to go on pounding this damn thing.' It does seem an eternity but suddenly Elsie says 'Ah, now enough,' and stirs in the vanilla and sultanas and puts the mixture near the hearth to rise. So the *breudher* is also baked and there is a right royal spread with the family sitting down to a Christmas breakfast of *breudher* and cheese, bread and butter, bananas, Scotch eggs, jam roly-poly and an astonishing assortment of savoury pastes and patés to apply on bread as required.

'Keep room for lunch,' Sonnaboy would tell the children while Cecilprins would try to look severe and say: 'Give all the buggers an opening dose for the New Year. Whole season won't stop eating.' Which was quite true because the round of Christmas visits had to be done and this meant a steady, unrelenting intake of cake and fruit and fizzes and biscuits and all manner of savouries. Each place, too, had its characteristic offerings. Anna always made love cake for Christmas. Beryl's sister, Juppie, was known for her asparagus and bread rolls. Florrie da Brea made some potent ginger beer and Leah's bacon and egg rolls were out of this world. Above all there was Florrie da Brea's 'miraculous' bottle which was the wonder of every Christmas. All Florrie bought for Christmas was one bottle of Johnnie Walker and every male who visited was treated to a single draught out of this bottle. Even Totoboy, who looked upon it as a sort of ritual peg. Over forty men would call and beam and sing out 'Happy Christmas' and dust cake crumbs on the floor and take a glass of whisky . . . and Johnnie Walker marched on. Florrie always had a drop more in her bottle for every new visitor and this was considered on par with the celebrated loaves and fishes. One drink was all anybody received and down the years, as the family grew, forty became fifty and then even sixty. But every male did receive his drink and the bottle lasted and was the most important Xmas topic. 'Going to Florrie's?'

'Yes, men. Have to wish the old lady, no?'

'Don't worry. Will get a drink.'

'That's what, men. How she can give everyone I don't know.'

'True, men. Real bottle that is. Saw on the sideboard yesterday. About quarter have. Pukka way to serve. Bloody bottomless bottle.'

Of course, Santa Claus had to come too, and in many Burgher homes it was Mrs Claus who performed the trick since it had to be between the hour of the return from midnight mass and around six a.m. As Beryl said, even if the children are dog-tired and go to bed at two, they are still up at dawn and if they don't find that Santa Claus has been and gone there will be a hullaballoo of earth-shaking proportions. And as Beryl also said, the men come back and open a bottle and go to sleep at the table, so who's going to put out the presents anyway.

After breakfast it's open house. People come, eat, drink and go. They bring roll packs of Chinese crackers and boxes of fireworks and little gifts. The postman, too, is on his special Christmas delivery and is greeted uproariously and plied with arrack and *breudher* and goes wobbling on his way. By 10 a.m. the poor man is seated on the side of the road, head in hands, bicycle tossed carelessly aside and too drunk to do any more.

Sonnaboy had the Christmas tree brought in from Nawalapitiya. It was no problem to bring it to Colombo in the Guards Van of the train and then tied alongside his bicycle to be carried home. A real cypress and a treat to festoon with jets and streamers and balloons and the big gold tinsel star. Carloboy stood beneath its branches and took a deep breath. 'Aaaah, real Christmas smell,' and everybody smiled and said, 'Yes, of course.'

Totoboy was in great form and said he would supervise the 'cracker business' after shrieks from the kitchen where Carloboy had tossed crackers into the fireplace. They ignited to spout fountains of hot ash and sparks on Iris who was, in turn, determined to put paid to this peace and goodwill business with a firewood stick. She had to be given a large arrack to calm her down and Totoboy took one look at the malevolent ash-spattered face that was his wife's, shut his eyes tight and declared hollowly that the last day had come. The dog (Sonnaboy had a cross-Airedale named Bess) didn't like crackers either. Bess gave a low howl and charged into Hatch's garden where that man's plump Australorp hens were ranging. This caused a stir that could have been heard all the way to St. Mary's. And all the while corks were popped and Beryl plumped for apple cider and Leah took some wine while even Colontota said he would try some apple cider 'because this is like fruit drink and no harm'. Bottles emptied with unbelievable swiftness and Cecilprins strolled in the garden and insisted that the lounger be put in the shade of the large sapodilla tree so that he could relax there. He had had three whiskies and said he was happy; so happy that he could scarcely think of lunch which was a most disjointed affair with the children eating first, then some of the womenfolk, because their men were still 'drinking like fish' and finally the rest sat down to ghee-rice and turkey, salt beef, gammon, roast beef, boiled tongue, stuffed tomatoes, curried pork and chillied potatoes and salads of peas, cucumber and carrots and as a whim (and because Beryl enjoyed the Jiggs cartoons in the *Observer*) corned beef and cabbage.

Sonnaboy went to Cecilprins. 'Papa, come and eat.'

Cecilprins smiled wearily, 'Tired, men, you just bring a plate of something here, will you. Nice under this tree. Better if had a jam furit tree, no? Like in our Boteju Lane house. You remember?'

Sonnaboy served what he could into a deep plate and brought it to the old man who nibbled at this and that and smiled and said, 'If your mama was here . . . my, would have done everything, no?'

Sonnaboy nodded. 'You eat all. I'll bring some more if want. And what about a small drink?'

'Later, men, later. You finish everything and buying again and then end of the month will come the bottle-selling time. Be a little careful, men. New school year also, no? See the expenses in January. School books also.'

This was no idle observation. January, the month after Christmas was affectionately known among the Burghers as the bottle-selling month. Empty bottles were the only encashable asset they had after the December revels. 'Bottle men' had their field days, going around with baskets on their heads buying up all the empty bottles which they in turn resold.

Anna peeped in on Cecilprins. 'Look, will you,' she told Totoboy, 'sleeping like a baby. And hardly touched any food. Sin, men.'

Leah told Beryl an hour later, 'Tell to see how Papa is, child. Now sun also hot outside.'

Cecilprins hadn't moved. In fact, he would never need to move on his own volition again and Christmas 1940 crashed around everybody's ears as Sonnaboy dazedly held his father's, hand and felt the cold stiffness and with an agonized howl beat his head against the arm of the lounger. While the men milled around, nerves snapping against alcohol and the stark reality of death and the children huddled fearfully in the hall and Diana wrung her thin hands and urinated on the sofa, Beryl ran out to fetch a doctor. Totoboy circled the garden aimlessly, then sat on the doorstep with his head between his knees and retched. The pandemonium grew as the truth sank in. Papa was dead. Anna, Leah and Elsie clung together to shriek in so disturbing a fashion that everybody in the lane charged in and the doctor arrived upon a scene of total chaos.

It was the case of the fabulous one-horse shay. Cecilprins was as tough a Burgher as the best of them. Born in 1854, he was eighty-six and had taken all that life threw at him and tossed it back. A stubborn man, warm, loving, set in many of his ways, yet his was the triumph of the ordinary and the enduring. Joy and sorrow had washed over him many times. He never sought after success or looked for favour. He never asked, never begged. He fathered thirteen children and never railed against Heaven for the trials he endured and the losses he bore. Quick to anger, quick to love, no pretensions, pride or pomp. And he had died with as much of the family around him, including his grandsons and (perish the thought) far too many granddaughters.

Sonnaboy pedalled madly to St. Mary's. His papa had to receive a blessing and the ministrations of a priest. He banged earnestly at the mission house door.

Father Robert of the Bambalapitiya parish was a dour man with a singularly one-track mind. In general he disliked human beings and considered that the species Homo Sapiens Bambalpitiensis was a flock that must stay within the fold. They—the sheep—must take due note of the fact that he was their spiritual shepherd and pay their respects to him every Sunday and First Friday and at all other pre-ordained Church festivals and ceremonies. They were to regard him as their resident priest and come to him in his domain. He took his duties seriously, but in the most absurdly literal sense.

'Myee, Father,' says Mrs de Run, simpering like the blazes, 'we never see you go anywhere. Why don't visit your parishioners once in a way?'

Father Robert would stare. 'Visit?' he would mumble, 'But you must understand that I am the priest sent to this church. My duty is here in the church. How can I go all over? Only on Mondays I go to the Archbishop's palace but that is our duty also.'

He was strictly a 'work to rule' priest and considering the rules that the archdiocese laid down, he remained glued to his church and never went to the mountain. Let the mountain come to him.

So when Sonnaboy grew tired of ringing the mission house bell and began banging on the door, Father Robert was most annoyed. Several old ladies had sent him Christmas platters and doubtless there was some *tara padre* curry too. This was snooze time.

'Who is it?' he asked shortly.

'Father, open the door. My papa died. You must come and give blessing.'

This was unwelcome news. 'Who are you? I have a headache.'

'Father, open the door.'

'I will not!' said the priest spiritedly, 'And kindly stop making all that noise. Who are you?'

Sonnaboy identified himself and the priest's frown deepened. This was the fellow who thumbed a nose at him and went off to Borella and got married.

'So what is the matter?'

'My papa is dead!'

'Yes, yes. So who is your papa? Does he belong to this parish?'

'He's in Kotahena. Came to stay for Christmas with us, and after lunch he just went and died. Father, open the door and come!'

'But he is not my parishioner. So why does he come to die in my parish? You go and tell the Kotahena priest.'

Sonnaboy heard and could not understand. The closed door infuriated him. 'Father!' he roared, 'You open this bloody door and talk to me.'

'Go away,' said Father Robert huffily, 'I know you engine driver fellows. Drinking all day and now coming to make a scene in the church. This is God's house.'

'You open this bloody door!'

Getting no answer, Sonnaboy stepped back, then hurled himself at the door which shot open with a crash of latches and hinges and was upon the priest before the man could say 'Quo Vadis'. Father Robert had always been a stick-in-the-mud man with a tiresome sense of authority that rubbed many the wrong way. But his cassock had been his shield. Old Jonklaas had once said: 'Like to catch and wring his neck. Bloody useless good-for-nothing bugger. Only sitting in the church and don't care what's happening outside.' But Jonklaas had also admitted that his hands were tied. 'Priest, no? Can't put a slap even.'

Sonnaboy had no such constraints. He seized Father Robert's shoulders with hands of iron and propelled him out into the street. 'Walk!' he roared, 'Or I will drag you by your bloody beard. My father is dead and you will come and do what the fuck you have to do, you heard!'

Father Robert rolled his eyes wildly. This was truly a fiend incarnate. 'Not a bloody sound from you! Just walk. I am behind you with my bicycle!'

And so Cecilprins was given a Roman Catholic send-off, albeit slightly belated, and when he was finally laid out for burial there was a look of amused satisfaction on his face. Christmas, naturally, was shelved and this time Viva and Opel and family came and also Terry, and, to his everlasting credit, Viva raised such a storm of prayers that even Cecilprins, wherever he was winging off to, must have turned back to stay awhile and listen. It was ironic. Maudiegirl's death saw her family torn asunder. Cecilprins' death brought them all together again and the brothers embraced and cried on each other's shoulders and all was well with the world again.

(Except, of course, Father Robert, who slunk away and rushed with reckless steps to his church and sank, breathless before the altar, groaning and wondering, no doubt, now a happy Christmas morning could turn into a nightmare by afternoon.)

The fears of Ceylon becoming part of the theatre of war magnified after Pearl Harbour and Japan's rampage in the East. H.M.S. Highflyer, the Royal Navy shore station in Colombo, became a hive of activity, and in Kollupitiya the R.A.F. base also saw large bodies of airmen who rode around in camouflaged trucks and half jeeps. Shore batteries were installed at Galle Buck and pillboxes lined the coast beside the railway to Galle, while in the north-east, the huge natural harbour of Trincomalee became the base of the Commander-in-Chief, East Indies Fleet. A submarine dock was built and China Bay became an R.A.F. preserve and the Army geared for anything and everything in Colombo and at Mutwal, where the Kelani River flowed into the sea.

Heather von Bloss was nineteen months old when the panic spread. The Japanese would certainly attack. Cedric Phoebus, who lived in 34th Lane, came to see Sonnaboy one day. 'Must see the lane, men,' he said, 'all the houses empty. Even where you stayed, people all gone. Pukka time to come and get for low rent. Only next door Ratnayake still there. Everybody bolting. Hellish buggers, no? Japanese going to bomb Colombo, it seems and everyone putting the *maaru* (doing the bolt).'

Sonnaboy plied Phoebus with a second drink. 'Where are they all going?'

'Don't know men, where running. Houseowners crying for tenants now. Those Joachims opposite, you remember? Went to Haputale. Rankines went to Nuwara Eliya. All going upcountry. I also going. You know your old landlord. You know what he's saying? Guess what?'

Sonnaboy couldn't and shook his head.

'If can find a tenant will give for thirty-five rupees. How that?'

Sonnaboy was visibly moved. 'I paid fifty, no, when I was there.'

'That's what!' Phoebus crowed triumphantly, 'So I'm thinking. This is Bambalapitiya, no? Not far from here RAF camp also. And near the bridge Army are in St. Peter's also. How if Japanese come and put bombs? But Wellawatte not so bad, no? And how much rent you're paying now? This is big house also.'

'Sixty-five,' Sonnaboy said, 'Too much, I know, but see the size, will you. Two storerooms also.'

'You come go now and see your old owner. Can get the house back for thirty. You say thirty-five too much. What men, you can save money, no? Get two bullock carts and shift in no time.'

Nobody in the family objected, of course. Beryl thought fondly of the long gossipy sessions with Ivy Ratnayake, who was, after all, a relation, and considered the move back eminently desirable. Sonnaboy and Phoebus inspected the lane of empty houses with sighs. 34th Lane seemed to be part of a ghost town . . . and this was true of much of suburbia. Everywhere, people were heading for the hills and those who remained were harassed by Air Raid Precaution Wardens and made to install blackout curtains and show no lights at night.

The 34th Lane house had its special attraction too. A deepset concrete storage room set into the rear of the kitchen. It was small, yet airy enough to accommodate the whole family at a pinch. It was, Sonnaboy pointed out, the perfect air-raid shelter. The house owner was overjoyed. He agreed to let the house for thirty rupees a month and sighed and said: 'All right, you pay fifteen for first month but if you damage the roof you have to repair.'

Sonnaboy said he would and pointed out that he was actually doing the landlord a favour. 'Actually, you must paint, not me,' he said, and the landlord said hastily: 'But you staying there, no? And anyway I am giving fifteen rupees.'

'Only paint money,' Sonnaboy said, 'Then what about the work, and in the sun also. But never mind. Where the keys?'

So the von Blosses moved back to Wellawatte, to a near-deserted 34th Lane where the Phoebuses, the Ratnayake's next door and the Melders at the top of the lane were the only residents, and Sonnaboy spent a morning on the roof painting a large red cross while Carloboy perched at the top of the ladder at gutter lever and bombarded his father with questions about why the Japanese would not bomb the house and why nobody else wished to paint the red cross on the roof. It was, as Sonnaboy told Ratnayake, just a precaution. The chore was not without its moments, though, for ther was a great hullaballoo around eleven when a long wailing blare sent Sonnaboy skittering for the ladder only to find that it had disappeared, whereupon he sat roaring at the edge of the roof with a pot of kicked-over red paint dripping all over the box hedge in the garden below and murderous yells to Carloboy to bring the ladder back. Beryl, on hearing the siren wail did what every mother was supposed to do. She took each of her children by the ear and and shoved them into the pantry shelter, wondering all the while what her husband was bellowing so lustily about. Carloboy, sitting in the cupboard, had quite forgotten about the ladder, which he had taken to the kitchen wall in order to inspect a house sparrow's nest. Sonnaboy, stuck on the roof, waved his paintbrush at the sky and howled blue murder.

The Wellawatte Spinning and Weaving mills had this bullhorn to summon labourers to work and indicate the end of shifts. The siren had that piercing timbre that was likened to a cross between the bellowing of an angry bull and the howl of a mad dog. This, civil authorities determined, would serve as an ideal air-raid warning. Trouble was that from time to time the warning would be sounded in order to keep citizens on their toes. Some assiduous fellow would sound the alarm at the ungodliest of times—like a couple of hours after midnight, or just when all good people were seated down to lunch or, as in this instance, when Sonnaboy was up on the roof and Carloboy had moved the ladder. It took all of ten minutes for the siren to go to work again, sounding the All-Clear and the family, trooping out of the shelter were greeted by a stream of deep blue language where the 'fucking ladder' and 'stuck up here on the bloody roof' featured prominently. The Phoebuses and Ratnayakes came to the gate to point and cackle making the air over the house curl up like a burning sock as Sonnaboy kicked the pot of paint for a six, flung the paintbrush at the chimney and screamed venom at the neighbourhood. Eventually the ladder was replaced and Sonnaboy descended amid cheers and the determination to skin Carloboy alive while the lad fled and wisely decided to stay under a bed while Phoebus said, 'So never mind, men, how to know siren will go?'

Sonnaboy was not mollified. 'And if planes came, fine thing, no? Everybody inside and I'm on the roof. You think Japs will keep quiet? How if they dive bomb or something?'

Nothing, however, that a little arrack did not settle, much to Beryl's annoyance. She was not happy. Of late, Sonnaboy was drinking too much; and with the war, the switch to the local arrack was yet another sign of the times. Quite suddenly, arrack was no longer infra dig. It was now the drink of polite society while whisky, soaring in price, was the special occasion drink. Oh, the times were certainly changing.

And the Japanese did attack, and it was Easter Sunday, 1942, and the *Sunday Observer* screamed in headlines that a large Japanese aircraft carrier had been sighted 800 miles south of the island and there were all manner of battle-wise statements from military types and a picture of Lord Louis Mountbatten who had actually set up an operational command headquarters in the Royal Botanical Gardens of Peradeniya.

Mountbatten, as Sonnaboy would relate, liked his eggs and Sonnaboy ought to have known, for there was that day when he had brought engine and train to the Colombo Fort platform and there was a terrific hustle and bustle as the Army and Navy trooped in and the stationmaster rushed to the engine to announce that Mountbatten would be a very very important passenger. 'Schedule is changed,' he said in hushed tone, 'Now you go express to Peradeniya where the admiral will get off. And don't jerk too much and whistle also. Admiral don't like when engines making unnecessary noise.'

To digress a little, the chronicler must state that the railway in Ceylon of those times and in Sri Lanka of this day, is not without its brigands. They are those who believe that anything that is consigned to the Goods Brake Van for carriage from point A to point B should be carefully assessed and removed if possible. For example Tommyboy Kelaart wishes to send his friend Bertie Oorloff in Colombo a fine bunch of bananas. Tommyboy is in Rambukkana, where, as everybody knows, the finest bananas in the land are grown. So he purchases a princely-looking bunch, each banana, for sheer size, looking positively obscene. He then lugs his gift to the station where the booking clerk admires them with reverence and books them for passage to Colombo and attaches a tag that says: BANANAS BUNCH ONE. Tommyboy's gift is then put into the Brake Van of the train to Colombo where it is ardently regarded by guard, underguard, porters, brake goods man and other railway types who all agree that as bananas, this bunch is hard to beat. Meanwhile Tommyboy telegraphs Bertie and impresses on him that the bananas he is sending certainly merit his attention. Bertie is impressed. Good old Tommyboy, he says, never forgets a pal. He tells his wife: 'That Tommyboy is sending us bananas. Big ones.'

'That's nice, dear.'

'Only thing is how to bring all the way from Fort Goods Shed. Will have to take a buggy.'

'So go and bring, dear.'

But somewhere between Rambukkana and Colombo, Tommyboy's bananas undergo a metamorphosis. Bertie, with buggy parked outside the goods shed railing, produces his pink goods ticket. He is ushered to a corner where his bananas await deliverence. And there he sees the most woebegone bunch of bananas he has ever clapped eyes on. Oh, the booking tag is there. BANANAS BUNCH ONE. But what, he asks the seven gods, are these mangy things? Even the labourers give him pained looks. What, they wonder, is this fellow going to do with this sorry emaciated bunch? When it was brought into the goods shed it was greeted with shouts of laughter. 'Look, will you. These are plantains?'

One said they reminded him of the penises of adolescent toque monkeys. 'Real monkey pricks.'

'For what things like this sending I don't know. Must be to insult, for sure.'

The goods shed clerk knew better, of course. 'From Rambukkana sending,' he said, 'guard must have put this and taken real bunch.' And this was true, for at Maho, the guard had arranged the switch. A porter was given five rupees and told to bring a bunch of bananas from the nearest market . . . and for five rupees all that worthy could find were the sorriest bunch ever. But they serve. Oh, they serve. After all, doesn't the tag baldly state BANANAS BUNCH ONE? In Colombo, the guard lugs Tommyboy's magnificent bunch away. Stationmaster Joseph is impressed. 'I say, men, pukka plantains. From where you bought?'

Guard beams. 'You want some to take home?'

So Tommyboy's bananas are carried to the Guards Inspector's Office where the bunch is cut into several combs and the driver gets a share, the stationmaster and underguard their share and everybody is pleased . . . all, that is, except Bertie who accepts the consignment, puts it red-facedly into the buggy and goes home to tell his wife that he is going to write Tommyboy a letter. This, he announces, is the end of a beautiful friendship. This is war. Tommyboy's bananas are an insult to human dignity. If this is Tommyboy's idea of a joke, he, Bertie, is not laughing. He is furious. He would like to take Tommyboy apart and dance on his several parts. Even his daughter's pimples are bigger than these bananas. Naturally Tommyboy rushes a protest. He swears on the Holy Shroud, that he sent the biggest, finest bananas in Rambukkana. Bertie writers back to inform Tommyboy what he could do in future with his bananas devoting two pages to a host of suggestions which, if suitably expurgated, could become a best seller titled *One Hundred and One Ways with Bananas.*

Well . . . to get back . . . Sonnaboy drove the train to Peradeniya where Lord Louis Mountbatten alighted and nearly started a fierce local war. His eggs had disappeared. Four dozen eggs, carefully packed and lovingly stored in the guards van had gone the way of Tommyboy's bananas. What was more, there was no substitute,

'What eggs?' the guard asked.

'The Allied Supreme Commander's eggs!' an aide-de-camp growled.

The guard thought this was funny. 'Big ones?'

The brake was searched, so was the Royal Mail bogey, the doglocker inspected and eventually the whole train fine-combed. No eggs. Mountbatten, as would be expected, was annoyed. His eggs were not booked as goods. All he had instructed was that they be placed in the brake for safety. Some military types came to the engine. Sonnaboy squinted at them. Fireman Jamis actually stood at attention thinking that this was the correct thing to do.

'What do you want?'

'Are you the engineman?'

'Why?'

'We are looking for eggs.'

'On the engine? What's wrong with you buggers? What eggs?'

They climbed on the footplate and winced at the coal dust and grease. The clinker was stoved against the firebox door and the fire roared angrily. On the platform the stationmaster was hopping and bobbing around as if he was in a Punch and Judy show. Even the platform flower-pots were searched.

'Oi,' said sonnaboy, 'if putting eggs here, will be hardboiled by now.'

Eventually Mountbatten stalked away with his party to climb into his Riley staff car and drive to his command post in the Botanical Gardens sans eggs. The Guard was served with a letter from the General Manger of Railways demanding explanation. He said he had no idea. His manifest had no listing of eggs. He considered that this was a persecution of sorts and intended to table the matter at the next meeting of the Guard And Enginemen's Union.

So, with such shennigans to relieve the tedium, Easter Sunday rolled up and all over, Burgher families dressed for church and hoped it would be a happy day despite the closing-in war and the shortages and this new business of having to queue for food and producing ration cards for oil and milk and sugar. Sonnaboy had to do a stint of arms drill and actually live in military camp as a lance corporal of the Railway Volunteer Force. He was proud of his stripes and boots and puttees and spent a lot of time polishing the brass buckles of his web belt and tunic buttons and teaching Carloboy the army way to shine boots—rub in the boot blacking very thinly, then spit on the treated area and rub in the spittle with one finger swathed in soft cloth with a circular motion. Carloboy set to work with a will. Pthoo! rub, Pthoo! rub while Beryl said it was sickening to watch and 'having shoe brush what is all this putting spit and for how long, I don't know, rubbing.' Sonnaboy would also take Carloboy to camp at times where the boy would be made to sing and everybody would get most rowdy over beer and hard Army biscuits and bully beef and the mess would ring to

'Lili Marlene' and such roistering rounds as:

The quartermaster jumped upon the sergeant major's back.

and that hot favourite of the times:

Hitler had only one big ball,
Goering had two, but very small,
Himmler, had something sim'lar,
But Mister Goebbels had no balls at all, tum-ti
tarum-pum-pum.

It was a hop and a skip to St. Lawrence's Church, which was in the next lane and Sonnaboy and Beryl rushed the family to the first mass of the day because Beryl insisted that she needed time to prepare the Easter lunch. All of the previous evening, eggs (not Mountbatten's) had been hardboiled and coloured and the baker had been relieved of his stock of hot cross buns. Sunday morning was smiling and clear-skied and as the dawn raised the haze of night, Sonnaboy, stepping to the gate said he saw aircraft flying high among the patchy clouds, so high that they looked like tiny toy planes winging noiselessly at about 65,000 feet.

The family took the short cut through a garden which had a board stating PRIVATE NO ADMITICEN and which everybody used since such boards with correct or incorrect spelling, were always ignored. A trek through the garden brought them to the bottom of St. Lawrence's Road and thus to the church where all the good people of Wellawatte converged in their Easter best, wearing white or butter yellow and the girls wore their Madonna expressions and carried candles done up with little satin bows and the men carried handsome black leather missals and Rona Redlich minced in on incredibly high heels and sat at the organ and began fiddling with piles of music sheets.

St. Lawrence's Church was an airy L-shaped building with half walls and wire grills, a few pews up front and chairs and benches making up the rest of the seating arrangements. It was not an imposing church. More like a sprawling dormitory and overcrowded with ornamentation which was nothing to write home about. The wooden altar and the carved, polished communion rails and the ebon prideaux were handsome enough, but Father Grero had no aesthetic sense. Statues with frightful faces were scattered everywhere, each reminding worshippers that Heaven must be a singularly unattractive place. St. Sebastian stood, an arm raised, for all the world like an advertisement for underarm deodorant. Arrows skewered his stomach and chest and gouts of red blood had been painted in with enthusiasm. The smile on the face was pathetic. The sort of smile that would say: 'Look, Ma, I'm a shishkebab.' St. Lawrence held pride of place, naturally, with an oversized painting of his martyrdom, where he lay on a rack, being roasted to a turn with a look that the painter hoped would convey ecstasy. The figures of the Stations of the Cross looked like a succession of the late Jim Henson's puppets, while large angels beside the altar with wings and scrolls and lopsided haloes stared blindly at the worshippers and looked for all the world like creatures in the last stages of some catatonic state or an atrophy of body and soul.

Father Grero believed that his flock, when in church, must be surrounded, enwrapped, toiled and moiled in all that the kingdom of God could throw their way. Pictures and images of saints were everywhere. Every pillar held its special ornamentation. There was Saint Cecilia making cows eyes at an organ; Saint Anthony with a wistful expression as though he had just been relieved of his gall bladder; Saint John embracing a cross and looking most uncomfortable. This Easter had the Tabernacle cloth in gold, banners of white and yellow and streamers of gold tinsel rustling from pillar to pillar. Bowls of white lilies filled the sanctuary and candles burned at every statue while old Muriel Rozairo went from niche to niche, kissing the clay feet of numberless saints and the Virgin and getting into everyones way with her circulating display of reverence for the graven images around her.

Father Grero came to the foot of the altar and the Easter Mass progressed with a lot of ringing of bells and standing and kneeling and the choir reminding the neighbourhood that Christ the Lord is Risen today. Leah and George were there and so was Anna, and

Mass over they met in the garden to wish each other a happy Easter when the air-raid warning sounded.

There was something urgent about that fiendish sound. What is more the smaller siren installed at the Wellawatte Police Station also began a fierce keening and far away there were strange pok! pok! sounds as though children were popping paper bags on some distant hill. Father Grero urged everybody to come into the church. Sonnaboy set a stubborn jaw. 'Every day the same story,' he growled, 'those ARP buggers blowing their whistles and sirens and everybody running and hiding. Damn nonsense. Just come go home. You wait and see, when Japanese come nobody will know and nobody will blow sirens when the bombs are falling.'

Beryl chewed a lip nervously. 'So never mind if bombs falling or not. We can wait until all clear and go home.'

'Yes, men,' old Mr Capper said, 'sense, no, your wife is talking. Come go inside and wait.'

Sonnaboy wasn't pleased. 'All balls!' he snorted, 'You think I'm afraid of these bloody sirens? You stay then if you want. I'm going home,' and with a face like a monsoon cloud be strode off while Beryl sniffed and drove the children into the church saying: 'One thing, your father . . . stubborn is not the word. Let go and do anything.'

Old Capper made clucking noises. 'Real one, your husband. Slightest thing get angry. How you put up with temper like that I don't know.'

Beryl sighed.

Sonnaboy strode home, found the doors locked and realised that Beryl had the keys. This enraged him, so kicking shut the gate he sat on the front step, glowering at the sky. Suddenly he saw a clutch of aircraft zoom out of a high cloud, plunging down, down, and he realised with a shock that the red rising sun emblem was painted on each underwing. Japanese planes, and roaring out of nowhere to meet them were British fighter planes. The air, from two thousand feet to as low as six hundred feet over the road swirled and smoked and there was a great thrumming and whining and the screech of metal and the staccatto crackle of turret fire. A dogfight, right over his house. And suddenly the distant thuds and booms were louder and he knew that they were gun batteries and shore emplacements and that this time the sirens had been for real. Far away were sounds of an urban frenzy. Screaming motors and was that a fire engine? He leaped to his feet and rushed to the road. Above the planes banked and swooped and tree tops swayed in the rush of their arcing and wheeling. He heard the phut-phut-phut of guns and saw long lines of red dust kick up on the road. Sonnaboy ran. He raced through the garden, up St. Lawrences Road and pounded into the church as though all hell was behind him. There, holding Beryl and the children close he told of the air battle and everybody listened ashen-faced and Mrs Van Starrex declared that she would faint, so there, and women squealed while the men raised hands to their ears and shouted 'Listen! Quiet!' and took each sound to be some dismal disaster of war. 'You can hear? Those are big guns. What was that? My God, something exploded, no? Don't know if bomb even fell. Or something blown up . . . there, bells. Must be ambulance.' Don't know how many dead no? And what is burning can't say. Good Lord, don't know if our houses gone. Planes come low and shoot, no?'

Father Grero insisted that everybody should pray instead of scaring each other silly, and one bright spark asked what would happen if a bomb fell on the church, whereupon Mrs Van Starrex kept to her threat and fainted, and Capper doused her with holy water which had absolutely no effect on her. When she did come to she was propped against the organ and vigorously fanned with hymnals and had to be assured every 25th second that no bombs were homing in on her.

An hour passed. Father Grero gave up on the mob and regarded his flock sourly. Of course, many decided that prayer would not be out of place but they all throbbed with excitement and paced around while old Farter Moldrich (so named because he had this tendency to wait for a moment of absolute silence and then break wind in a long drawn-out manner) was describing how shrapnel from bombs and shells could make a man look like minced meat and how several bombs dropped in a close pattern could cause a firestorm and other delicious bits of information that made the women white in the face and clutch their children to them and

Mavis Ludekens embraced an altar boy and screeched: 'We all die for sure, we all going to die for sure!' until her husband pushed her into the confessional, sat her down and snarled: 'So die! But don't make such a bloody noise!'

Another hour passed. Leah was discussing Easter lunch with Beryl. George sat, picking his nose and grunting at everybody who tried to pick a conversation with him. Men strolled around the garden, heads turned to the sky. Sonnaboy had seen Japanese raiders right over his head. They hoped to see some sign of battle too.

Leah was telling Beryl: 'Fine one, that George. Telling yesterday go straight to the market and buy a chicken for lunch. How, child, to go straight the way he is telling? So I told, how to go straight men, must turn, no? when come to top of the lane and again turn to Manning place and then again turn to the poultry place and if turning all over like that how to go straight? And he saying you're a damn fool, men, in front of the children also. One thing, I don't know what's wrong with these men. Just see how Sonnaboy went. Very good if planes fell on his head. And how the way he came running? All big talk only. So how, anymore children coming? Don't allow, men. Already have four, no? Last week he's coming home and grumbling that three girls coming one after the other and next time must get boy. Easy for them to say, no? We are the ones with all the pains and the big stomachs and all. I told George no more nonsense. Enough, men, two. Think of all that have to do even for these two. And who knows with this war and all, how we will manage? One thing, George is careful. Yesterday also he said good if have no more children. And Ivor also sickly. Giving, men, all the nourishment but always getting something. And if get cough and cold will go on for how long I don't know. Whole night going hacka-hacka-hacka and crying and no sleep for anyone. One thing, children are real problem, men. Elsie won't keep quiet. If the children are too much, she hammers. Whole trouble is we are too kind. Everything seeing to. Asking anything we are giving. And George won't even correct them. Telling you're the mother, you correct. Fine thing, no? Everything on my shoulders putting. But one thing, thank God, they are all right in school. Nuns saying that

Marlene is very good and learning nicely. How your lot? That Carloboy looks a real devil, no? But must be bright. For that my Ivor. Very slow, men. Only likes to torment his sister and hiding her pen and homework book and then big fights. So are you coming in the evening? Made some cake and some tinned fish sandwiches if anybody comes. What else to do; nowadays can't throw money, no? George will pull a bottle. I don't know how these men can drink like this. One thing, that Viva won't touch, child. Only other day I was telling how if our buggers are in Bandarawela? In that cold everyday will be drinking. But see Viva—in all that cold, won't touch, men. And lucky devil . . . company house and van and no Japanese to come and bomb or anything . . . .'

. . . And on and on and on while the Japanese flew over Colombo and dropped a bomb on the lunatic asylum in Angoda because that place was very big and imposing and one madman died and another escaped in the confusion. The pilot must have thought the asylum a building of some importance. The Royal Air Force rose to meet the raiders and another bomb was dropped in Ratmalana, near the airport and one RAF Flying Boat tried to take off too quickly and careered all over the runway with its controls jammed and there were a few road mishaps as vehicles roaring for cover, tore into each other . . . and then, unaccountably, the Japanese called it a day and flew away, never to return.

Another fifteen minutes passed. Anna was filling in the family on her many clashes with the cookwoman and how Mister Colontota had taken to smoking Sportsman cigarettes. 'Must see the dance, men,' she said, 'taking one cigarette and cutting in half with a blade. Keeping half on the altar and smoking half. Then waiting three hours and smoking the other half. Real fusspot, men. If give a glass of water to drink must see how holding glass to the light. If have tiny speck of anything, saying, Anna, what is that? I ask what, what, and pointing and saying there, and I look and can't see anything. Have some dirt, he saying and now have to boil and strain the water. One thing, he's careful. Must see the fuss to eat anything. If too much salt, bad. Too much ginger, bad. And can't cook any beef also.'

'So he is Buddhist, no,' Leah said, 'So you come for lunch when you want to eat beef. Whole thing is you won't come out, no? Only coming to church. What you are doing the whole day in that house I don't know. And no children also.'

'How to come, men. If leave and come that cookwoman Sumana will finish everything and rob also. Can't leave that devil for a minute. Last week brought four limes and told to keep in salt pot. Next day no limes. I asked what woman you did with all the limes, and all finished she saying. How to use and finish four limes in one day, men? Must have taken home or given to the nextdoor people. Always going to the wall and talking with the nextdoor servant.'

And the All-Clear sounded and everbody went home and the island of Ceylon had had its first air raid; and that, as every historian will say, was the only time in two World Wars that the island was attacked. A few hours of half-hearted target practice. Only the madhouse suffered. The Japanese planes returned to the carrier and never looked towards the island again. A strange war, to be sure.

In 34th Lane, however, the von Blosses home became the cynosure. For, on reaching home, Sonnaboy found sixteen spent bullets neatly embedded in his front door and the children picked up many more, brass gleaming wickedly, that lay in the road and in the private garden. This was certain evidence of the dogfight that had raged overhead and Phoebus considered the bullet-studded door and said: 'How if were in the veranda?' and Sonnaboy smacked a palm and said, 'Veranda? My God, men, sitting I was on the step. Then when planes coming low I ran to the church.' Everybody said it was a mercy for, had Sonnaboy remained on his front step he may have been struck by the bullets that had ripped his door.

Hitler, of course, lost, and Japan received an atomic strike and while all Europe and the rest of the world was in post-war ferment, Sonnaboy decided that he was taking no chances about his next baby. 'Dammit,' he told Totoboy, who seemed to be pulling boys out of a hat, 'this one must be a boy.' He consulted a Tamil guard who said that the Hindu god of a forest shrine in the deep south-east was pretty good at this sort of thing. 'You go to Kataragama,' the man advised, 'and put some money near the statue and tell that you want a boy and you'll see.'

'But wife already pregnant, men.'

'So all the better. You go. Bathe in the river and break a coconut and give about ten rupees and just ask Kataragama god to give a boy baby.'

'But I'm Catholic, no?'

'So? You think only Hindus go there? Everybody going. Sinhalese and Christians and Buddhists and even Muslims. if you are thinking like that then go to your church and pray for a boy and ask your god to give a son.'

'I don't know men . . . you are sure about this Kataragama?'

'Sure, I'm sure.'

So Sonnaboy made a pilgrimage to Kataragama—a trip that shocked the family, and on his return he was taken to task by his sisters and Father Grero and stubbornly told them all to go to hell. For one thing, home was not a happy one. There were whispers. Beryl, it was said, was seen too often in the company of a dapper fellow with a thin moustache and heavily pomaded hair. Sonnaboy was a creature who could not relate to situations like this. He took seriously to drink and this made him a menace in his best moments. Soon, he began to have his doubts about the child Beryl bore. Was it his . . . or was it that—who was that fellow people were chinwagging about—Kinno Mottau?

Surly, suspicious, ugly after arrack, he began to look for and find enemies everywhere. Moving out of 34th Lane into Mahadangahawatte Lane, he took savage satisfaction in assailing Beryl with his penis. He used it as a weapon on her, constantly taking, constantly impregnating her. So followed David and Michael (two boys for the price of one Kataragama pilgrimage) and Beverley Annette, and Beryl aborted the next and rushed into Kinno's bed to voice her sorrows and found herself carrying his child, which scared her stiff. She turned to a neighbour for help and was advised to take a decoction, which she did. This made her bleed tremendously and go poker stiff. She barely lived, but pulled through after the dead foetus was removed and after two weeks in hospital, was sent home to a murderously angry Sonnaboy who dragged her into the bedroom, threw her across the bed and raped her. And this was the nature of their relationship for many more years and she bore him two more boys and a girl while an abandoned infant was also brought into the home— Boniface—who was formally adopted and everybody asked why and Sonnaboy told everybody, grimly, to mind their business. The chronicler has detailed this at the beginning of this chapter so little more needs be said, although it can be said that the scurvy-ridden infant was accepted by Sonnaboy just to burden his wife still more. There was no more love. Just Sonnaboy and his arrack; Beryl and the children.

Leah and George watched their children grow up. Marlene became a journalist, writer and well-known author. Her books are read in Sri Lanka to this day.

Anna and Mister Colontota decided, like ·Sonnaboy, to adopt a child and accepted into their home the infant son of the cookwoman. They were so proud of their Sunil, who grew up to be the blackest-hearted scoundrel in Wellawatte. He is believed to be wandering the backstreets of Colombo to this day, a vagabond, a syphilitic and a thief.

Totoboy's children fared well. Fortune married a railway engine driver while Brennan, Winston and Cyril all settled in white-collar jobs, then emigrated to England.

Viva took his brood to Australia; Sonnaboy took his brood to England—all except Carloboy and Marie who remained in Sri Lanka.

Elsie's children had their ups and downs. Ian became a marine draughtsman and architect. Noella went, everybody said, to the dogs, eventually becoming mistress to a Tamil thug who beat her daily and gave her two bastard daughters. Beulah drifted aimlessly, a gaunt-faced, unlovely harridan. Dorcas shone for a moment. She married, bore a daughter and then cancer claimed her. Thelma married a rich Sinhalese landed proprietor, while Caroline Daisy graduated, taught at a convent, married a legal type and after he had died, went back to being her natural self—a lesbian.

The island, too, saw its traumas. After the war came independence and the need to give the native Sinhalese a place in the sun. In the 1970's the island was renamed the Republic of Sri Lanka. One Prime Minister decreed that Sinhala had to be the official language of the country and the government. Burghers were told, learn Sinhalese, or else. The age of the favoured English-educated was over. Schools were nationalised. Sinhala was the medium of instruction henceforth. Burghers in their thousands left the island.

Sonnaboy was told to take a qualifying examination in Sinhala.

'For what? he demanded,'to drive an engine?'

So he quit and emigrated to England.

The 1970s saw a Burgher exodus. Australia accepted the bulk of them, while others went to England and Canada and others found employment and an opportunity to settle in New Zealand, the USA and Western Europe. But many remained, and even those who went away always returned, if only to holiday and see old friends and go to the churches of their youth and kneel at the graves of their fathers and grandparents and think of the old happy days under the jam fruit tree.

Oh, many remained, just as Carloboy did. Sonnaboy died in England but Carloboy's brothers and sisters would come occasionally to Sri Lanka and talk loud and long of life in Blightly and bring cheap Carnaby Street watches to distribute to all and sundry. His aunts, Elsie, Anna and Leah all passed on and are doubtless gossiping, ninety to a dozen, under the shade of some jam fruit tree in Paradise.

Terry and Totoboy died too and it is said that doctors still wonder how Totoboy had lived for so long with a liver that had shrunk to the size of a postage stamp. Dunnyboy died too and everybody said it was a great mercy. Viva, who went to Australia, was last reported trying out every one of Heinz's fifty-seven varieties and doubtless praising the Lord with each can he opened.

Oh, there is so much more to record. One cannot consider so many lifetimes and actually reach any satisfactory conclusion. But the Burghers are quite the most unique segment of all the peoples of Sri Lanka. Gloriously, historically unique. The chronicler has failed to record much. Many other luridly colourful vestiges of Burgher life still remain to be written, especially that of the railway community, to which Sonnaboy and his family belonged. This, the writer promises, will be another story. But for now, it is time to write Finis.

As the chronicler lays down his pen, he looks out of his window where, in the garden, a jam fruit tree sighs in the wind. It stands there in enduring memory of the Sonnaboy and the Cecilprins of this story.

Let a line be added: For all the Burghers in Sri Lanka and in their adopted countries the world over, God bless you, everyone. And look me up, drop in, anytime.

We can still 'put a party'.